CROSS-CHANNEL AVIATION PIONEERS

CROSS-CHANNEL AVIATION PIONEERS

Blanchard and Bleriot, Vikings and Viscounts

Bruce Hales-Dutton

AIR WORLD

CROSS-CHANNEL AVIATION PIONEERS

First published in Great Britain in 2020 by
Air World
An imprint of
Pen & Sword Books Ltd
Yorkshire – Philadelphia

Copyright © Bruce Hales-Dutton, 2020

ISBN 978 1 52677 559 7

The right of Bruce Hales-Dutton to be identified as Author of this work has been asserted by him in accordance with the Copyright, Designs and Patents Act 1988.

A CIP catalogue record for this book is available from the British Library.

All rights reserved. No part of this book may be reproduced or transmitted in any form or by any means, electronic or mechanical including photocopying, recording or by any information storage and retrieval system, without permission from the Publisher in writing.

Typeset by SJmagic DESIGN SERVICES, India.

Printed and bound in the UK by TJ Books Limited.

Pen & Sword Books Limited incorporates the imprints of Atlas, Archaeology, Aviation, Discovery, Family History, Fiction, History, Maritime, Military, Military Classics, Politics, Select, Transport, True Crime, Air World, Frontline Publishing, Leo Cooper, Remember When, Seaforth Publishing, The Praetorian Press, Wharncliffe Local History, Wharncliffe Transport, Wharncliffe True Crime and White Owl.

For a complete list of Pen & Sword titles please contact

PEN & SWORD BOOKS LIMITED
47 Church Street, Barnsley, South Yorkshire, S70 2AS, England
E-mail: enquiries@pen-and-sword.co.uk
Website: www.pen-and-sword.co.uk

Or
PEN AND SWORD BOOKS
1950 Lawrence Rd, Havertown, PA 19083, USA
E-mail: Uspen-and-sword@casematepublishers.com
Website: www.penandswordbooks.com

Contents

Introduction		vi
Prologue		viii
Chapter One	The Beautiful Voyage	1
Chapter Two	Unfaithful Wings	14
Chapter Three	'Which Way is Dover?'	29
Chapter Four	After Blériot	44
Chapter Five	Triumph and Tragedy	56
Chapter Six	Lunch in Paris, Tea in London	71
Chapter Seven	Exploiting the Practical Possibilities	79
Chapter Eight	On Silver Wings	94
Chapter Nine	The Flight of the Dragon	108
Chapter Ten	Air Bridge	121
Chapter Eleven	A New Era in Air Travel	136
Chapter Twelve	The Great Race	153
Chapter Thirteen	A Lot Less Bovver	168
Chapter Fourteen	The *Radio Queen* and other Tales	184
Chapter Fifteen	Pollution-Free	191
Chronology		204
Bibliography		207
Index		209

Introduction

For more than a century the English Channel, the stretch of water that separates England and France, has acted as a yardstick for judging aviation achievement.

At its narrowest point the Channel may only be twenty-two miles wide yet its symbolic significance is out of all proportion to its size. For many years, aviators from around the world have realised that a successful cross-Channel flight qualifies them to be taken seriously as pilots, aircraft operators and inventors.

Cross-Channel Aviation Pioneers represents an attempt to chronicle the achievements of those brave and skilful men and women who have blazed a trail with new ways of traversing the Straits of Dover. As such it is a logical follow-up to *Trans-Atlantic Pioneers* published in 2019. Essentially, this, too, is a book about civilian rather than military operations.

As might be expected, this is a story rich in 'characters'. They range from the crabby Jean-Pierre Blanchard who was so reluctant to share his success with his sponsor, John Jeffries; the debonair but unlucky Hubert Latham; the determined gambler, Louis Blériot, who rode his luck to everlasting fame; the aristocratic but ultimately tragic Charles Rolls; the diminutive John Moissant who took his cat along for the ride; and the feisty Harriet Quimby, journalist and screenwriter, whose success in becoming the first female pilot to cross the Channel was overshadowed by the loss of the *Titanic* the day before.

More recently there was Taffy Powell who invented cross-Channel aerial car ferry services and built a special terminal to handle them; the laconic Sir George Edwards, whose vision and determination led to the first turbine-powered airliners and Sir Christopher Cockerell, whose hovercraft made him possibly the last of the lone British inventors.

And even though cross-Channel flight has become a routine part of many international air journeys, the early years of the present century have been

INTRODUCTION

rich in daredevils, like Felix Baumgartner, Yves Rossy, Jonathan Trappe and Franky Zapata who found novel ways to make the crossing and show their disdain for the risk involved.

No doubt there will be more cross-Channel pioneers eager to test themselves and their ideas. But they will do well to respect the Channel and its capricious weather. Asked by a reporter what it felt like to have conquered it, Anglo-American balloonist Jonathan Trappe retorted: 'We have not conquered the Channel. We have only had the honour to float in the skies above the cold waters for one quiet day. Today and forever, the English Channel remains unconquered.'

Bruce Hales-Dutton
West Malling
March 2020

Prologue

The sun rises on another day. Gradually, its rays reveal a landscape of grassland, marshes and densely wooded areas.

On the lower slopes of the range, below the grassy spaces where the wild horses graze, are forests of yew and sweet-chestnut and elm. The thickets and dark places hide grizzly bear and hyæna as grey apes clamber through the branches.

This vision of a land before history revealed in the late nineteenth century continued,

> a broad and sluggish Thames flowed through its marshes to meet its father Rhine, flowing through a wide and level country that is under water in these latter days, and which we know by the name of the North Sea. In that remote age the valley which runs along the foot of the Downs did not exist, and the south of Surrey was a range of hills, fir-clad on the middle slopes, and snow-capped for the better part of the year. The cores of its summits still remain as Leith Hill, and Pitch Hill, and Hindhead.

This was what many millennia later would be known as south-east England. Scientific and geological analysis has provided a broad canvas of knowledge about it but human imagination was required to paint in the detail. And who better than Herbert George Wells, teacher, journalist and novelist who was a native of this place, albeit in another time, to wield the brush?

According to Wells, writing in *A Story of the Stone Age* which first appeared in 1897, it was '50,000 years ago, if the reckoning of geologists is correct'. He was basing his ideas on late Victorian research which visualised a land later called 'Dogger Land' which occupied what's now the North Sea

PROLOGUE

and the English Channel. It was, Wells wrote, 'a time when one might have walked dry-shod from France (as we call it now) to England'.

Indeed, research has shown that what's now known as Britain was once a peninsula attached to the north-west of the European land mass. It was a time when Britain was home to a fragile and scattered population of about 5,000 hunter-gatherers. They were descended from the early humans who had followed migrating herds of mammoth and reindeer onto the jagged peninsula.

When the last Ice Age ended, around 10,000 years ago, it left behind an area of cold dry tundra that grew warmer and wetter as the ice caps melted. The Channel was then dry land although it was slowly being submerged as sea levels rose. But around 8,000 years ago it's thought that a single catastrophic event finally caused the two land masses to break apart.

Landslides in Norway triggered one of the biggest tsunamis ever recorded when a landlocked sea burst its banks. The water gushed out and turned low-lying plains into what's now the North Sea and marshlands to the south to form the English Channel. The ridge of chalk, which for 10 million years had joined the peninsula to the main land mass, was finally ruptured.

It's hard to imagine the violence of this event. 'The waves would have been maybe as much as 33ft high,' said geologist David Smith of Oxford University. 'Anyone standing out on the mud flats at that time would have been dismembered. The speed [of the water] was just so great.'

Britain had become an island. It was, says, Jean-Marc Puissesseau, chairman and chief executive of the ports of Boulogne and Calais, the first Brexit.

Chapter One

The Beautiful Voyage

How many ways are there to cross the English Channel by air? The answer, as history has shown, is that nobody really knows. The fact is that, even 100 years after the first powered aerial crossing, there are probably many ways of crossing the Straits of Dover which separates England and France that have yet to be invented.

On Sunday 4 August 2019 a 40-year-old jet-ski champion and engineer from Marseilles added his name to the roll of cross-Channel aviation pioneers. In doing so, Franky Zapata joined a list of flyers stretching back 234 years to January 1785 when Jean-Pierre Blanchard and John Jeffries made the first aerial crossing. They went by balloon; Zapata chose a 'hover board', a jet-powered platform just big enough to accommodate its pilot standing up to control his machine at speeds exceeding 100 mph.

Zapata's extraordinary device looked as though it had just left the pages of a sci-fi comic. But then no doubt Louis Blériot's spindly, wire-braced monoplane with its bicycle wheels probably looked just as alien to onlookers when the Frenchman arrived in Dover in July 1909. Indeed, Zapata invoked the spirit of his countryman when he spoke of opening a new era in aviation.

Since the days of Blanchard and Jeffries the Channel has provided a yardstick for judging aviation achievement. Jonathan Trappe, who flew the Channel suspended from a cluster of helium balloons, put it this way:

> the English Channel continues to call to us. I don't know if it is a siren's song, or if crossing that ribbon of water will be like breaking the ribbon at the finish line. With good luck, I will find out today.

At its narrowest point, the Dover Strait, the Channel is just twenty-two miles wide. Yet the prestige attached to crossing this strip of water is out of proportion to the distance involved. There has always been something symbolic about making the trip, especially if it's done in a new way.

CROSS-CHANNEL AVIATION PIONEERS

Yet, despite its significance in separating the British Isles from the European land mass, the English Channel or *La Manche* looks like any other stretch of water no matter which side you view it from.

But had it not been for a geological accident eight millennia ago it would have been very different: we could have walked across.

No doubt there have been many nervous travellers who wished it was still possible to do so. Others probably gazed wistfully at the gulls soaring effortlessly over the often choppy stretch of sea. But the world had to wait until 1784 for the first aerial crossing of the English Channel by humans.

Many centuries before, hot air balloons were reputedly in use in places as far apart as China and South America. There has been talk of man-carrying smoke balloons during the Yin dynasty of the twelfth century BC and it's been suggested that in China during the fourth century BC fire balloons were used for signalling in warfare. Legend also has it that balloons were used by priests of pre-Inca civilisations. Peruvian funereal rites involved sending corpses out over the Pacific by hot air balloon.

Whether or not the human-carrying balloon was invented in the ancient world, it was unquestionably two French brothers who first demonstrated its potential to a mass audience in the revolutionary age of the late eighteenth century. And it wasn't long before the possibilities it offered for a new form of transport were soon evident.

The first public demonstration of a hot air balloon by Joseph and Étienne Montgolfier in June 1783 was followed five months later by the first manned ascent and then, after a year and a half, by the first aerial crossing of the English Channel in early 1785.

The Montgolfiers relied on hot air generated by an on-board fire but it wasn't long before a safer and more efficient lifting agent became available. This was hydrogen, although the British scientist Henry Cavendish called it 'phlogiston' or 'inflammable air' when he discovered it in 1766. But it was not until 1783 that it was first used as a lifting agent for balloons. That put it in direct competition with hot air.

The Montgolfier family was an old-established one able to trace its roots back to mediaeval times. They began paper manufacture in the fourteenth century and their business prospered so that it received royal patronage in the eighteenth century. By that time Pierre Montgolfier was in charge of the firm and his two sons, Joseph, born in 1740, and Étienne five years his junior, began to consider the possibilities of flight.

There is a certain amount of speculation surrounding the events that led to their experiments with hot air balloons and, inevitably, legend plays its part. One story has it that the behaviour of garments drying in front of the fire suggested the possibility of levitation by hot air. It's also thought that Joseph's urge to experiment was inspired by Joseph Priestley's paper *Experiments and Observations on Different Kinds of Air* which appeared in France in 1776.

Although Joseph Montgolfier learned how to produce hydrogen he soon discovered its limitations with the paper vessels he was using initially. He turned to hot air, although he appears not to have realised that air expands when heated and that its weight drops as its volume increases. He assumed that the process of combustion produced a special type of gas and that the most effective way to produce it was by burning a mixture of damp straw and wool.

Following a series of successful small-scale experiments with paper bags, Joseph's ambitions soared. He suggested to the governments of France and Spain that his invention offered a means of prising Gibraltar out of the clutches of the stubborn British defenders by means of an airborne assault using balloons.

By this time Étienne had become an enthusiastic and active partner in Joseph's experiments with successively larger vessels offering greater lifting power. This work led to a 22,000-cubic-foot envelope made of cloth lined with paper and comprising numerous sections. According to Étienne, these sections were fastened like garments 'with buttons and buttonholes'.

On 5 June 1783 a big crowd gathered in the square at Annonay near Lyons in southern France to witness the balloon's ascent. On Joseph's signal, the eight men holding down the vessel released their grip and the balloon soared rapidly upwards. It came down a mile and half away ten minutes later. But for the loss of gas through the buttonholes and 'other imperfections' it could have flown further, Étienne later claimed.

When the news reached Paris 500 miles away the scientific community greeted it with some scepticism. The Paris Academy assumed the Montgolfiers had used hydrogen and immediately commissioned Jacques Charles and the brothers Aine and Cadet Robert to produce a better balloon. The resulting craft had an envelope made of silk coated with a solution of rubber which they hoped would make it less permeable.

The initial method of providing the gas was complex and cumbersome requiring iron filings to be mixed with sulphuric acid. Many problems had to be overcome – not least the leakage of gas from the envelope – before the tethered balloon was allowed to rise in a public demonstration on 27 August 1783. Watched by a huge crowd, the balloon, named *The Globe*, ascended from the Champ de Mars, where the Eiffel Tower now stands, to a height of 3,000 feet where it disappeared into a rain cloud. It appeared a few minutes later before it was finally lost to sight over the Paris skyline.

The Globe came down forty-five minutes later near the village of Gonesse fifteen miles from the centre of Paris, which, 217 years later, was the site of the Air France Concorde supersonic airliner crash. There the terrified villagers attacked the limp balloon envelope with muskets and pitchforks, tearing it to pieces.

Étienne Montgolfier was in Paris to watch *The Globe*'s ascent and, later, he and his brother moved their operations to the capital. There they resolved to construct the biggest balloon yet. It would have an envelope of linen in a paper sandwich that, when expanded, would be 74-feet tall and 43-feet in diameter.

The balloon was scheduled to be demonstrated to King Louis XVI and Queen Marie Antoinette at Versailles on 19 September. They only just made it. A week before they'd agreed on a preview to members of the Academy. The Montgolfiers burned 50lb of straw and several pounds of wool to inflate their envelope; the speed of inflation compared to Charles' hydrogen balloon amazed the watchers.

But a sudden storm arose and the high wind destroyed the balloon. But, aided by a team of helpers, the Montgolfiers built a replacement in time for the Royal demonstration. This time a spherical envelope 57-feet tall and 41-feet in diameter and made of stronger cloth with paper backing on the inside was specified. The outside was elaborately decorated in blue and gold and displaying the royal insignia.

It was completed in just four days leaving just enough time for a trial ascent the day before the Versailles spectacular. Pre-launch rumour suggested the balloon would be carrying a man but the king himself vetoed the idea as too dangerous. As a compromise a wicker cage carrying a sheep, a cockerel and a duck was suspended from the balloon. After a sumptuous banquet the king and queen made a pre-launch inspection of the craft but the smell of the fuel, to which the brothers had added some old shoes and decomposing meat, quickly drove them to a more remote vantage point.

Meanwhile, the balloon was straining to be free. A huge crowd was watching as three cannon shots signalled that it was time for the craft to be the released. Immediately, it soared majestically into the sky, rising to a height estimated at 1,700 feet before drifting away in the breeze. Eight minutes later it made a gentle landing in the forest of Vaugesson just two miles from Versailles.

THE BEAUTIFUL VOYAGE

Joseph Montgolfier was disappointed. He'd expected it to reach 12,000 feet and stay aloft for twenty minutes. Everybody else, though, including the Royal Family, was highly impressed. The three passengers were probably happy too. They'd arrived in one piece, although the cockerel was said to have been kicked by the sheep before launch.

Fresh from this triumph, the Montgolfiers announced their intention of building a man-carrying balloon. The king remained dubious and decreed that, if the brothers were resolved on such a risky venture, the craft should carry aloft two criminals who, should they survive, would be pardoned.

This notion outraged a young Parisian doctor and scientist called Jean-François Pilâtre de Rozier. Described as a headstrong man of action and the Don Juan of the Paris salons, de Rozier had closely followed the activities of the Montgolfiers and had worked with them. He believed that the honour of making the first flight should most emphatically not be given to criminals. He found an influential ally in the Marquis d'Arlandes, a somewhat hot-tempered and arrogant major in the Garde Royale who had good connections at Court. He offered to try to change the king's mind on condition that he could accompany de Rozier in his great venture.

Eventually the king agreed to the flight and de Rozier was free to make history. He joined forces with the Montgolfiers to work on a new and stronger balloon. The envelope was 75-feet-6-inches tall and 49-feet in diameter, around which was constructed a cloth-covered wickerwork balustrade. The wrought-iron fire basket was suspended from the envelope by chains.

On 15 October 1783 de Rozier made the first ascent, albeit tethered to the ground by ropes. Watched by the now customary large crowd, he ascended to 84 feet, the limit of the rope. By continually feeding the fire with straw he was able to remain aloft for over four minutes. Longer and higher ascents were made over the next few days. On one occasion, de Rozier was accompanied by d'Arlandes.

The historic first free flight was scheduled for 21 November but in a further captive ascent the envelope was damaged by strong winds. It was hastily repaired by a team of voluntary seamstresses. By the time the repairs had been completed the weather had improved. De Rozier and d'Arlandes stepped into opposite sides of the gallery to maintain balance and at 1:54 pm the great blue-and-gold craft rose impressively from its launching stage. Estimates of the height reached vary with some reports suggesting it reached 3,000 feet.

'I was surprised at the uneasy silence which our departure caused,' d'Arlandes wrote later. 'I therefore took out my handkerchief and waved it.'

This earned him a rebuke from de Rozier who instructed him to put more fuel on the fire instead of doing nothing.

The craft's survival was continually threatened by the fire which sustained it in the air. The aeronauts had provided themselves with sponges to stifle any fires in the envelope or the ropes that might be set off by sparks from the fire. But this couldn't prevent small holes being burned in the envelope nor the breakage of ropes. It was time to descend. D'Arlandes wrote later

> I felt the balloon pressing softly against my head. I pushed it back and leapt down to the ground. Looking round and expecting to see the balloon still distended, I was astonished to find it quite empty and flattened. On looking for Rozier I saw him in his shirt sleeves creeping out from under the mass of canvas that had fallen over him.

Man's first flight had lasted twenty-five minutes and covered just over six miles, terminating at Butte-aux-Cailles where the aeronauts were mobbed. In the ensuing confusion, de Rozier's coat was ripped off and divided up by the souvenir-hunting crowd. It seems d'Arlandes was the first of the duo to recover and he rushed off to the Paris Academy to tell his story of the historic flight.

This success galvanised the champions of the hydrogen balloon into action. Charles, together with the brothers Aine and Cadet Robert, launched a public subscription to fund the construction of a man-carrying craft. The results represented a huge advance on the Montgolfiers' hot air vessel and set the standard for balloon design for years to come.

The envelope comprised sections of rubberised silk sewn together to form a perfect sphere 27-feet-6-inches in diameter. These sections were alternately coloured red and yellow. Crucially, the envelope incorporated a valve at the top which would be opened to release gas to enable the aeronaut to descend at will. At the bottom was an open neck to facilitate inflation and to allow for expansion.

Cord netting attached to a wooden ring encircling the envelope at the centre was in turn attached to ropes from which the wickerwork car was suspended. The car itself was an elaborate device that resembled a chariot from the ancient world but which carried Charles and Aîné Robert aloft. The first manned ascent by a hydrogen balloon took place on 1 December 1783 from the gardens of the Tuileries. It was estimated that 400,000 people, half the population of Paris, turned out to watch.

THE BEAUTIFUL VOYAGE

Among them was Joseph Montgolfier who was given the honour of releasing a small balloon to gauge the wind strength. At 1:45 pm the brightly coloured main balloon and its baroque and gilded car rose swiftly upwards to a height of 1,800 feet.

The crowd, which hitherto had been silent, broke into a roar of approval. Charles said later: 'Nothing will ever equal that moment of joyous excitement which filled my whole being when I felt myself flying away from the earth. It was not mere pleasure; it was perfect bliss.'

Two hours later the balloon made a soft landing in open ground after a flight of twenty-seven miles. But that wasn't enough for the exhilarated Charles. He was determined to make another ascent but this time solo. Robert disembarked and Charles flew for another thirty-five minutes and three miles.

A craze for ballooning now broke out among the Paris intelligentsia. The Montgolfiers, however, resolved to go one better with an even bigger hot air balloon. When fully inflated it would be 131-feet tall, have a diameter of 104 feet and a capacity of 700,000 cubic feet.

Its launch was repeatedly delayed by damage caused by bad weather but, on 19 January 1784, the craft finally staggered into the air weighed down with a load of seven men. Further damage to the envelope cut the voyage short and the balloon was forced to descend after just fifteen minutes in the air.

The techniques of ballooning developed rapidly during 1784 culminating in a 150-mile flight by Cadet Robert and M. Collin-Hullin. The year also saw the first ascent by a man who would soon win undying fame. In August French aeronaut Jean-Pierre Blanchard decided to leave France and go to England where the competition was less intense.

Indeed, the initial reaction on the other side of the Channel to the aeronautical activities in France had been one of scepticism. Even the president of the Royal Society, Sir Joseph Banks, failed to get it. At first he saw ballooning more as a way of easing the burden of conventional earthbound transport. Attached to coaches or carts, balloons would make them lighter and easier to move.

Erasmus Darwin, the eighteenth-century physician, natural philosopher and grandfather of the better-known Charles, thought that a small balloon attached to a wheelbarrow would make it easier to transport heavy loads around his estate in Ireland. This, he suggested, would enable one man to shift ten times his normal weight in soil, wood or bricks.

But Benjamin Franklin, America's ambassador to France, concentrated minds with his suggestion that 5,000 balloons each carrying two men could carry an invading army across the Channel. He did not add that the wind would have to be blowing in the right direction to ensure success.

By that time ballooning had evolved into a professional activity with a cadre of experienced practitioners willing to take wealthy clients for a flight. Blanchard, though, wasn't the first to make a balloon ascent in Britain. Vincenzo Lunardi, a Tuscan who anglicised his Christian name to Vincent, had come to London to work for the Neapolitan ambassador.

Lunardi became interested in ballooning and raised money by public subscription to fund the construction of his first craft. After numerous false starts he made his first ascent from Moorfields, London, on 15 September 1784. It was England's first balloon ascent, the first in Britain having been made by James Tytler from Edinburgh. Then, on 4 October, Charles Sadler became the first Englishman to go aloft. Balloon madness had extended from France to Britain.

Blanchard went up for the first time from Oxford on 16 October 1784. He was accompanied by the scientist Dr John Sheldon, who had paid for the trip, a collection of scientific instruments and a small dog. The balloon was also encumbered by a pair of flapping wings made of silk stretched over a wicker work frame and a hand-operated propeller with eight-foot blades, both of which were intended to provide forward motion.

Weighed down by this gear, the craft rose sluggishly and Blanchard feared it wouldn't clear surrounding trees and buildings. His response was to throw out all of Sheldon's instruments and the balloon landed at Sunbury. There Blanchard disembarked his passenger and took off again, finally landing at Romsey in Hampshire, seventy-three miles from London. Whether or not Sheldon felt short-changed isn't recorded but he never ventured aloft again.

Blanchard was invited to dine with the Duchess of Devonshire and he arranged for a special ascent of a balloon carrying her colours. He met Joseph Banks and several influential balloon enthusiasts who had formed an unofficial balloon club. Among them was the American-born but London-domiciled John Jeffries who ran a successful medical practice in Cavendish Square.

Jeffries regarded balloon ascents as potentially part of a scientific exploration of the secrets of flight, the nature of the upper air and the formation of weather. Anxious to be elected a Fellow of the Royal Society, Jeffries set out his ideas in a paper for Banks and agreed to produce reports of his ascents for the Royal Society.

In his first flight with Blanchard, Jeffries took with him numerous scientific instruments which enabled him to collect much data about prevailing weather conditions and samples of air. The trip lasted two hours and ended in a village near Dartford. It set the two men planning a far more ambitious voyage. Which of them first suggested the idea of a cross-Channel flight isn't known but it was undoubtedly Jeffries who made all the arrangements and agreed to put up the £700 required to cover the cost of the venture.

Crossing the Channel was an obvious objective for late eighteenth century balloonists. According to Richard Holmes in *The Age of Reason*

> it carried the distinct undercurrent of an arms race: which nation could command the new element of the air in the event of an invasion? The challenge quickly became an informal national competition with attempts from both British and French sides of the water. It was seen simultaneously as a scientific, a diplomatic and a sporting battle.

The other main contenders were Pilâtre de Rozier and James Sadler. Each was struggling to get finance for the venture but foreknowledge of their plans prompted Blanchard and Jeffries to make their attempt on the channel crossing as soon as they could and before Christmas if possible. Inclement weather conditions, however, prevented this.

The voyage was delayed for several more days by the mean-spirited and cantankerous Blanchard's attempts to avoid sharing the honour of making the first aerial channel crossing with his patron. Blanchard declared it would be a solo attempt and he tried to deny Jeffries access to the craft when it arrived at Dover Castle. Jeffries responded by recruiting a gang of local heavies to force the issue, which was only resolved by the intervention of the castle's governor.

But Blanchard had another trick up his sleeve. He intended to wear a lead-weighted belt under his coat and claim that the balloon wouldn't be able to support the weight of two people. Jeffries saw though the trick and calmly asked Blanchard to dispense with his personal ballast.

In response Blanchard flatly refused to carry any scientific instruments other than a compass and a barometer. They also carried nine bags of sand ballast, anchors, cork lifejackets, a bottle of brandy, biscuits, a bag of apples and the English and French ensigns. There was also a large inflated bladder containing a number of letters described as being 'from people of the first distinction in this country to several French nobility'. The flippers or oars plus propeller which Blanchard continued to hope would enable him to steer independently of the wind were also installed.

CROSS-CHANNEL AVIATION PIONEERS

The morning of 7 January 1785 was clear and cold after a frosty night. The 9.00 am, discharge of the three guns at Dover Castle was the signal for Blanchard and Jeffries to begin inflating the balloon with hydrogen. This was to take two and a half hours during which time the cargo was added.

A contemporary account notes that the aeronauts were wearing frock coats, dimity waistcoats, nankeen britches, white silk stockings and shoes festooned with black silk ribbons. Jeffries had an expensive beaver hat to keep out the cold, together with fine chamois leather gloves to improve his grip. Blanchard was wearing a silk covered hat decorated with a small ostrich feather.

At 1.07 pm another gun was fired from the Castle – said to be the one known as Queen Elizabeth's Pocket Pistol, a cannon that was made in Utrecht in 1544 by Jan Tolhuys as a gift for King Henry VIII. The spectators who had gathered on the Castle slopes and along the seafront were hushed. Slowly the balloon rose from the Castle grounds and the crowds began to cheer. Blanchard stood up and bowed, then removed his hat

Jeffries' account of the next two hours makes light of the hazards the pair encountered during what he called 'the magnificence and beauty of our voyage'. As it happened the pre-launch shenanigans between the two aeronauts had represented a bizarre prologue to a perilous journey which had moments of high comedy. This started when both men accidentally dropped overboard each other's national flag and apologised profusely for doing so.

At first the balloon drifted eastwards over the treacherous Goodwin Sands but, as the wind changed, it headed towards Calais. But it was rising so sluggishly that it seemed unlikely it could reach France. By the time they were two-thirds of the way across the channel the aeronauts had off-loaded all their ballast and jettisoned their provisions. Five or six miles from the French coast the craft was descending rapidly towards the sea. The aeronauts had to find other ways of lightening the vessel. The wings and propeller were discarded but even that wasn't enough. As Richard Holmes wrote: 'They now began to perform a kind of aerial striptease.'

Out went what Jeffries called 'our silk and finery'. Blanchard removed his greatcoat and threw it over the side. 'I was compelled to follow his example,' Jeffries wrote later. 'He next cast away his trowsers [sic].' The pair donned their cork jackets yet, despite the seriousness of their plight, 'I believe both of us, as though inspired, felt ourselves confident of success in the event.'

THE BEAUTIFUL VOYAGE

Only the brandy and the letters remained. The aeronauts were now freezing in the January cold in just their underclothes and cork jackets. But a miracle happened. The craft was just 120 feet above the water when it steadied and began to rise again as it caught the onshore wind.

So much so, in fact, that it was carried over the French coast and, clear of the coastal updraught, the balloon began to descend rapidly towards a thick forest. A violent crash seemed inevitable but Jeffries realised the travellers had one last card they could play. 'It was contained within ourselves,' he wrote.

According to Richard Holmes, 'Seizing the leather bladders hung in the balloon's rigging as flotation devices they carefully urinated into them and threw the contents over the side.' Jeffries later claimed that they lightened the balloon by 'no less than five or six pounds.'

The next problem was landing safely. 'We landed most tranquilly,' Jeffries wrote, 'into the middle of the forest …. almost as naked as the trees, not an inch of chord or rope left, no anchor or anything to help us, nor a being within several miles.' Still wearing his chamois leather gloves, Jeffries was able to grab the branches of passing trees and bring the voyage to a gentle halt.

It took twenty-eight minutes to let the gas out of the envelope to enable the aeronauts to manoeuvre the gondola to the ground. The pair were down but too stunned and shaking with cold to congratulate each other on their achievement. Soon they were 'surrounded by footmen, horsemen &c. and received every possible assistance from them.'

The well-wishers included local magistrates who provided them with clothing to cover their nakedness. Jeffries reported being provided with a horse 'and had a fine gallop of seven miles'. The two men were invited to a grand reception in Calais town hall. Blanchard was awarded the Freedom of the town. The car from their balloon is preserved in the Calais Museum and a marble-topped balloon-shaped monument was erected at the spot in the Forêt de Guines where they landed

The aeronauts were later presented to King Louis who made Blanchard a generous cash award and awarded him a pension for life. Jeffries, the sponsor of the voyage, got nothing. The travellers later received the plaudits of the Académie des Sciences and a standing ovation at the Opera. They were personally congratulated by Pilâtre de Rozier who asked them to give a lecture at his science museum at the Rue Saint-Honoré.

The British Ambassador, the Duke of Dorset, promised Jeffries he would be elected a Fellow of the Royal Society on his return to London which he duly was. He received the Freedom of Dover and local dignitaries, including the Lord Warden, Frederick North, Earl of Guilford, suggested that a monument should be erected to both men. This never materialised. Jeffries' detailed report of the voyage for the Royal Society was published in 1786.

Two months after the flight Jeffries returned to Dover. He wrote in his diary:

> At noon visited the cliff and spot of our departure on our late aerial voyage into France. The recollection of it was awfully grand and majestick [sic] and my heart filled, I hope, with sincere and grateful acknowledgements to the kind protections of that day.

The Cross-Channel Aeronauts

On the face of it Jean-Pierre Blanchard and John Jeffries were an ill-matched pair. Yet it's possible their cross-Channel voyage may not have happened without the sharp contrasts in their characters. Where Jeffries was generous, tolerant and coolly analytical, Blanchard was selfish, cantankerous and unwilling to share the honour with his patron. He was also short in stature. Despite his unlovable character and the extravagant claims he made about some of his exploits, Blanchard was undoubtedly a skilled and brave aviator.

He was born near Rouen, France, in 1753 into an impoverished family. He became fascinated with the idea of flying from an early age but when Joseph and Jacques Montgolfier succeeded in launching the first manned balloon ascent in 1783 Blanchard became obsessed. His ambition was to cross the Channel and, by training and working hard to raise finance, he became a professional balloonist.

He came to England in 1784 thinking that it would be easier to raise money there. He met Jeffries who was a member of an influential but unofficial balloon club. Blanchard invited Jeffries to make an ascent from Grosvenor Square, which generated a great deal of interest. Spectators included the Prince of Wales, the future Prince Regent and King George IV

Jeffries was born in Boston, Massachusetts, in 1744 and later felt obliged to become an exile in London. He'd left the American colony following the trial of British soldiers implicated in the Boston 'Massacre' of 5 March 1770, when five civilians were killed and six others were injured. Jeffries had been a principal witness for the defence. The defence lawyer was John Adams, a future American president. Six of the soldiers were acquitted while two others were found guilty of manslaughter and were punished by having their hands branded. This caused a great deal of public disquiet and is said to have been one of the immediate causes of the War of Independence.

Jeffries was wealthy and had a scientific interest in the possibilities of aviation and was happy to accept Blanchard's invitation. Despite Blanchard's extraordinary attempts to cut his patron out of their venture, Jeffries did not hold it against him, at least in public. His account of their cross-Channel voyage was peppered with references – quite possibly ironic – to 'my gallant captain' and 'my little hero'. From then on Jeffries' feet remained firmly on the ground.

Not so M. Blanchard. In all, he made sixty-three balloon ascents. After his return from France, he spent some of his reward money on establishing a balloon academy in London's Stockwell Road. His attempts to attract interest through parachute descents by animals ended in failure and the wrecking of his establishment by a disappointed crowd.

Yet Blanchard did achieve many distinctions overseas. He became the first man to make balloon ascents in Germany, the Low Countries, Switzerland, Poland and Bohemia. In 1785 he set a distance record of 300 miles from Lille, France, but his biggest triumph, apart from the channel crossing, was making the first manned flight in the New World when he ascended from Philadelphia on 9 January 1793.

Blanchard died in 1809; Jeffries survived him by ten years.

Chapter Two

Unfaithful Wings

He was young, good looking, elegantly dressed and apparently fearless. In early twentieth century society he could have passed for a big game hunter, racing motorist or aviator.

In fact, Arthur Charles Hubert Latham was all three. Usually known by the last of his Christian names, Latham has gone down in aviation history as the pilot who, but for a cruel twist of fortune, could have beaten Louis Blériot to the honour of being the first to fly the English Channel in an aeroplane.

After the first aerial crossing by the Franco-American duo of Jean-Pierre Blanchard and John Jeffries in January 1785, the world had to wait another 134 years to acclaim the next cross-channel aviation pioneer.

Of the two balloonists whose ambitions to make the first cross-channel flight were frustrated by Blanchard and Jeffries, James Sadler gave up in the face of difficulties that delayed his plans. But Pilâtre de Rozier, one of the first two men to fly, did not.

Unlike Blanchard and Jeffries, de Rozier chose to cross the channel from France to England. His intention was, no doubt, to restore French prestige, although author Richard Holmes has speculated that he might also have wanted to demonstrate that Britain was vulnerable to invasion by air.

Indeed, any bellicose aspirations behind the voyage might have been heightened by the threatening appearance of the device with which de Rozier planned to make his attempt. It actually comprised two balloons in one: a spherical hydrogen-filled envelope on top of a thin, tubular hot air balloon. It was intended to combine the best features of both but its appearance was described as 'oddly menacing, like a warlike mace or club'.

Pilâtre and his co-pilot, Pierre Romain, stood in a circular gallery feeding fuel into an open brazier beneath the hot air balloon. The brazier could be lowered or jettisoned for landing or in the event of an emergency. The craft's novel design was de Rozier's answer to Blanchard and his wings and oars. But it was actually a potential death-trap combining naked flame with highly inflammable gas.

The cross-channel attempt was scheduled for 15 June 1785. But the weather was unfavourable and de Rozier's English fiancée, Susan, pleaded with him not to go. 'It is too late!' was the aeronaut's response.

At 7:15 am the balloon rose up from its launching place at Boulogne. At first it seemed to be going well as the craft reached a height of 5,000 feet. But then it seemed to hesitate and drift back towards France, losing height all the time. Watchers on the ground later reported seeing de Rozier frantically pulling on the rope that operated the gas valve on top of the balloon which appeared to have jammed open.

Sparks from the brazier twinkled around the balloon and flame was seen to appear at the top where the hydrogen was venting. Then the whole thing just folded up on itself and dropped to earth. Pilâtre de Rozier, the first man to fly, tried to jump clear at the last moment but both aeronauts were killed, their bodies horribly broken. They had come down not far from the spot where Blanchard and Jeffries had landed in triumph six months earlier. They were buried that evening in the local church yard at Wimereux.

Later speculation suggested that their loss hadn't been due to the sparks from the brazier igniting the escaping gas but to a build-up of static electricity. The valve was made of copper and the envelope, elaborately decorated with gold sheets, could well have acted as a condenser.

Whatever the cause, the first-ever fatal aviation accident sent shock waves through the scientific community and changed public attitudes to manned flight. Susan Dyer saw the wrecked balloon plunge to earth and was so overcome that she collapsed and apparently died soon afterwards. There was a suggestion that she had committed suicide because she was pregnant with de Rozier's child. Erasmus Darwin was moved to write a poem in which he compared the heroic de Rozier to 'hapless Icarus on unfaithful wings'.

The deaths of de Rozier and Romain sent shock waves through the aeronautical and scientific communities in France and Britain. In fact, it was not the only fatal ballooning accident to occur at this time and the result was that the pastime fell out of favour in Britain. From then on, any balloon flying in British skies was assumed to be French and therefore hostile, although the much-feared aerial invasion by Napoleon's army failed to materialise.

James Sadler continued his experiments and made, ultimately unsuccessful, attempts to cross the Bristol Channel and the Irish Sea.

CROSS-CHANNEL AVIATION PIONEERS

In 1817, however, Sadler's son Windham did make a successful crossing from Ireland to Wales. Seven years later Windham died in a balloon accident in the Pennines. James Sadler never flew again.

Just as the honour of making the first crossing of the English Channel became a competitive event, the first journey across the twenty-two miles of water by aeroplane also become something of a race.

A publicity-seeking firm of champagne manufacturers from the Loire valley had offered the equivalent of £500 in 1906 for the first aeroplane flight across the Channel but there was no machine capable of meeting the challenge and therefore no takers.

Lord Northcliffe, proprietor of the *Daily Mail*, later raised the stakes by offering a cash prize of £1,000 for the first heavier-than-air craft to cross the Channel. It was said that Northcliffe was obsessed with aviation. He went to the international aviation meeting at Reims in 1909, met Wilbur Wright and appointed Harry Harper as the *Daily Mail*'s air correspondent. It was a world first for the title Harmsworth had founded in 1896 and was now turning into the best-selling newspaper on the planet.

To British aviation Alfred Harmsworth, the first Viscount Northcliffe of St Peters in the County of Kent, was the individual who probably did more than any other to champion its early development. Through the cash prizes awarded by the *Daily Mail*, Northcliffe inspired the early aviators to ever greater efforts. Among them was the £10,000 offered for the first flight from London to Manchester, the £1,000 for the first cross-channel flight and the £10,000 for the first non-stop crossing of the Atlantic.

Latham's biographer, Barbara Walsh, believed Northcliffe's motive was as much political as journalistic. She was convinced that the British authorities were blind to the 'frailty of the safety barrier of high seas that lay between them and Europe'. Walsh wrote that

> For too long, public representatives had assumed that British invulnerability could never be shattered by an airborne attack from a foreign power, particularly Germany, and it was high time their complacency was shattered. In truth, once the first aviator conquered the straits, Northcliffe's favourite slogan, 'England is no longer an island' would be proven without doubt.

He took every opportunity to deliver this message and jolt the country out of its lethargy through the columns of his newspaper. As a result, recipients of the *Mail*'s largesse would include such great names of pioneer aviation as Louis Paulhan, Louis Blériot, John Moore-Brabazon, Thomas Sopwith, John Alcock and Arthur Whitten Brown and Amy Johnson.

Between 1910 and 1930 the *Mail* handed out over £60,000 in prize money. Some of the losers also received consolation awards like the £5,000 which went to Harry Hawker and Kenneth Mackenzie Grieve for the gallant failure of their bid for the trans-Atlantic prize in 1919. Three of the winners of *Daily Mail* prizes, Alliott Verdon Roe (Avro), Sopwith and Hawker would become aircraft manufacturers.

In 1909 there were three contenders for the *Mail*'s cash. They were Louis Blériot, Hubert Latham and Comte Charles de Lambert. The favourite was probably Latham. He was born in Paris, the son of an English father and a French mother, and was educated in Paris and at Oxford. Lionel Latham, scion of a family with numerous successful trading enterprises, married Magdeleine Mallet, daughter of one of the most prestigious banking families in France in 1880. Hubert was their second child.

He was introduced to ballooning by his cousin, Jacques Faure. Early in 1905 the pair began making plans to fly from London to Paris. Their intention to use a small petrol engine for steering was frustrated by customs officers' demand for them to pay an excessive export levy for it.

They began their journey at 6:45 pm on Saturday 11 February from Crystal Palace. They took off into a bright but bitterly cold moonlit night. Within an hour they had reached the coast at Hastings but their height diminished as they crossed the sea and by the time the French coast came in sight they were so low that balloon's guide rope was dragging in the water.

Once they had crossed the coast Faure and Latham, cold and tired, considered landing then and there but, after a discussion, they resolved to continue to their original destination. By 1:00 am they could see the lights of Paris. Latham was all for a spectacular ending to the voyage by landing in the centre of the capital in the Place de la Concorde. But, mindful of the hazards posed by tall buildings, the more experienced Faure insisted that they land outside the city, on the plain at Aubervilliers. They had completed the journey in the record time of six hours and thirty minutes.

Paris greeted the pair of aeronauts as heroes. The Aero Club de France threw a reception for them and speeches were made comparing their exploit with that of Blanchard and Jeffries.

Meantime, Latham's family was urging him to settle down in a respectable profession but Faure introduced him to the Antoinette Motor Company and the eccentric but gifted engineer Léon Levavasseur. This was to be a turning point in Latham's life.

The company had been founded by industrialist Jules Gastambide in 1906 with himself as president and Levavasseur as technical director. The red-bearded engineer designed the world's first V8 engine, a liquid-cooled unit originally intended for aeronautical use but later used in speedboats. As the engine had been financed by Gastambide, Levavasseur suggested that the engine be named after his patron's daughter, Antoinette.

Levavasseur experimented with the construction of aircraft and in 1906 the Antoinette Company was contracted to build a machine for pioneer airman Captain Ferdinand Ferber. Louis Blériot was a vice-president of the company but quit in 1908 when his protests that building aircraft would put Antoinette in competition with its customers were ignored.

Latham had become associated with Antoinette initially to assist with trials of a new racing speedboat but when the company entered the flying training business, based at an army camp at Châlons, he was one of its first pupils.

According to Barbara Walsh, Latham was an excellent front man for the Antoinette Company. 'So,' she observed,

> when they were looking for someone who could be their PR man, head up their sales campaign for their aeroplane and make a bid for the Channel flight they called on Latham and asked if he'd like to fly an aeroplane.

The school incorporated a rudimentary flight simulator comprising half a barrel mounted on a universal joint with flight controls, pulleys and poles projecting from either side to provide balance while the instructors applied external force. On 17 August 1909 Latham was awarded Aviator's Certificate number 9 by the Aero Club de France. Within months of learning to fly Latham had become the company's principal instructor. His pupils included a cousin of King Alfonso of Spain who became his country's first military pilot.

By the spring of 1909 the Antoinette Company's experiments with aircraft had resulted in a large, graceful monoplane designed by Levavasseur. The pilot was perched on rather than in the narrow fuselage and therefore exposed to the full blast of the airstream. Latham made several impressive flights in this aircraft. In May 1909, three months after joining the company, he flew for 37.5 minutes at a speed of 45 mph at a height of just over 98 feet. A week later he set the European non-stop flight record at an hour and seven minutes which seriously challenged the Wrights' world record.

During this flight he took his hands off the steering wheel, took a cigarette out of his silver case and calmly smoked it in an ivory holder. This delighted Levavasseur because it demonstrated the machine's stability. Then, on 6 June, Latham won the *Prix Ambroise Goupy* for flying a straight-line course of nearly four miles in four minutes, thirteen seconds.

These flights convinced Levavasseur that Latham was his best pilot. Furthermore, based on the length of the flights Latham was conducting, Levavasseur was satisfied that his Antoinette IV monoplane was sufficiently reliable for a forty-five-minute to one-hour continuous flight and could therefore attempt to fly across the English Channel

Latham was also confident of his ability to fly the Channel. On 11 July he gave the *Daily Mail* the required twenty-four-hours notice of his intention to make the attempt. 'When it is actually realised,' observed the journal *Flight*,

> that a man has seriously notified his intention of attempting to achieve a feat which has never before been accomplished in the history of the world and of doing so within 24 hours, the project comes from the clouds with a run, and it is, indeed, no wonder that Calais and Dover should have been seething with excitement ever since.

The *Mail*'s Harry Harper was among the journalists who gathered at Sangatte near Calais where Latham had established his base. The former theatre critic had been instructed to install himself in Calais' Terminus Hotel for as long as necessary to cover the story. Harper recalled in 1949 that Latham 'always flew with such abandon that one French journalist wrote that every time he went up he had "death at his elbow"'.

The British newspapers went to great lengths to assure their readers that Latham spoke English with the ease of someone born to it and that he had completed his education at Oxford. According to Barbara Walsh,

> Puffing up such stories allowed their aeronautical correspondents to appeal to their readers' partisanship and public opinion was soon swayed into taking this young man into their hearts. Here was a stalwart son of Anglo-Saxon descent, his blood only slightly diluted on his mother's side and whom the British could claim to be as good as their very own.

Further down the coast from Sangatte, de Lambert had set up his camp at Wissant, accompanied by his wife and daughter. There he had assembled his two Wright Flyers, No. 2 and No. 18. He had been one of Wilbur Wright's first pupils at the flying school he established at Pau. According to *Flight*, he was 'indifferent' to the *Daily Mail* prize. The journal reported: 'The count has no intention of unduly hurrying his attempt at crossing and intends to practise very thoroughly in the vicinity before he steers for England.' *The Times* reported that the count was keeping his plans 'more or less secret'.

Indeed, de Lambert seems to have been something of a mystery figure. He was said to have been a member of an aristocratic French family who fled the country at the time of the revolution. His wife had connections to the English aristocracy. 'Those in the know,' wrote Barbara Walsh

> reckoned it was not altogether surprising that he and Latham were now setting themselves up as sporting rivals for the *Daily Mail* prize. They both belonged to the same elite crowd of socialites which had competed for motor yacht prizes in the 1905 Monaco Regatta at the time Latham first put the Antoinette engines through her paces so successfully.

But de Lambert was, by the standards of the day, an accomplished and experienced aviator. In March 1909 he had flown a Wright machine for just over twenty-five kilometres in twenty-seven minutes and in July set a record by flying between Juvisy aerodrome and Paris in fifty-nine minutes and thirty-nine seconds.

However, he soon eliminated himself from the cross-Channel race by crashing one of his machines and failing to prepare the other in time. *The Times* reported that another competitor, Arthur Seymour, had declared his intention of making the Channel crossing. 'Mr Seymour is said to have purchased a Voisin aeroplane but it is regarded as doubtful if he will make an attempt to cross the Channel.' Barbara Walsh dismissed him as 'a complete novice and still taking flying lessons'.

For a while Latham, therefore, seemed to have the field to himself. But what about the Wright brothers? They appeared to be obvious front-runners, having flown for thirty-eight minutes, enough for a Channel crossing. But they weren't interested. In 2009 aviation historian Philip Jarrett told the BBC

> The Wright brothers weren't into flying for prizes or taking unnecessary risks, so they weren't going to do it. At the end

of 1908 when the prize was first offered there probably wasn't anyone else who could have done it – which shows that Lord Northcliffe was far sighted. But, by the middle of the next year, there were two or three people who had a reasonable chance of doing it – but only two or three people in the whole world.

Latham made several practice flights in his Antoinette VI and on one occasion crash-landed in a cornfield. This damaged his machine but not severely. Soon it was only the need for favourable weather that was holding up Latham's cross-Channel flight and gaining the honour he coveted.

Latham's extensive family connections gave him access to valuable assistance on both sides of the Channel. The French navy put a warship at his disposal and Latham was able to charter from the Port of Calais a rescue tug called *Le Calaisien* which was equipped to haul him and his machine on board should the worst happen during the flight.

Flight reported that Latham's chosen landing place was Rope Walk Meadow on Shakespeare Cliff, Dover. But for two telegraph poles this location was described as 'fairly convenient'. The town's mayor was said to have postponed an overseas trip so as to be present to welcome the successful flyer. The British Motor Boat Club had made arrangements to patrol the course in English waters. The Royal Aero Club also offered to provide a rescue tug.

Sir William Crandall, chairman of the Dover Harbour Board, also promised help. His son had been friendly with Latham when they were up at Oxford. Crandall senior told the *Daily Mail*:

> I know him [Latham] very well. He is a dear, good fellow, modest and unassuming, as plucky as possible and one of the best motor drivers in the world. If I was a betting man I would put my money on him ... .

Latham, however, was a betting man. He told *The Times'* reporter that six months earlier, before he had learned to fly his Antoinette, he had laid a wager that he would win the *Daily Mail* prize. The size of the bet was apparently not reported.

The weather remained unfavourable for many days and Latham had to renew his intention to compete for the *Daily Mail* prize. The crowds gathered daily in the hope of seeing Latham make his bid. On one occasion a spectator remarked to his wife and children that 'Latham has the jitters'. The aviator heard him, instantly swung round and delivered a well-directed uppercut that sent the man sprawling. Latham calmly lit a cigarette and declared: 'I'm not a showman. I never asked you to come here. Now get out of my field!'

After many weary days of waiting, 'which taxed the patience of aviator and spectators to the utmost,' *Flight* reported

> the weather was at last propitious for an attempt on Monday 19 July and at 20 minutes past 6 in the morning, three guns booming from the destroyer *Harpon* [other reports say it was a torpedo boat and give the name as *Harpoon* or *Tarpon*] which was steaming at half-speed below the cliffs at Sangatte, definitely informed all concerned that M. Levavasseur, who was on board, had decided that conditions were good enough, and that the flight should be made.

A major innovation was the wireless service between Sangatte and the roof of the Lord Warden Hotel, Dover, provided by the Marconi company. A 4:30 am on Tuesday 19 July the weather on both sides of the Channel was reported to be misty but about half an hour later conditions were improving noticeably. By 5:48 they were reported as 'nearly ideal' although there was still some mist.

Ten minutes later Antoinette VI was wheeled out of its shed and prepared for the flight. By 6:12 am it was being pushed along the road to the starting point at Blanc Nez. Latham, clad in a blue knitted jersey and goggles, mounted his aircraft and took off for England. *Flight* reported that 'the machine, after running down the slope at Blanc Nez, at last disappeared from sight and by the half hour, had all been well, he would have been on the point of landing at Dover'.

The wireless messages between Sangatte and Dover succinctly unfold the story:

> Sangatte, 6:42 am– He has gone.
> Sangatte, 6:46 am– He is making wide sweeping circles.
> Sangatte, 6:50 am– He is out of sight…
> Sangatte, 6:53 am– Look out for him and tell us at once.
> Dover, 7:23 am– Anything yet?

Latham had climbed to 1,000 feet and was passing the *Harpoon*. He tried to photograph the ship but his engine started to misfire. He tried all the electrical connections within his reach as well as the fuel and air supplies to the engine. It was in vain. He had to bring his aircraft down on the water to as smooth a landing as he could manage. He had flown for no more than eight miles from the French coast.

In a 1951 *Flight* article, aviation historian Colin Boyle noted,

> It was characteristic of Latham that he had made no effort to see if the monoplane would float or not; he had merely assumed that it would. Fortunately, the event proved him correct; in the calm sea it floated easily and while he waited to be rescued, he again casually rolled and smoked a cigarette. He was taken dry-shod from the cockpit of the Antoinette.

The Times reported that

> The intrepid aviator, safely sitting on the wing, plucked out of the sea while quietly smoking a cigarette. He had escaped possible disaster with nothing worse than a pair of wet boots.... Far from being a failure, this safe drop to the sea from a height of some 150 ft marks one of the most brilliant achievements in the history of aviation!

The machine was in the water for about half an hour before it was hoisted aboard *Le Calaisien*. Latham himself had been rescued by the *Harpoon*. Both vessels returned to Calais where, according to *Flight*, 'the aviator received a welcome of tremendous enthusiasm, being called upon, among other things, to kiss the queen of the port, a buxom, red cheeked fisher-girl'.

Later, Latham told *The Times* reporter the story of his flight

> I was about 600ft above sea level when leaving land and gradually attained an altitude of 1,000ft, my speed being from 40 to 45 mph. I had travelled about seven miles out to sea when the engine stopped and I was obliged to glide down, which I did in one straight line without undulations. I struck the water so gently that only a tiny splash was caused and I merely felt some spray in my face. The machine floated splendidly, as I expected, and I kept my feet dry by raising them on the framework. After a few minutes the *Harpoon*'s

boat came to me bringing ropes which I fastened above and below the centre of gravity and then we towed the aeroplane alongside the destroyer.

The machine was salvaged. Subsequent examination of the engine showed that a piece of wire had worked its way into it and caused the misfire. The aircraft itself was badly damaged. That evening, Latham was back in Paris demanding that the Antoinette Company provide him with a replacement.

Latham had wasted little time in getting Antoinette VII assembled at Sangatte following its arrival on 21 July. It was similar to its predecessor but had a bigger engine and wings. It had never been properly tested, although Latham did take the opportunity of a brief flight while he waited for the weather to improve.

On the morning of 25 July Leon Levavasseur had risen at 2:00 am and again at 3:00 but had not thought the weather suitable for another attempt and did not, therefore, wake Latham. Accordingly, the pilot was not roused until 5:00.

The following day's *Times* reported that Levavasseur had confiscated Latham's alarm clock to ensure he got a good night's sleep. 'Incredible as it may sound,' the newspaper noted

> though there was flat calm at 3 o'clock, M. Levavasseur did not apparently realise the fact and allowed M. Latham to sleep on. At 4 o'clock he again completely misjudged the weather conditions and the thing ended in M. Latham's not being aroused until 5 o'clock, 20 minutes after M. Blériot had actually left the coast of France and just as the breeze began to rise with the sun. The man who had undoubtedly led the van in the attempt to fly across the Channel was thus robbed of a splendid chance of carrying out his project.

According to Harry Harper, Levavasseur woke up just in time to see Blériot's monoplane leaving the French coast. He rushed to wake Latham and his crew to see if it might be possible to catch Blériot. By the time Antoinette VII was ready to take off, a gusty wind had risen, accompanied by heavy rains. Harper wrote: 'Any attempt at a take-off would have been nothing less than suicidal.'

Latham was bitterly disappointed but he sent a telegram to his rival congratulating him on his success and saying he hoped to join him at

Dover shortly. Blériot replied with the sporting offer of sharing the prize money with Latham if he could get across the Channel that day.

Boyle wrote: 'This Latham was only too anxious to do but Levavasseur restrained him for the wind had now risen again. Blériot had seized the only interval in several days of storm.' It was one of several pieces of good luck enjoyed by Bleriot that day.

Two days later the weather cleared and late in the afternoon, Latham set out on his second attempt to fly the English Channel. The news of his departure was transmitted to Dover where 40,000 people were said to have gathered on the cliffs to watch him land. When he was spotted approaching the English coast the ships sounded their sirens and the crowd cheered itself hoarse. But fortune was still against Hubert Latham.

With success almost within his grasp the Antoinette engine failed again and once more he was forced to land in the sea, almost at the foot of the white cliffs of Dover. It was another heroic failure. This time he suffered injuries. The machine landed heavily in the choppy water and Latham was thrown forward on impact, hitting a strut. His goggles were smashed and shards of glass cut deeply into his nose and forehead. After his rescue he was attended by Dr J.C. Ridgway, house surgeon from Dover Hospital, who put five stitches into his face.

Almost another year would pass before the Channel was flown again. Latham was keen to make yet another attempt but the directors of the Antoinette Company had already spent a large sum of money on the cross-Channel project and lost two machines. They were not inclined to risk a third venture, particularly as the world's first aviation meeting at Reims was imminent and they wanted to send all their available machines there.

In fact, Latham participated in twelve other competitions throughout Europe and, in late 1910 and early 1911, four in the United States at Baltimore, Los Angeles, San Francisco and New York. There he participated in the second Gordon Bennett International Gold Cup race as a member of the French team. This represented the first competitive outing for the improved Antoinette VII powered by a 100 hp V-16 engine.

Latham's attempts on the Channel may have been fruitless but they transformed him into a heroic figure whose coolness and recklessness made him the idol of the crowds. At the Reims aviation meeting of August 1909 he took the altitude record, albeit with a modest 508 feet, although he claimed to have reached over 1,000 feet. He also made a flight of ninety-six miles – Henri Farman beat him with a flight of 112 miles – and he set a record for the 100 kilometres (62 miles) closed circuit, which he covered at an average speed of 42 mph.

The success of this meeting inspired several others. In October 1909 two were held in England, at Doncaster and at Blackpool. Equinoctial gales were blowing, however, and for two days there was no flying at all. Latham was at Blackpool where he was the star of the show. As the crowd grew restive due to the lack of activity, Latham announced that he would take up his Antoinette.

The wind was blowing at over 20 mph and gusting at up to more than 40. The other aviators tried to persuade Latham not to go up but he was determined to fly. With some difficulty he got his machine into the air. Spectators and pilots watched in horrified admiration as Latham circled the field, his big monoplane shivering in the gusts that blew across the field. At times he was scarcely making any headway against the wind but with it he approached 100 mph. This flight made Latham the hero of the meeting.

He continued his attempts on the height record and, by the end of 1909, had raised the world figure to 1,485 feet. According to aviation historian Colin Boyle, writing in *Flight* in 1951,

> he was now, beyond all doubt, the pilot of the year. He had learned to fly only in February, but his two great attempts on the Channel crossing, his magnificent rough-weather flying at Blackpool, and his repeated raising of the height record made him the darling of the crowds who attended the flying meetings.

Despite his daredevil approach to aviation Latham did not meet his end in a flying accident as might have been expected. In 1912 he was big game hunting in the French Congo when he was killed in circumstances that have never been satisfactorily established. The official version is that his rifle jammed at a critical moment and that he was tossed three times by a wounded buffalo. It seemed that luck had again deserted him at a critical moment.

Although Latham is the forgotten hero of pioneer aviation, he made a significant contribution to its development. 'We should acknowledge that Latham made his mark,' wrote Barbara Walsh.

A statue was later erected at Cap Blanc Nez from where Hubert Latham had come very close to achieving real immortality. The fact was, though, that Louis Blériot's luck was a lot better than his.

The Antoinette Monoplanes

The Antoinette Monoplane made famous by Hubert Latham and his exploits was an elegant machine with some novel features. These included its V8 engine and use of wing dihedral.

The fuselage featured a V-shaped cross-section and resembled a narrow boat hull tapered at both ends. It consisted of a lattice girder, the fore part of which was covered with a veneer of sheet cedar. The section behind the pilot's seat was covered in rubber-proofed fabric which extended over the top side of the fuselage to form a kind of flat deck. The machine was supported on the ground by a pair of small pneumatic-tyred wheels attached to an axle with pneumatic suspension. An ash skid projected forward to prevent the propeller blades hitting the ground. A light skid at the rear, also made of ash, protected the lower rudder.

The tail consisted of two fixed planes and three moveable ones to provide rudder and elevator control. The rudders were mounted above and below the horizontal tail plane.

The pilot controlled the aircraft using two hand wheels vertically mounted each side of the seat. The right-hand wheel operated the elevators, while the one on the left operated the wing warping to control roll. The rudders were operated by foot controls. Two smaller wheels adjacent to the main ones adjusted engine throttle and ignition.

The large, thick wings were built up on two transverse main spars with a framework of transverse ribs concave in section and spaced about eighteen inches apart. The spars were constructed on the lattice-girder principle and were attached to the fuselage by substantial metal brackets. The rear pair were pivoted to allow for wing warping. Further support was provided by wires attached at one end to a wooden post projecting up from the fuselage ahead of the pilot and at the other to the main wing spars. Upper and lower wing surfaces were covered in rubber-proofed fabric.

The machine's designer, Leon Levavasseur, had opted for the stability provided by a modest degree of wing dihedral even though the principle had been eschewed by other constructors. The Wright brothers had used dihedral in their early gliders but abandoned it in later designs.

Antoinette monoplanes were powered by water-cooled V8 engines although V16s were also used. The cylinders were separate steel forgings and were complete with head and valve chamber. They were encased in copper water jackets.

A feature of the design was that very little water was carried, the idea being that it would be allowed to convert into steam and condensed back into water by a tubular aluminium condenser mounted outside the fuselage. The fuselage covering was cut away to facilitate air circulation around the radiator.

The engine itself was mounted at the front of the fuselage and supported by a pair of transverse girders. The crank chamber was cast in such a way as to extend it to the propeller boss. The two-bladed six-feet diameter propeller was fastened directly to the crankshaft.

Specification – Antoinette VII
Length 40 ft
Wingspan 46 ft
Wing area 365 sq. ft
Height from centre of propeller boss 6 ft 9 in.
Weight without pilot 1,040lb
Powerplant Antoinette water-cooled V8.

Chapter Three

'Which Way is Dover?'

It was 05:20 hr on Sunday 25 July 1909 and history had just been made.

And legends were about to be created. For there was a great deal of what we would now call 'spin' given to the story, which means, over a century later, it's sometimes difficult to separate fact from fiction.

Had the first man to cross the English Channel by aeroplane really asked the way to Dover before taking off from France? Had his engine been cooled at a critical point in the flight by a fortuitous shower of rain, enabling him to continue? Was he really met at Dover by a customs official concerned that the world's first international overwater air traveller might have brought contraband with him?

But whichever way you looked at it, the main facts were clear enough: the dapper little man with the sad eyes and droopy moustache had done it. Louis Blériot had proved that Britain was no longer an island. He had just made, one newspaper, declared, 'the flight that changed the world'.

And underlying the achievement was the fact that Blériot was not only a man of many parts – businessman, aviator, designer and constructor – but also one who combined a fierce determination with the instincts of a gambler. For Blériot had taken neither map nor compass with him. His plan had been to steer in what he reckoned to be the right direction for Dover. And he was well aware that the little three-cylinder engine he was relying on to keep him airborne was far from reliable.

Harry Harper, the *Daily Mail*'s air correspondent, reported that the engine had never run for longer than about twenty minutes without overheating and losing power. But Harper, who was in France to cover the flight, also recalled that, 'Blériot's luck as a pioneer had always been proverbial. He had emerged safely from crash after crash in experimental machines'.

The big gamble certainly paid off. Just over thirty-six minutes after leaving France, Louis Blériot had written his name indelibly in the history books when he came down near Dover castle.

It was far from a perfect landing – the machine suffered a broken undercarriage and propeller – but then Blériot's total flying experience wouldn't have been enough for him to be allowed to go solo had he been learning to fly today.

Yet he had crossed twenty-two miles of sea in a flimsy wire-braced machine with bicycle wheels and a wheezy motor-cycle engine with little more than two-thirds the power of a Morris Minor.

Even so, in the weeks leading up to his historic cross-Channel journey, Blériot had been preparing with a series of long flights. He remained aloft for fifty minutes at a meeting at Juvisy aerodrome watched by a crowd estimated at 10,000, although the flight was terminated by fuel starvation. Later, he flew from Étampes to Artenay, a distance of twenty-five miles, and then from Douai to Arras and back. Another flight, from Douai in his monoplane, was cut short after twenty minutes when his motor started misfiring.

In its issue of 17 July 1909, *Flight* reported on Blériot's longest cross-country flight to date, which, the journal observed, had been undertaken in an 'almost casual manner'. Blériot had flown the twenty-five miles from Orleans to Étampes, albeit with one brief stop to prove that he could land and take off again, in a time of forty-four minutes. During this flight he passed the Bordeaux express train. The journal noted that

> Heads were thrust out of carriage windows, first in alarm, then in amazement as the astonished occupants had the experience of witnessing under unique conditions the new locomotion which needs neither road nor rail. It was an inspiring moment as Blériot, gracefully increasing his altitude to clear the telegraph wires, sailed calmly over the railway high above the train, waving his hand to the excited and cheering passengers.

Before his cross-Channel flight, Blériot established himself at Les Baraques, a small village just outside Calais. He was accompanied by his wife and Alfred Leblanc, a balloonist who had assumed the duties of manager, Anzani, manufacturer of the engine and several mechanics.

Alice Blériot supported her husband loyally but she was unhappy about his aerial activities and was generally in tears when he was flying. It was also stated that during his final trial flights before the cross-Channel attempt Blériot had injured his leg and this was still causing him pain on the morning of the flight. In fact, he was seen to be walking with the aid of a stick. There was also a story that arch-rival Hubert Latham had overslept and missed the opportunity to steal a march on Blériot with a second attempt.

Inevitably, there was a substantial press corps camped on the coast eager for any snippets of information to pass on to their readers. Among them was the *Mail*'s Harry Harper who had been there for five weeks. Although he didn't know it at the time, Harper was about to make history himself. The Marconi Company had been given permission to create a wireless station on the French coast with a tall pole supporting an aerial. From there messages were relayed to a corresponding station on the roof of the Lord Warden Hotel at Dover.

It was the first to be operated in connection with a pioneer aeroplane flight and had already been used during Latham's first cross-Channel attempt a few days earlier. Perched on the roof of a building overlooking the beach at Les Baraques (now Blériot Plage), almost halfway between Calais and Sangatte, Harper was about to make the first-ever outside wireless broadcast. 'What I was saying,' he wrote forty years later, 'was immediately wirelessed to Dover and from there went straight on by 'phone to newspaper offices in London.'

Harper said:

> I 'phoned down to the Marconi man below brief word pictures of the scene I was watching – how Blériot was now seated in his cockpit, how his little three-cylinder Anzani air-cooled motor was being run up, and how the airman was just now taking off on a trial flight.

Blériot's machine had been accommodated in a tent a mile or so away and Harper watched as it was wheeled to the starting point by several helpers. Blériot himself, clad in cork jacket, overalls and a cloth flying helmet, was standing in the cockpit holding on to one of the kingposts that supported the wing and directing operations.

The trial flight, between Les Baraques and Sangatte, had convinced Blériot that the time was right for the attempt. There was a wind blowing and the weather was far from ideal with, he estimated, gusts of 10 knots. Off Dover the breeze was reported to be double this speed with cliff currents said to be particularly strong. In mid-Channel the winds had dropped. In consultation with Alfred Leblanc, Bleriot decided there was just time for him to make the flight before conditions made it impossible.

Flight observed that

> taking the weekend as a whole, it has been one of the windiest periods of a particularly unsettled summer, and the previous day had in particular seemed hopeless for any cross-Channel flight. Half a gale had indeed been blowing and a heavy sea running only a few hours before, and hence it is hardly to be wondered at that the feat was as totally unexpected as it was.

Blériot had, indeed, set off almost without warning although there had been an enthusiastic crowd present to cheer him on his way. Generally, though, 'the world and his wife were mostly abed', particularly on the English side of the Channel. Blériot had risen at 02:30hrs feeling, *Flight* reported, 'not very well'. He had taken a short car ride to clear his head and that was why 'he was able to snatch the one brief fine moment that presented itself between the daytime storms of Saturday and Sunday'.

Meanwhile, Blériot's wife had boarded the escorting French torpedo boat, the *Escopette*. There had been a row between Latham and Bleriot about which of the escort vessels, the *Escopette* or the *Harpoon* which was to shadow Latham, should leave harbour first. Latham's biographer, Dr Barbara Walsh, says that at one point Blériot insisted the matter be resolved by calling the Minister of Marine.

Walsh wrote that, just before midnight, with the flights just hours away, a compromise was reached. The *Escopette*'s captain was to be ready to put to sea by 02:00hr when he received a message that one of the aviators was ready to take off. He would then follow whichever was the first aviator to take off.

Although no precise timings were apparently recorded – the aviator had no watch – Blériot was airborne at 04:35 local time (on his timing, accounts differ). He had soon outdistanced the *Escopette* and found himself on his own for ten minutes. The weather became turbulent and visibility declined. Blériot later recalled thinking: 'I'm alone. I can see nothing at all.' He was even more terse in the sketch map he later drew for the *Mail*, using just one word to describe his predicament at this time: 'Rien.'

The log of wireless messages exchanged between Sangatte and Dover noted that:

> 04:36 – Blériot has started; look out for him. We saw him at 04:35. He started from Le Baraques

'WHICH WAY IS DOVER?'

    04:40 – He is nearly halfway across
    04:47 – He has outdistanced the boat
    04:50 – He is out of sight of French coast.

Harry Harper said that Blériot told him later how, that just he was nearing mid-Channel, good fortune came to his aid again.

> His engine began to show the familiar symptoms and the monoplane started to lose altitude, the waves of the Channel drawing unpleasantly close below. But just when things were looking really serious a rainstorm swept up the Channel and the colder rain helped to cool the overheated little engine.

Under the circumstances Blériot had done the only thing possible and carried straight on. What he didn't know was that he was being blown eastwards in a loop which would result in a landfall near Deal, further up the coast than he'd planned. Turning west, he flew along the coast towards Dover to a gap in the cliffs where his friend Charles Fontaine of *Le Matin* was waving a large Tricolour. This gap led to the pre-arranged landing place at Northfall Meadow which was a short distance from the walls of Dover castle. This flag would accompany Blériot for the rest of the day and would figure in many of the photographs of him after his achievement.

Meanwhile, the wind had been rising all the time and was now blowing in heavy gusts. One of these caught Blériot just as he was landing with the result that he came down rather heavily, damaging his undercarriage and breaking his propeller. It was, by the aviator's own reckoning, 05:12 hr. It would be another twenty minutes before rumours that Blériot had landed had reached the wireless station at Sangatte.

At Dover Blériot remained seated in his cockpit as seagulls wheeled overhead and he quietly contemplated what had just happened. Few were up and about that early on a Sunday morning but several people said later that they'd heard the sound of the machine's engine before they spotted the machine itself.

The night watchman at the Premier Pier told *The Daily Telegraph*

> I suddenly saw a peculiar object away to the eastward, moving very rapidly across the sky. As it came closer I could hear the whirring of the motor and I judged that it was one of the flying men who had made a start and had practically got across.

The chief officer of the local coastguard station said that he could hear a 'continual buzzing' when the machine was several miles away. When it did come into view 'the speed was almost incredible'. As it happened, PC John Stanford and a few soldiers from the nearby garrison were among the few eyewitnesses to the landing of Blériot's machine. Even M. Fontaine had not actually been there to see it.

There was, though, one who watched the historic arrival but one remained silent for ninety-four years when Bridget Toynbee shared her recollections of the day with the author in a hundredth birthday interview for the journal *Pilot*. She said: 'The day before, my mother said to our coachman: "will you get up very early tomorrow and bring round the brougham."' The next morning, she was roused early, dressed in warm clothes and sent off. 'I was wrapped in a shawl and all alone with the coachman – my mother was tending to my sister who was very ill,' Bridget told the author.

They drove the five miles from the family home at Ringwold, where Bridget's father was a magistrate, to a field near Dover Castle. 'I seemed to be the only child there,' she remembered. She said

> Then there was this extraordinary noise: wheeeeee! And out of the sky came a monstrous bird which landed beautifully in this big field. Out came a little man dressed in leather – leather coat and goggles – but I don't remember a hat or a helmet. The worst thing about it was that when we got home and told what we had seen nobody believed us!

Looking back, Bridget realised that her father must have been aware that something momentous was about to happen – the whole area was buzzing with rumours of the forthcoming flight – and wanted at least one member of his family to see it happen. 'It was wonderful to have been there to witness that historic event,' Bridget added.

When Blériot returned to Calais aboard the *Escopette* that evening, he told Harry Harper all about the flight. 'I remember him saying how amused he had been when, soon after he landed at Dover, a decidedly worried looking Customs officer had appeared on the scene complete with a batch of forms,' the reporter recalled forty years later. He wrote

> he wanted to make certain Blériot had not brought any contraband goods across the Channel and one of the forms the airman was called upon to sign was to the effect that

the 'vessel' of which he was described as 'the master', was free from anything in the nature of infectious diseases.

Flight reported that there were several customs men on the scene and that they had 'very properly' been among the first to accost the pilot 'after his unconventional descent on British soil'. The journal added: 'With fitting forbearance, however, they recognised that it was only "one of those flying men" and therefore made no attempt at an inspection for contraband.'

The journal also estimated that, allowing for his involuntary diversion, Bleriot had flown a distance of thirty-one miles and that his average speed had been about 45 mph. His height above the sea had varied between 150 and 300 feet. This was much lower than Latham's altitude during his first attempt. Bleriot believed that, shortly after take-off, his speed had been nearly 50 mph, which moved *Flight* to comment that only an experienced pilot would feel safe at such a velocity. Safety, it observed

> lies in speed, there is much reason to believe, but that is a different kind of safety, and is hardly in the reckoning if the pilot himself is not at home in the air under such conditions. M. Blériot is now a master of the upper element but he worked hard for his degree; on no occasion has his knowledge and skill stood him in better stead than during his Channel flight, for there he met with difficulties which must surely have brought a less experienced pilot to sad grief.

The journal was less sure about the aviator's safety precautions, arguing that there should have been more rescue vessels stations in mid Channel. 'To this extent,' it noted

> M. Blériot's flight may possibly be regarded as somewhat foolhardy, and the fact that he so quickly outpaced [his escort] certainly rendered his position extremely hazardous had any accident happened; M. Blériot himself admits as much. But fortune favoured him so that he kept his course.

As news of Blériot's achievement spread so more crowds gathered around his aircraft and its landing place. The aviator became concerned for the safety of his machine and, later in the day, Eddie King of the Dover Marquee company had a tent erected to cover it. The public was charged 6d [3p] for admission to view it and the proceeds, amounting to £60, were donated to a local charity.

Flight noted that

> on retiring to bed on Saturday night, it is certainly no exaggeration to estimate that not more than one man in a thousand in these islands, or for that matter, throughout the world, really credited in his heart of hearts the possibility of aeroplaning across the Channel during the recent summer. By mid-day on Monday, at latest, the continents of North and South America, of Australia, Europe, and the leading centres in Asia, were agog with the news of the actual realisation of that ambition.

The following day the machine was taken to London to be exhibited at Selfridge's department store in Oxford Street. The astute H. Gordon Selfridge, ever alert to publicity opportunities, had done a deal with the *Daily Mail* to allow members of the public to see the aircraft which had just crossed the Channel. He agreed to pay £200 to the charity of the newspaper's choice, the London Hospital.

By 10:00 hr on the day after the historic flight the machine was on view in the newly opened store's sports, motor requisites and motor clothing department. It was estimated that at least 120,000 people had filed past it – 18,000 on Monday, 26,000 on Tuesday, 36,000 on Wednesday and 40,000 on Thursday. On Wednesday a party of MPs visited the store and spent a considerable time examining the machine. It remained on display until the Thursday after the cross-Channel flight. It was also displayed at the White City.

Later it was whisked away to Paris where it was suspended outside the offices of *Le Matin*, which had supported Blériot. The newspaper later bought the machine for 10,000 francs to 'place at the disposal of the State'. It emerged that Blériot had received offers of ten times as much from potential buyers in England.

Press coverage of Louis Blériot's exploit was extensive on both sides of the Channel. In France it was ecstatic as each newspaper's account of the journey endeavoured to outdo the next with leading articles hailing the flight as a great French victory. *The Times* noted that Paris had been overwhelmed by 'Blériot fever' and that everything else had been forgotten, including the appointment of a new cabinet.

'WHICH WAY IS DOVER?'

Inevitably, the French press compared Blériot's achievement with those of other notable Gallic pioneers like Jean-Pierre Blanchard who had been the first to fly the Channel, Zedee, inventor of the submarine, as well as Pasteur and Curie.

Coverage was no less muted in Britain, although the Northcliffe newspapers were obliged to hail the new hero of the hour and dump Latham whom they'd previously championed. Blériot was now portrayed as the somewhat naïve ('which way is Dover?') but hardworking family man with a wife and five children who'd made the flight despite his injured foot.

According to Barbara Walsh, Blériot was the brave bumbling amateur, the antithesis of the cool, sophisticated Latham. Clearly, 'spin' was not a twenty-first-century invention.

Conspiracy theorists were also active, wondering why Latham's associates at Antoinette had failed to rouse him early enough on 25 July and then insisted that the weather was too bad for a successful cross-Channel attempt. Were the directors of the company motivated solely by concern for Latham's safety or were they reluctant to risk losing another aeroplane? Or was there something else? Latham's reaction varied between anger and despair.

By 08:30 hr he had locked himself in his room and asked not to be disturbed. He kept repeating to *The Times*' correspondent: 'Why won't they let me start? It's so cruel. I have often flown in as strong a wind as this.'

Generally, though, such negative thoughts were swept away by enthusiasm for Blériot's achievement. When he and his wife arrived in Paris they were greeted by what *Flight* described as a 'surging crowd of people who simply swamped the extra force of police which had been detailed to keep the road clear'. As soon as the train had surged into the station a great crowd had pressed around the couple. As a result, they had difficulty in fighting their way to the delegation from the Aero Club de France which was there to greet them.

The road from the station to the club's headquarters was lined with cheering crowds and waving *Tricolours* were much in evidence. On arrival the guests were welcomed by the club's president, the Comte de la Vaulx, who presented Bleriot with a gold medal. Later in the day, there was another presentation, by staff at Blériot's factory.

But perhaps the greatest social whirl was in London where the centrepiece of the celebrations was a lunch at the Savoy Hotel at which Lord Northcliffe presented the £1,000 prize to Blériot. Northcliffe was also waiting at Victoria Station to greet the guests of honour on their arrival from Dover. A motorcade had been arranged to convey them to the luncheon.

CROSS-CHANNEL AVIATION PIONEERS

Among the many notables present at the Savoy was Richard Haldane, Secretary of State for War in the Liberal government; yachtsman and tea magnate Sir Thomas Lipton; Major Baden Baden Powell, balloonist and brother of the hero of Mafeking; Colonel John Capper, superintendent of the Royal Balloon Factory; Polar explorer Ernest Shackleton; the Honourable Charles Rolls; Frank Butler, wine merchant and balloonist; Gordon Selfridge; Moberly Bell, managing director of *The Times*, and Harold Perrin, secretary of the Royal Aero Club. Altogether, there were about 150 guests.

In his carefully crafted speech to the gathering, duly reproduced in full in the next day's *Times*, Northcliffe declared that in Blériot and Shackleton, France and Britain were able to acclaim typical heroes of their respective countries. He also compared Blériot with other French innovators and played up the importance of the *Entente Cordiale* by saying that the peace of the world depended on the maintenance of good relations between the two countries. Northcliffe added that he was proud that his newspaper had 'in a most humble and unexpected manner' become associated with Blériot.

Flight reported that the prize was presented to Blériot in the form of two £500 notes 'contained in a letter case enclosed in a handsome silver cup'. At this point in his speech Northcliffe switched to French. In response, Blériot spoke a few sentences in which he downplayed the magnitude of his achievement. 'In that, needless to say, his words carried no conviction to the enthusiastic assembly,' *Flight* reported.

The social whirl continued with a civic reception at Dover, a celebratory dinner at which the Royal Aero Club presented Blériot with its Gold Medal and unanimously elected him a member of the club, and a reception organized by representatives of his own company in London.

Once the initial excitement had subsided, many commentators expressed apprehension about where it might lead and how the world had been changed, not necessarily for the better. *The Times* quoted M. Quinron, president of the French Aerial League, as saying: 'The sea is no longer a barrier. Relations between nations will undergo a change. The strategic and political situation of certain peoples will be transformed.'

Even Alberto Santos-Dumont was making no secret of his opposition to the use of the aeroplane as a weapon of war. Now forced to abandon flying because of the onset of multiple sclerosis, the man generally recognised as the first to fly an aeroplane in Europe planned to return to his native Brazil and devote the rest of his life to promoting the peaceful uses of aviation.

'WHICH WAY IS DOVER?'

But an editorial published in its 31 July edition, *Flight*, which had only been established earlier that year, considered the implications of Blériot's achievement in an assessment of the flight in more technical terms. It observed that the public was used to balloon flights while the achievements of the Wright brothers, while highly impressive, were 'apt to be looked on as mere mid-air gambols over a playground'.

The journal went on

> but the world knows the Channel. Even those who have not crossed it can appreciate the position of affairs, because they understand that we in this country dwell on an island. Now, the nearest distance that a crow can fly from France to England is about 16 miles, therefore before a machine can essay to journey by air from France to England without alighting—for it could not reach the farther coast once it did come down on the surface of the waters—the means and the mechanism must be very much more substantial and serviceable things than are mere toys.
>
> Within 30 hours of M. Blériot's achievement the whole civilised world was made aware of the fact that the age of aerial locomotion by mechanical means is no longer of the distant future but is in very much of this year in which we are living. As to the technical phases of the latest and most dramatic feat so far recorded in connection with heavier-than-air machines, it is interesting to find that it stands to the credit of a machine in which the principle of automatic stability has been carried very far indeed; also that, while being exceedingly speedy, the machine in question employs a very modest amount of horsepower, and besides, is itself of very small dimensions as these things go.

A twenty-first-century view of the Bleriot XI was given to *Aeroplane* readers by Rob Millinship, one of the team of pilots flying one of the gems of the Shuttleworth Collection. 'It is almost unflyable,' he said. 'Never mind crossing the Channel, I wouldn't cross the River Trent in it.' This was partly due to its being 'wildly underpowered' and also to the difficulty maintaining directional control via the system of wing warping. Millinship explained:

> if you try to roll left it will go right. If you put the stick to the right, the left wing warps downwards, but because it such

a steeply cambered wing you get all the trailing edge going down, which produces more drag than lift.

Yet Louis Blériot managed to overcome these difficulties. The *Daily Mail's* Harry Harper was undoubtedly right when, forty years later, he summed up Blériot's achievement this way: 'What the flight did more than any other had done was to mark clearly and definitely the dawn age of the age of the air.'

Louis Blériot – The Man and His Machines

Louis Blériot had been born at Cambrai on 1 July 1872, the oldest of five children. He was said to be a precocious child who left home at the age of ten to attend a boarding school. When he was fifteen he moved to the Lycée at Amiens, where he lived with an aunt.

Blériot spent a year at the Collège Sainte-Barbe in Paris before passing a demanding entrance exam which allowed him to study at the prestigious École Centrale in Paris for the next three years.

After compulsory military service, Blériot landed a job with Bagues, an electrical engineering company based in Paris. It was while working there that he developed what would become the first practical automobile headlamp. With this achievement to his credit, he was able to quit his job and start his own business supplying headlamps to the two foremost motor manufacturers of the day, Renault and Panhard-Levassor.

One day in 1900 Blériot was enjoying his lunch break when he saw a beautiful young woman dining with her parents. He decided then and there that this was the woman he was going to marry and bribed a waiter to tell him her name. The following year, he and Alice Vedene, the girl in the restaurant, were married.

Louis Blériot's business was successful and he used the money he earned from it to fund his early aviation experiments. When he was thirty, Blériot taught himself to fly in an aircraft of his own design. Through much trial and plenty of error, he developed his skills as both pilot and designer.

His first series of experiments using ornithopters were all unsuccessful. But in 1905 Blériot met Gabriel Voison and was greatly impressed by his floatplane glider. He commissioned Voison to create what became known as the Blériot II. This machine crashed, nearly killing Voison, but Blériot's enthusiasm remained undiminished.

He later teamed up with Voison to start a company called the Ateliers d'Aviation Edouard Surcouf, Blériot et Voisin. The pair then developed two versions of aircraft powered by lightweight Antoinette engines. But neither the Blériot III nor the Blériot IV was successful and Blériot later dissolved his partnership with Voison.

He then established Recherches Aéronautiques Louis Blériot. It was to represent a major milestone in aviation development because it resulted in the world's first successful powered monoplane.

The Blériot VII made its first flight on 16 November 1907. It established the configuration that would be followed by most other manufacturers in which horizontal and vertical tail surfaces were mounted at the rear of the fuselage.

Blériot used this machine to make two more flights of over 500 metres on 6 December which also included an 89-degree turn. This was considered to be a most significant achievement at that stage of French aeronautical development.

The Blériot VII evolved into the XI which created a sensation when it appeared at the first Paris Aero Salon in December 1908. The aviation community was stunned by its compact dimensions and simplicity of design.

The fuselage comprised an ash framework having a square section at the nose with the side members meeting at the tail. The convex section wings were built around two wooden spars measuring 3 inches by ¾-inch section. Curved wooden ribs, mostly made of wood ¼-inch thick, were arranged along the wing spaced 7 inches apart. Some were of aluminium reinforced with wood but those closest to the fuselage were made of channel-section wood.

A key feature of the design was the quickly detachable wings in which the main spars projected beyond the main ribs to locate in metal sockets attached to the fuselage framework and secured with bolts. The wings were braced above and below the fuselage by wires attached to steel structures located ahead of the pilot's cockpit.

The single-piece rudder was mounted at the extreme end of the fuselage and pivoted to provide directional control. The convex section tail plane was mounted beneath the rear fuselage ahead to the rudder.

Its outer sections pivoted to provide elevator control. The tail plane's span was about two-thirds that of the wings.

The main undercarriage comprised a pair of bicycle wheels on hinged forks with diagonal steel tubes running from the wheel hubs to a sliding collar on the main vertical member which continued to run upwards to support the engine bearers. Substantial elastic bands provided the suspension medium. A similar-sized tail wheel was located ahead of the tail plane.

The pilot sat on a board raised a few inches above the main fuselage girder with his back resting against a leather strap. A foot-controlled bar operated the rudder via a system of wires, while vertical lever provided control for the wing-warping.

The Anzani W-3 was an air-cooled, naturally aspirated three-cylinder unit displacing, 3.377 litres and developing 25 hp. The cylinders were arranged in a fan formation and projected above the crank. The inlet valves were automatically operated but the exhaust valves were uncovered by the pistons at the end of their stroke. The engine was attached to the fuselage by four channel-section steel brackets bolted to the faces of the crankcase and drilled for lightness. The wooden two-blade propeller was 6 feet 8 inches in diameter.

Fuel and engine oil tanks were mounted in the fuselage between the cockpit and engine. For the cross-Channel flight, a flotation bag was installed in the rear fuselage.

The cross-Channel flight resulted in orders for copies, which sold for 10,000 francs apiece. Several modern replicas of the Blériot XI have been built. For the 1965 film *Those Magnificent Men in Their Flying Machines*, some of which was filmed in Dover, a two-seat replica was constructed together with a modern engine. In 1984 Patrick Lindsay flew this machine across the Channel. The wife of the chairman of Dover District Council also had a ride that day.

On 25 July 2009, the hundredth anniversary of Blériot's epic flight was marked by the flight of another replica. Edmond Salis made the crossing from France and landed at the Duke of York's Military School not far from Northfall Meadow. Royal Aero Club Chairman David Roberts brought with him a blade from the original propeller of Blériot's machine.

One of the most impressive achievements undertaken with a Blériot monoplane was made by Norwegian Tryggve Gran who flew his Gnome-powered XI-2 from Cruden Bay near Port Erroll, Scotland, to Jaeren near Stavanger, Norway, on 30 July 1914. He covered the 290 miles in four hours ten minutes. Two years earlier, Gan had been a member of Robert Falcon Scott's Antarctic expedition and was a member of the group which found the bodies of Scott and his party. Gan later enlisted in the RFC.

Specification – Blériot XI
Length 25 ft
Wingspan 28 ft
Wing area 150 sq. ft
Weight without pilot 484 lb
Maximum speed 47 mph
Service ceiling 3,281 ft
Power plant Anzani W 3 air-cooled with 3 cylinders in fan formation.

Chapter Four

After Blériot

Blériot might not have opened the flood gates with his Channel crossing, for it was a year before any other aviator attempted to emulate him, but he certainly opened up a range of possibilities.

To Lord Northcliffe, who put up the £1,000 prize for the first Channel crossing by aeroplane, it was probably immaterial which of the competing aviators actually pulled it off. Both the leading contestants were foreign – although Northcliffe's newspaper, the *Daily Mail,* made much of Hubert Latham's English family connections – and both were piloting French-built machines.

In fact, it's unlikely that any British pilot would have had the skill or experience to contemplate such a journey at that time. And, less than a year after Cody's first flight at Farnborough, there was certainly no British-built machine capable of making the crossing.

But Blériot's success was grist to Northcliffe's mill. It provided a big boost to his campaign to make the government aware of Britain's vulnerability to attack from the air. His newspapers weren't alone. Indeed, the more thoughtful commentators drew attention to the fact that while Britain had invested huge sums in creating a powerful modern navy this fleet could be rendered obsolete virtually overnight by an enemy able to launch a massive armada of aeroplanes to overwhelm the nation's defences and rain bombs down on its citizens with impunity.

The fact was that Blériot's flight had brought the world into the air age when suddenly anything seemed possible. From a twenty-first-century vantage point this fear of attack from the air may seem to have been greatly exaggerated. But it had originated with Napoleon and by 1909 Europe was again on the brink of war.

The fear of devastating attack from the skies was maintained during the 1920s and '30s by supporters of air power such as Douhet and Trenchard and repeated by politicians. Baldwin's mantra 'the bomber will always get through' sent a chill through the nation.

AFTER BLÉRIOT

Even so, few people in 1909 could have imagined that in little more than 30 years, as the *Daily Mail*'s Harry Harper put it, 'armadas of bombers would be laying waste cities and munition areas, that pilotless flying bombs would be streaming across the Channel or that huge rockets would be crashing down in the London area'.

Within days of Blériot's Channel flight, Parliament was debating the government's approach to aviation. Over the years the House of Commons has varied its times of sitting so that in 1909, unlike today, MPs sat during August. But that year there was a session on August Bank Holiday Monday. This was unusual but then so was the subject being debated.

The result was that MPs unanimously voted the sum of £78,000 to be spent by the government on aeronautical development for military and naval purposes during the coming year. War minister Richard Haldane, however, made his sceptical attitude towards both dirigibles and aeroplanes at their current stage of development fairly clear.

He thought it unlikely there would ever be substantial private ownership of dirigibles, but added 'no doubt a few country gentlemen will have their aeroplanes'. But he acknowledged it would be 'very foolish if we were to neglect these possible instruments of war, and it is vital that we should push ahead'. The journal, *Flight* regarded the allocation as a step in the right direction but not quite enough. It commented

> We who know the vast field to be covered will realise that such a sum is not enough for the work that has to be undertaken to enable Britain to make up lost ground; but we who know also how tedious has been the toil to convert the authorities, and how niggardly have been the results to date, must feel something like a thrill of joyous surprise when we learn not only that so appreciable a scale of expenditure is to be embarked on by way of a beginning, but also that the Commons passed the vote unanimously, not a voice being heard against it.

Yet it was Louis Blériot himself who was one of the first to visualise the peaceful uses of aircraft. Soon after his historic flight, the French aviator was telling Harry Harper he was confident

> that the ability to travel through the air at speeds impossible by land and sea would, in the end, prove a boon rather than

a menace to mankind, promoting world understanding and making the peoples of the globe less and less inclined to resort to the folly of war.

One of the many social functions arranged in Blériot's honour was a banquet organized by the Aeroplane Club. In his speech, the Lord Mayor of London said that Blériot's flight was the harbinger of a 'stupendous change in locomotion'. He added:

> In the not very distant future we should be able to hail an aeroplane, and say, 'I should like to be taken to the Champs Elysees, Paris,' and we should arrive there in the course of a few hours.

On this occasion, Bleriot seems to have been non-committal. He said that the science of aviation was developing 'at gigantic speed' and would continue to do so by means of constant emulation, which would be the result of well-organized competitions and encouragements offered by 'the numerous institutions and individuals concerned in aviation'. Within the near future, he added, such progress would be made that would enable aviation to be regarded as a practical science and not merely a sport.

At the time of his Channel flight Blériot had invested about 780,000 francs of his own money to fund his aviation experiments. It paid off, though: one result of his Channel crossing was that his company, *Reserches Aéronautiques Louis Blériot*, saw an immediate transformation in its business as his company began receiving orders for Type XI aircraft.

Although Blériot was reported to have promised his wife that he would not fly again after his Channel crossing, he participated in the *Grande Semaine d'Aviation* at Reims in August 1909, where he set a new world speed record, and continued to attend other aviation meetings. Up until December he had several narrow escapes but his legendary good luck eventually failed him. While flying in gusty weather conditions at Istanbul, Blériot's machine made a crash landing on the roof of a house. This left him with internal injuries, several broken ribs and a three-week stay in hospital.

Between July of 1909 and the onset of the First World War in August 1914, over 800 aircraft were turned out by the Blériot factory. Most of them were Type XI monoplanes, or variations on the design, which found customers from all parts of the world. Blériot machines were also used by the newly formed air forces of Russia, Austria, Britain, Italy and France.

AFTER BLÉRIOT

In addition, Blériot aircraft and their pilots dominated many major European air races and other competitions. By July 1910 Blériot Type XIs held world records for duration, distance, speed and altitude. But the innovative design of the monoplanes which had made them so successful was also to cause controversy.

Following accidents involving four Blériot machines the French Army placed a brief ban on the use of monoplanes in 1912. It was alleged that the machines suffered from an inherent weakness which caused the wings to fail in flight. The ban was lifted after the landing wires were strengthened. A similar ban was imposed in Britain and although the cause was not directly related to Blériot aircraft and the prohibition was short-lived, monoplanes remained out of favour for some years.

Further controversy for Blériot ensued when he and five other French aircraft manufacturers were involved in a five-year legal issue with the Wright brothers who alleged infringement of the patents covering their wing-warping control system. The Wright brothers claim was finally dismissed by the courts in France and Germany.

In late 1909 Blériot established a flying training school for pilots at Étampes near Rouen. Early the following year he opened a second at Pau in the south-west. Between 1910 and 1914 the schools trained around 1,000 pilots. Nearly half of those holding an Aero Club de France brevet at the outbreak of the First World War had trained at Blériot flying schools.

There were also schools in Britain: in September 1910 one was opened at the newly established Hendon aerodrome near London and by July 1914 a fourth was in operation at Brooklands. A small factory was also opened at the Surrey site, which produced about twenty Blériot training monoplanes.

In 1913 Blériot acquired the assets of the Deperdussin company following the arrest on fraud charges of its founder Armand Deperdussin. In the process the company's name was changed from *Société de Production des Aéroplanes Deperdussin* to *Société Pour l'Aviation et ses Dérivés*, generally referred to by its acronym of SPAD.

Mass production in French factories and worldwide exports ensured that the company prospered during the First World War. Production licences were sold in several countries, resulting in the establishment of a larger British factory at Addlestone near Brooklands and a further production line opened at the Curtiss Elmwood plant at Buffalo, New York.

SPAD's best known products were probably the highly successful VII and XIII fighters. Among the most successful aces who flew them were Georges Guynemer, Rene Fonck (the conflict's highest-scoring Allied pilot),

Eddie Rickenbacker and Francesco Baracca, whose prancing horse insignia was later carried on the racing cars created by Enzo Ferrari.

By 1927 Blériot had long since retired from flying himself but he was at Le Bourget aerodrome in May to acclaim Charles Lindbergh following his solo flight from New York. The two great pioneers were later photographed together.

Blériot remained involved in the aviation business until his death from a heart attack in Paris on 1 August 1936. He was accorded a funeral with full military honours and buried at the *Cimetière des Gonards* in Versailles. A stone memorial, roughly in the planform of Blériot's machine, marks the spot near Dover Castle where he landed after his greatest achievement, his cross-Channel flight of 25 July 1909.

The English Channel was not crossed again by aeroplane for almost a year. On 21 May 1910 French aristocrat Jacques de Lesseps made the crossing in one of the first Blériot XIs powered by the highly successful Gnome rotary engines which he called *Le Scarabée*. He had actually been planning to make a double crossing but the weather was against him. After several days waiting for conditions to improve, de Lesseps finally ran out of patience and took off from Les Baraques the day after the funeral of King Edward VII.

He was, however, delayed by fog on the French coast and was therefore able to make only one flight, landing safely in St Margaret's Meadow, Dover. The following day's *Times* carried a short report which said little more than that his flight had repeated that of Blériot and had taken thirty-seven. It had been intended that de Lesseps would be supported by the *Escopette*, the French warship which accompanied Blériot on his journey a year earlier. But, according to *Flight*, 'owing to the thick fog, each sighted the other but once for a brief moment in mid-Channel.' De Lesseps landed in a large meadow some distance inland from the South Foreland Lighthouse.

Because of the weather the watchers on the cliffs at Dover had almost given up all hope of seeing de Lesseps' machine arrive. But then, the coastguard officer, who'd been the first to sight Blériot when he made his successful crossing, announced that he could hear an engine. A few minutes later, the machine, flying at a height of around 1,000 feet, emerged from the fog, heading for the Langdon Battery, further along the cliffs than Northfall Meadow, where Blériot landed. The crowd followed as quickly as it could. *Flight* reported that

> It eventually transpired that the descent was accomplished after a long gliding descent of over two miles in a meadow

belonging to Wanstone Court Farm, about three miles east of Dover and about a mile inland. There M. de Lesseps was welcomed by Mr R. Clayson, of St Margaret's, who happened to be in the field, while the ladies of the farm provided the aviator with refreshment.

The flight had won for de Lesseps the 12,500-franc Ruinart Prize, donated by the Ruinart champagne company. Blériot was ineligible for this award because of mistakes he made in completing the registration paperwork. Among the first to congratulate de Lesseps was the Hon. C.S. Rolls, who was awaiting a favourable opportunity to fly from Dover to Calais and had himself entered for the Ruinart Prize.

De Lesseps' flight was re-created on 20 and 21 May 2010, when a pair of replica Blériot monoplanes, flown by Pascal Kremer, Henk van Hoorn and Goy Feltes, made the Channel crossing. De Lesseps' grandson, Michael, was also in attendance.

Jacques de Lesseps was the son of the diplomat and entrepreneur Ferdinand, who was responsible for building the Suez Canal. Jacques had become fascinated by aviation and in September 1909 was enrolled at the Issy-les-Moulineaux flight school on the outskirts of Paris. He was awarded his pilot's licence in January 1910 but not before he had become the first aviator in the world to fly and land at night.

Later that year he was invited to participate in the first-ever International Air Congress in Canada held between 24 June and 2 July at Montreal. He took his two Blériot monoplanes to North America and it was at the controls of *Le Scarabée* that he made the first flight over of the city of Montreal. He repeated the feat at Toronto and while there he met Grace McKenzie, daughter of a wealthy railroad tycoon.

De Lesseps had travelled to North America with his friend Hubert Latham mainly to participate in the international air show at Belmont Park, New York, and other events. He was also one of several aviators to fly around the Statue of Liberty, which, in 1886, had been inaugurated by his father in the presence of President Grover Cleveland.

Later he returned to Toronto where he became engaged to Grace MacKenzie. They were married in London in January 1911 before moving to Paris where their four children were born. Jacques de Lesseps died in October 1927 while on a survey flight in Canada.

Significant as the flights of Blériot and de Lesseps undoubtedly were, they were well and truly put in the shade by the Hon. Charles Rolls.

CROSS-CHANNEL AVIATION PIONEERS

He was a pioneer motorist who became interested in ballooning, eventually making over 150 ascents, many with his great friend John Moore-Brabazon. Both men turned to heavier than air flight and Rolls went to France where he met the Wright brothers. When the Short brothers of Battersea and Eastchurch acquired a licence to build the Wright Flyer, Rolls became an early customer. He gained Royal Aero Club pilot's certificate Number 2 in March 1910. Moore-Brabazon already held licence Number 1.

Both men were active flyers at the Royal Aero Club's flying ground at Eastchurch on the Isle of Sheppey in Kent. Early in 1910 Rolls established a base for himself at Dover with the intention of improving on Blériot's achievement. Rolls planned to fly to France and back to England non-stop.

Rolls had a hangar built at Swingate and it was completed by 20 May. Speculation about its purpose was settled the following day when a flying machine marked 'Hon. C.S. Rolls' was delivered and four mechanics began to assemble it. The job was completed by 24 May but strong winds prevented test flying. At 17:00 hr, the machine was wheeled out of its hangar but it took some time to get the engine running smoothly. Two hours later the aircraft was drawn by two horses to its launching rail and the aircraft took off. Rolls flew eight circuits around Swingate Downs for about twenty minutes before landing near the hangar.

Further trial flights followed over the next few days. One of them ended when engine trouble intervened; a landing skid was damaged in a heavy landing. On another occasion a water pump developed a leak. There were more setbacks on the day scheduled for the flight with fog, wind and an engine which refused to run cleanly.

More controversially, the Admiralty revoked consent for Royal Navy torpedo vessels to act as picket boats for the flight, obliging Rolls to seek aid from harbour building contractors Pearson & Son. The national press had a field day criticising officialdom, but eventually the tugs *Lady Curzon* and *The Gnat* were positioned at points seven miles and fourteen miles along the flight route.

Rolls arrived at Swingate at 18:00 hr but was cagey about his intentions, telling the large crowd which had gathered that he planned to make another trial flight. Clad in overalls, padded coat, cap and goggles, plus a cork life-jacket, the aviator climbed between the struts and wires of his aircraft. The engine was started and the aircraft launched so that by 18:30 Rolls was airborne and heading for the coast.

Bob Hollingsbee of the Dover Society related what happened next. 'Out in the Channel,' he wrote, the Dover Harbour Board tug, *Lady Curzon*, steamed steadily in the same direction, a pennant flying to signify all was well. About an hour later the tug was spotted steaming back towards Dover, but of Rolls there was no sign. By 19:40hr many spectators had abandoned hope of seeing Rolls return, but suddenly a speck appeared in the sky and a rush of people – estimated at several thousand – headed for the cliff edge and had to be checked by waiting soldiers of the Royal Garrison Artillery. Rolls crossed the recently completed Admiralty Harbour, to the accompaniment of ships' sirens and whistles, and circled above the town before landing outside his workshop. Once again soldiers came to the rescue to control the big crowd in case of damage to the frail aircraft.

The flight was a complete success. Rolls, having crossed the French coast near Sangatte, flew a third of a mile inland to drop a letter to the French Aero Club with the message: 'Greetings to the President of the Aero Club of France. Dropped from a Wright aeroplane crossing from England to France. Charles S. Rolls, Vive l'Entente.'

Captain Moore, the official Royal Aero Club timekeeper, noted that Rolls had taken off at 18:30 hr, crossed the coast four minutes later, reaching the French coast at 19:15 (UK time) and landed in Dover at 20:06. A few days later the *Dover Express* published a letter from Rolls thanking two local farmers, Mr Spanton, of Lenacre Court, and Mr Eastes, for use of their land at Swingate, as well as others, including the military, for their assistance.

In addition to making the first double Channel crossing, Rolls had become the first Briton to fly the Channel, the first pilot to cross from England to France and the first to land at a pre-arranged spot without damage to the airframe. It was, commented aviation historian Dallas Brett, 'a most memorable and praiseworthy achievement carried out in a workmanlike manner without unnecessary fuss'.

There was no monetary prize on offer but Rolls was awarded the Royal Aero Club's Gold Medal and King George V and Queen Mary sent congratulatory telegrams. In Britain, Rolls' achievement was hailed with relief: at last a Briton had done it. *Flight* felt the achievement should

> go very far towards silencing the critics who are so fond of croaking about an effete and played-out people. At long last,

and in eminently dignified fashion, it has been demonstrated to the world that we have among us flying men who can do all that the limitations of the present-day aeroplane will permit, and that we can also build as good machines as those produced in other countries.

Indeed, the journal ranked Rolls' achievement ahead of Louis Paulhan's historic London to Manchester flight. Acknowledging that Rolls wasn't the first to make a cross-Channel flight, it pointed out that

> there was no chain of motor boats placed at intervals across the Channel to render first aid to the aviator in case of accident; no escorting torpedo craft to watch over his safety. Apart from the greater magnitude of the actual performance ... the undoubted risks of such a journey were recognised and accepted in that spirit of calculating pluck and confidence which is one of those characteristics that have made the Briton respected all over the world.

But, of course, Rolls' double Channel crossing represented more than just a demonstration of British pluck. A one-way flight had been something of an experiment, but a double crossing had really shown the practical possibilities of aerial transport. There were also those who saw more darker portents. *Flight* commented

> Now that Mr Rolls has conclusively proved that there is nothing impossible in the idea of a sudden raid by aeroplane, and the Army authorities have satisfied themselves that it actually is possible for a dirigible balloon to make an air voyage without mishap, it is permissible to hope that considerably more enthusiastic development of aircraft will be followed up quickly by the State, even if only in the interests of national defence.

Like the original Flyer, Rolls' machine was launched from an 80-feet-long rail. At one end of it rose a pylon about 18-feet tall with a pulley at the top over which ran a rope. The rope ran down inside the pylon with a half-ton weight attached to its end. A trolley, which was essentially a railway sleeper attached to a set of wheels, supported the aircraft itself.

AFTER BLÉRIOT

To launch, the rope was passed over the pulley at the top of the pylon, under a further pulley at the pylon end of the rail and then along the rail and back to the aeroplane to which it was attached by a quick-release mechanism.

The main drawback of this arrangement was that once the whole thing had been set in position, using a sturdy horse to move it, the wind might well have changed and everything had to be shifted again. Once the engine was warmed up and running flat-out, the pilot operated a trigger which released the weight, pulling the machine rapidly along the rail. In his autobiography published in 1956, Moore-Brabazon explained what happened next: 'You were doing about 40 mph and you had to do something about it by pulling your elevator. After that, if you got into the air, well, it was your job to get on with it.'

Indeed, with no recognised techniques to fall back on, the pioneer airmen were very much on their own to discover for themselves the rudiments of control. Moore-Brabazon recalled that it was 'in essence an adventure into the unknown'. It was not unusual for the machine on reaching the end of the rail to fail to soar into the air. In such cases it would fall back on to its trolley and probably break its undercarriage skids leading to more repair bills.

These bills were very much the bugbear of pioneer aviators. Moore-Brabazon called them 'frightful'. He wrote: 'Every time you went out something was smashed and had to be put right.' It was rumoured that Charles Rolls' weekly repair bill often reached £200.

Sadly, Rolls did not have long to enjoy his triumph. A month after his double Channel crossing he was killed when his machine came apart in mid-air at the Bournemouth aviation meeting in August 1910. A statue created by sculptress Kathleen Scott, wife of Robert Falcon Scott, Scott of the Antarctic, to commemorate Rolls' achievement, was unveiled at Dover by the Duchess of Argyle in April 1912.

The popular Rolls was widely mourned, not least by his friend John Moore-Brabazon. The two men had first become acquainted at Cambridge and Moore-Brabazon acted as Rolls' mechanic when he went motor racing. 'He became my greatest friend,' Brabazon wrote later. 'He was the strangest of men and one of the most likeable,' he recalled.

> He was tall and rather thin and his eyes stood out of his sockets rather more than was normal. He was rather fond of a Norfolk jacket and always wore a high stiff white collar ….

He didn't suffer fools gladly and his sense of humour was rather crude … . Really Charlie Rolls' only fault – if it can be called that – was extreme parsimony. He simply hated spending money.

Rolls' double Channel crossing, plus the lure of a generous cash prize, inspired aviators to emulate his feat. Towards the end of the year a number of the era's leading pilots were gathering at Dover to meet the next major cross-Channel challenge.

The Hon. Charles Rolls

Racing driver, balloonist, pioneer aviator, co-founder of one of the world's most famous engineering companies, Charles Stewart Rolls was born in London in 1877 the third son of John Rolls, the first Baron Llangattock, and Lady Llangattock.

Charles Rolls developed an interest in engines at an early age and gained a BA degree in applied science and later an MA in engineering from Cambridge University. He was a keen cyclist but in 1896 bought his first car, a Peugeot Phaeton, and campaigned against the restrictions imposed on motor vehicles by the Locomotive Act, becoming a founder member of the Automobile Club of Great Britain.

Rolls also competed in some of the earliest motorsport events and was the first British driver to race in Europe where he participated in some of the notoriously dangerous city-to-city races on public roads which were later abandoned in favour of events on closed circuits. In the 800-mile Paris-Madrid race in 1903 Rolls was one of several drivers whose names would become associated with major car manufacturers. The race was abandoned at Bordeaux due to a series of accidents including one which claimed the life of Marcel Renault.

Although Rolls spent some time working for the London and North Western Railway at Crewe, it soon became clear that his talents lay more in salesmanship than engineering. In January 1903, helped by £6,600 provided by his father, he started one of Britain's first car dealerships, C.S. Rolls & Co. of Fulham, London, which imported French Peugeot and Belgian Minerva cars.

AFTER BLÉRIOT

The following year Rolls was introduced to Frederick Royce who was just beginning to build quality cars. Royce the artisan had little in common with Rolls the aristocrat, yet they became friends and agreed that Royce would build cars and Rolls would sell them. Rolls-Royce was born. The first fruit of the partnership was the Rolls-Royce 10hp car, which was unveiled at the Paris Salon in December. Two years later the two principals formalised their partnership by creating Rolls-Royce Limited, with Royce appointed technical managing director and Rolls providing the financial backing and business acumen.

Rolls had also developed an interest in ballooning and in 1901 co-founded the Aero Club. In 1905, when he was at the New York motor show promoting Rolls-Royce cars, he was introduced to the Wright brothers. This meeting sparked Rolls' interest in heavier-than-air flight. In 1909 he bought the first of six aircraft built by the Short brothers under licence from the Wright brothers. He made than 200 flights with this machine, including the first non-stop double crossing of the English Channel by aeroplane.

But he was not flying this aircraft at the Bournemouth aviation meeting. Instead, he was at the controls of a French-built Flyer which had been modified against Wilbur Wright's advice. Rolls had added wheels and an auxiliary elevator in the tail. It was this second elevator which collapsed in a steep dive during a spot-landing competition at Bournemouth with disastrous consequences.

In its obituary of Rolls published on 13 July 1910, *The Times* noted:

> Mr Rolls is the tenth airman who has met with a fatal accident in a motor-driven flying machine, and he is the first Englishman who has sacrificed his life in the cause of modern aviation.

Moore-Brabazon added: 'This terrible disaster to aviation and also the loss of so dear a friend sickened me and my wife of aviation altogether and I never flew again until the war.'

A stained-glass window in Eastchurch parish church was dedicated as a memorial to Rolls by the Archbishop of Canterbury in 1926. Another window remembers Cecil Grace who was lost in an attempted cross-Channel flight in 1910.

Chapter Five

Triumph and Tragedy

One thing the pioneer cross-Channel aviators had in common apart from their 'unconquerable spirit', as one aviation historian put it, was their sheer lack of experience.

Of course, that was inevitable given that powered flight was barely a decade old in the second decade of the twentieth century. But the very idea of pilots whose lack of flying hours would hardly qualify them for their first solo flight today tackling a twenty-two-mile ocean crossing in a flimsy, low-powered machine seems almost suicidal.

T.O.M. Sopwith, for example, had never undertaken a cross-country flight, yet he was happy to enter for a contest that would involve not only flying the Channel but also a lengthy Continental journey.

Henri Salmet, although chief instructor at a flying school, was happily contemplating a flight that would make him the first pilot to fly from London to Paris and back in a single day more or less on the spur of the moment.

And when he landed in a Kentish cornfield, diminutive US-domiciled French-Canadian John Moisant revealed that the first flight across the Channel with a passenger was only his sixth time aloft.

In fact, Louis Blériot had no sooner landed at Dover on 25 July 1909 when Baron Maurice de Forest, racing driver, aviator and Liberal politician, was offering a substantial cash prize for a repeat.

Writing to the *Daily Mail* on the day of Blériot's flight, but before he was aware it had been completed, de Forest, French-born but a naturalised British subject, said he was 'uneasy' about the speed of aeronautical development. 'I think,' he said,

> that the extraordinary progress accomplished in aviation during the last year decidedly places the practicability of an invasion of this country through the air within the bounds of a perfectly reasonable and not far distant possibility.

TRIUMPH AND TRAGEDY

He added: 'I think that the feeling of apprehension increases when it is observed that the candidates for the *Daily Mail* prize at present in the field are all foreigners about to complete on foreign-built machines.' He therefore stipulated that his prize would be awarded to the first Briton to cross the Channel in a British-built machine.

When it became clear that the Channel had been conquered by a foreigner he doubled the prize to £4,000. *Flight* called it 'a most munificent offer to encourage flight in this country'.

But de Forest added a further stipulation: the flight had to be completed before the end of 1910. It was, said aviation historian Dallas Brett, 'an idea which fired the imagination'. The flight, he wrote, 'involved the Channel crossing, itself a hazardous feat, followed by a long flight to the eastward, unhampered by restrictions and limited only by the pilot's endurance and the tank capacity of his aircraft.'

It was certainly not an undertaking to be treated lightly. Indeed, the event would end with the destruction of four aircraft and the loss of one of Britain's most accomplished pilots. But the nation would also be able to acclaim a new aviation hero.

The contestants began to gather at Dover towards the end of the year. Claude Grahame-White and his Bristol biplane were joined at Swingate Downs by C.H. Greswell (Bristol-built-Farman) and Robert Loraine (Bristol). They were all to be out of luck. High winds damaged their machines so badly that they couldn't start.

Grahame-White managed to repair his machine but crashed during a test flight. He was able to extricate himself from the wreckage but fainted shortly afterwards from loss of blood caused by his injuries. He was taken to the Lord Warden Hotel where he ordered a new machine but his doctor refused to allow him to start the race. Army officer Lieutenant Maitland was also eliminated by a crash. But T.O.M. Sopwith with his ENV-powered Howard Wright biplane, Frank McClean (Short-Green) and Cecil Grace (Short-built Farman) were preparing for the flight at Eastchurch on the Isle of Sheppey.

On 18 December the gales abated and Sopwith decided to seize the opportunity. His lack of experience meant that he had yet to complete a cross-country flight, yet he was planning to fly across the Channel and beyond.

As the sun rose Sopwith attempted a short practice flight in his newly delivered machine. He discovered it was sluggish off the ground when taking off downwind so, when starting his attempt to win de Forest's prize at 08:30hr he headed upwind. It was a good decision; the machine lifted off well. Sopwith circled the airfield for fifteen minutes to gain height before setting off at 1,000 feet for Dover, which he reached thirty minutes after taking off. A further twenty-two minutes later he was crossing the French coast a few miles west of Gap Griz Nez.

Unlike some of his predecessors, Sopwith had equipped his machine with a compass. But he found it offered little help and he decided to steer by the sun in the general direction of Châlons, where he planned to land. But the sun was soon covered by cloud and Sopwith inadvertently swung to the north of his intended course. When he crossed the Belgian border, conditions became increasingly gusty and his machine began to buck alarmingly in the disturbed air. At one point, he was almost flung out of his seat and onto the wing.

As the country below appeared to be increasingly hilly, Sopwith decided to land. He had covered 169 miles in the three-and-a-half hours since taking off from Eastchurch. He could have gone further. *Flight* observed that

> This enforced termination of the grand achievement was more disappointing as, of the 20 gallons of petrol which Mr Sopwith carried with him, no less than 11 gallons still left a sufficient quantity to have easily accomplished a further 300 miles under decent weather conditions. Except for the uncertainty of the country and treacherous winds which were undoubtedly due to the hilly district, not a hitch occurred with either the machine or its gear. The ENV engine went through without a misfire from first to last during the journey ... and the only regret is that Mr Sopwith was unable, by reason of the eccentricities of his compass and the disappearance of the guiding sun, to continue with his original intention of getting to Paris, which would have given him, from the start from Eastchurch grounds, a distance of about 240 miles.

It was, though, a 'splendid achievement' by a relative novice and it would win him the £4,000 prize.

Less fortunate was Cecil Grace. He had taken off from Eastchurch at noon on the 18th and averaged 60 mph on the run to Dover. There he found a thick mist was covering the Channel and the wind was rising. He had little choice but to land at Dover which he did shortly before Grahame-White suffered the accident that ended his attempt to claim the prize before the contest had started.

TRIUMPH AND TRAGEDY

Four days later the weather was still misty and windy but Grace was impatient to get going. At 0900 hr on 22 December he took off from Swingate Downs and headed out over the Channel. He landed at Les Baraques where he decided the weather was too bad for him to continue. With time running out, Grace decided to head back to Dover to prepare for another attempt. Accordingly, he arranged with the captain of the steamship SS *Pas de Calais* that he would use the vessel's smoke to guide him across the water.

But the ship was late leaving port and Grace was left to fly alone into the fog. His machine was heard passing the North Goodwin lightship and shortly afterwards was sighted by the crew of a fishing boat. But Cecil Grace was never seen alive again. A cap and goggles were recovered from a Belgian beach a fortnight later and identified as his. He was the second Briton to die in an aviation accident.

Earlier in 1910, John Moisant became the first airman to cross the Channel with a passenger. On 17 August, Moisant, born in Illinois the son of French-Canadian immigrants, took off from Calais in his Blériot XI carrying his French mechanic, Albert Fileux, and his tabby cat Mademoiselle Fifi. They landed in a cornfield near Deal.

Standing beside Fileux, Moisant told reporters:

> I took up flying as a hobby eight or nine months ago. This is the sixth time I have been in the air and the machine I'm using is the only one I've ever flown in.

The French newspaper *France Patrie* hailed Moisant's 'energy, audacity and intrepidity'. The British were also impressed by the American aviator who was small in stature – 5 feet 3 inches – but big in heart. 'One would expect,' observed the *Westminster Gazette*, 'that this journey of his across the Channel would knock his nerves up but he maintains a calm equal to that of the Trafalgar Square lions.'

Sopwith might well have reached Paris had his navigation not gone awry and it was not until April 1911 that the first flight between the two capitals was actually made. Yet it had not been planned. Pierre Prier, chief pilot instructor at Blériot's Hendon flying school, made the trip on the spur of the moment as the result of a casual remark.

His route from Hendon took him over Chatham, Canterbury and Dover before crossing the Channel. In France he overflew Calais, Boulogne, Abbeville and Beauvais. He had encountered mist over the Channel yet was able to maintain an accurate course to cover 230 miles in three hours fifty-six minutes at an average speed of 62 mph. His flight was not only the first between London and Paris but it also set a world's record for distance flown in a straight line.

Within the year an attempt would be made to make the return journey between the two capitals in a single day. Henri Salmet, Prier's successor at Hendon, had for some time nourished an ambition to go one better. As he wanted to see Blériot on business, Salmet resolved to go as soon as the weather permitted. When he awoke on Thursday 7 March 1912 Salmet saw that conditions were ideal. 'I think,' Salmet said later, 'it being fine, I will go.'

Salmet had, however, made some preparations for his flight. He had varnished the fabric on the wings of his Bleriot monoplane to tighten it and make it waterproof. Early on the 7th he telephoned the coastguard at Eastbourne for a weather report, then, putting an inner tube around his waist to act as a lifebelt, he took off at 07:45 hr.

By the time he had reached the coast he was flying at an altitude of 4,000 feet but the wind was now strengthening. When he was two miles out he decided it was too gusty for him to continue at that height. Coolly, he turned back for the coast to gain height before setting out again at about 7,000 feet. Salmet may have been a relative novice but he knew enough to equip his machine with a compass. However, as his machine was constantly buffeted by the wind the needle kept swinging ten degrees either side of his intended course, rendering it virtually useless.

By now he was flying blind and after an hour and forty minutes he decided to come down to a lower altitude to establish his position. From about 650 feet he was able to recognise the landmarks he had already established on his map. After a while he sighted the Eiffel Tower and, shortly afterwards, Issy aerodrome. His first act on landing was to wash his Gnome engine, which he had prepared himself, with paraffin from a can he always carried.

As it happened, Salmet had arrived at Blériot's headquarters before the telegram he'd previously despatched to announce his visit actually arrived. It was lunchtime and the place was practically deserted. But when Salmet telephoned Blériot asking to meet him, Blériot replied that he would come later in the afternoon. Salmet then told him that would be too late. 'I want to get back to London today.'

That was enough for Blériot to drop everything and drive to Issy where he greeted his visitor: 'Bon jour, Salmet. Toutes mes felicitations',

Salmet later recalled: 'In his great joy he grasp [sic] both my hands and squeeze [sic] so hard that he hurt much.' The two pilots then retired to the aviators' café for lunch.

Salmet left Issy at 14:15 hr. But the wind was mostly against him and it took him nearly four hours to cover 136 miles, reducing his average speed to just 34 mph. Nearly out of fuel, he was forced to land at Berck-sur-Mer. 'I am very cross against the weather,' he recalled later. By the time he found a supply of fuel it was too late for him to continue his journey so he was obliged to spend the night in Berck.

After signing autographs for the many spectators who had gathered to watch his departure, Salmet took off again just before 10:00hr. But his engine started to misfire. 'My magneto is wrong,' he said later. 'I put it right and I start again at 10:12.'

He crossed the Channel from Cap Gris-Nez to Folkestone in just fifteen minutes, flying at about 85 mph. But the weather deteriorated and he was forced to land at Chatham. He took off for Hendon the following morning at 06:15hr but encountered fog near Maidstone and landed in a field, breaking his propeller. A replacement was sent from Hendon and he was off again despite unfavourable weather.

Salmet struggled as far as Beckton gasworks where he attempted to land in a football field. But it was shorter than he thought and, while he was trying to avoid hitting a goal post, a gust of wind caught his machine and flipped it on its back. After struggling for days to return to Hendon, Salmet was so disgusted with the turn of events that he walked away from his wrecked machine without a backward glance.

Although Henri Salmet failed to fulfil his ambition that day, his consolation prize was the first aerial crossing of the Channel between Eastbourne and Dieppe, a longer journey than Dover to Calais.

It was less than a month later that the first British pilot flew between the two capitals. Gustav Hamel made the trip with a passenger, and a female passenger at that. The lady was Eleanor Trehawke Davies, about whom very little seems to be known other than that she was a regular visitor to the major aviation meetings and managed to persuade some of the leading pilots of the day to take her up. One of them was Gustav Hamel, of whom *Flight* observed somewhat archly that 'he has flown so far and so often'.

Hamel took off from Hendon at 09:38hr on 2 April in a two-seater Blériot powered by a 70 hp Gnome engine. His passenger was given the job of maintaining the air pressure in the petrol tank but she failed to work the hand pump properly and very nearly let the machine down in the sea.

Fortunately for the pair, the aircraft was flying at 7,000 feet when the engine stopped and Hamel was able to glide safely down to a landing near Ambleteuse. After paying a call on Louis Blériot at Hardelot, the pair continued to Paris where they landed at Issy-les-Molineux at 17:55 hr.

At the age of thirty-two, Davies had become the first woman to fly the English Channel. Two weeks later her achievement was emulated by Lady Victoria Perry, daughter of Lord Limerick. In 1913 Davies became the first woman in Britain to loop the loop. Although she never qualified as a pilot, Davies owned two Blériot monoplanes, one of which she donated to the Royal Naval Air Service just before her death in 1915.

A fortnight after Davies' first cross-Channel flight a glamourous American became the first female pilot to fly the Channel. Harriet Quimby was a journalist and Hollywood screenwriter who became interested in aviation in 1910. The following year she became the first woman in the USA to qualify for an aviator's certificate. She later became a professional air show pilot whose trademark flying gear comprised trousers tucked into high lace boots, plum-coloured satin blouse, necklace and antique bracelet. Because of her petite stature and fair skin, the press called her 'the Dresden China Aviatrix' and 'the China Doll'.

Harriet Quimby had strong views about the role of women in aviation. She wrote:

> In my opinion there is no reason why the aeroplane should not open a fruitful occupation for women. I see no reason why they cannot realise handsome incomes by carrying passengers between adjacent towns, why they cannot derive incomes from parcel deliveries, from taking photographs from above or from conducting schools for flying.

In 1912 Quimby decided to come to England to fly the Channel. Her Blériot monoplane powered by a 50 hp Gnome engine was delivered to her at Deal where she began her preparations. She was assisted by Gustav Hamel who test flew the machine once it was assembled. Hamel, unsure of a woman's ability to make the flight, offered to dress in Quimby's purple flying suit and make it for her. She refused.

Harriet awoke at 03:30 hr on 16 April to ideal flying conditions: a generally clear sky and, most importantly, no wind. But it was clear she had no time to waste before the wind strength increased.

Quimby wrote later:

The sky seemed clear, but patches of cloud and masses of fog here and there obscured the blue. The French coast was wholly invisible, by reason of moving masses of mist. The wind had not come up yet. The smooth grounds of the aerodrome gave me a chance for a perfect start.

Hamel had warned her that she was in for a chilly flight and she prepared accordingly. Under her satin flying suit she wore two pairs of silk combinations covered by a long woollen coat with a raincoat over that. Around her shoulders was a long wide stole of sealskin. 'Even this did not satisfy my solicitous friends,' she recalled. 'At the last minute they handed me up a large hot-water bag, which Mr Hamel insisted on tying to my waist like an enormous locket.'

Quimby's account of her flight continued

It was 05:30 hr when my machine got off the ground. The preliminaries were brief. Hearty handshakes were quickly given, the motor began to make its 1,200 rpm and I put up my hand to give the signal of release. Then I was off. The noise of the motor drowned the shouts and cheers of friends below. In a moment I was in the air, climbing steadily in a long circle. I was up 1,500 ft within 30 sec. From this high point of vantage my eyes lit at once on Dover Castle. It was half hidden in a fog bank. I felt that trouble was coming, but I made directly for the flagstaff of the castle, as I had promised the waiting *Mirror* photographers and the moving-picture men I should do.

In an instant I was beyond the cliffs and over the channel. Far beneath I saw the *Mirror*'s tug with its stream of black smoke. It was trying to keep ahead of me, but I passed it in a jiffy. Then the quickening fog obscured my view. Calais was out of sight. I could not see ahead of me or at all below. There was only one thing for me to do and that was to keep my eyes fixed on my compass.

My hands were covered with long Scotch woollen gloves which gave me good protection from the cold and fog; but the machine was wet and my face was so covered with dampness that I had to push my goggles up on my forehead. I could not see through them. I was travelling at over a mile a minute.

The distance straight across from Dover to Calais is only 25, and I knew that land must be in sight if I could only get below the fog and see it. So I dropped from an altitude of about 2,000 ft until I was half that height. The sunlight struck upon my face and my eyes lit upon the white and sandy shores of France. I felt happy but could not find Calais.

Being unfamiliar with the coastline, I could not locate myself. I determined to reconnoitre and the wind had risen and the currents were coming in billowy gusts. I flew a short distance inland to locate myself or find a good place on which to alight. It was all tilled land below me, and rather than tear up the farmers' fields I decided to drop down on the hard and sandy beach. I did so at once, making an easy landing.

Then I jumped from my machine and was alone upon the shore. But it was only for a few moments. A crowd of fishermen – men, women and children each carrying a pail of sand worms – came rushing from all directions toward me. They were chattering in French, of which I comprehended sufficient to discover that they knew I had crossed the channel.

Quimby had indeed flown the Channel, taking an hour and nine minutes to do so. Yet her accomplishment was only briefly covered by the press. The reason is not hard to find: the liner *Titanic* had sunk two days earlier and the story was still dominating the headlines. Even though Quimby had become the first female pilot to fly the Channel, aerial crossings were becoming more routine and consequently less newsworthy.

Such was the increasing reliability of aircraft that machines could be flown from factories in France – still the leading manufacturer of both airframes and engines – to their customers in Britain. So it was that when the government ordered one of the latest two-seater Deperdussins for use by the Royal Navy at Eastchurch it was decided to fly it across. Lieutenant Longmore RN was at the factory in Issy le Molineux to watch the final stress tests on the machine when the wings were loaded with 2,500lb of sand. After successful test flights the machine was ready for its delivery flight on 13 April with M. Prevost, Deperdussin's chief test pilot in command and Lieutenant J.C. Porte RN in the passenger's seat.

Ten miles short of Calais they had to land for a plug change but mist was descending over the Channel and Prevost and Porte were uncertain about continuing. In the end they decided to trust their compass and go at noon.

TRIUMPH AND TRAGEDY

After an uneventful crossing, landfall was made at Deal and the aircraft landed at Eastchurch after a flight of three hours forty-five minutes. It was the first long-distance delivery flight of an aircraft from factory to customer.

A fortnight later, on 2 May, W.H. Ewen collected a 45 hp Caudron single-seat monoplane from the factory at Crotoy intending to fly it to Hendon where it would join his flying school. He took off at 09:32 hr and landed at Calais thirty-three minutes later, having flown fifty miles at about 90 mph in the speedy machine with its futuristic streamlined fuselage. In mid-Channel, however, he flew into cloud and his compass needle started fluctuating wildly. A brief sighting of the sun put him on the right course and he was able to make a safe landing at Dover where he stayed the night. The following day the weather deteriorated markedly and he decided to land at Chatham. From there he decided to send the machine the rest of the way to Hendon by train.

Meanwhile, Hamel and Eleanor Trehawke Davies continued their Channel-hopping, completing three crossings in as many weeks, although they had to make several forced landings due to weather and fuel feed troubles. Their final journey in this series, on 21 May, from Issy to Eastchurch, was completed in four stages.

The popular Claude Grahame-White made several cross-Channel ferry flights but even more noteworthy was James Valentine's achievement. On 4 July he took off from Dover with the intention of making three crossings in two days. His Deperdussin monoplane took thirty-five minutes to reach Wissant. From there, he left almost immediately and flew non-stop to Hendon. The following day Valentine arrived at Abbeville where he stayed the night before travelling on to Paris.

A graphic and colourful description of what it was like to fly the English Channel in those pioneering days came from a passenger in a Caudron seaplane which was being ferried from the factory in France to the Naval Wing of the newly formed Royal Flying Corps at the Isle of Grain.

Well-known display pilot Sidney Pickles was at the controls and W.R.M. Oddey occupying the passenger's seat when they took off on 23 June 1913. All went well until the machine crossed the coast at Gap Griz Nez when it encountered thick cloud. There was no sign of the English coast. A ship came into view, Oddey wrote, and was soon obscured by the mist. But still there was no sight of land. He went on

> It seemed years since we started and the memory of the French coastline had almost faded out of the sense of reality, so long

> did it seem since we had left it. Occasionally I would notice that the machine would rock quite a lot and then fly steadily for a while until it had another spasm. Ordinarily I should have been much interested in the performance and possibly a little alarmed. But, under the present circumstances I think I was willing to accept anything that fate might ordain, were it only a change.

Just after 19:00 hr Pickles tapped Oddey on the shoulder and indicated land ahead. Keeping Dover to their left, the pair headed for Margate where Pickles landed on the sea to refuel. It was nearly dusk when the machine took off again and by 20:24 hr it was passing Herne Bay pier. Oddey's narrative continued

> Presently came Sheerness with the lights of the town and the steamers and the three flashing buoys, making a scintillating picture. Suddenly, three searchlights shot their beams across the water and, passing over a little bay, Pickles switched off and made a smooth landing on the Medway precisely at 21:00 hr.

By April 1913 Gustav Hamel had a dozen Channel crossings to his credit. His thirteenth would form part of what was considered his greatest flight. His plan had been to fly from Dover to the German city of Cologne and he took with him a passenger, Frank Dupree. The fuel tank of his 80 hp Gnome-powered Bleriot carried forty gallons of petrol, enough for five and a half hours flying.

The Channel crossing was uneventful and landfall was made at Dunkirk. After several hours' flying wind and rain was encountered which caused Hamel to deviate from his course. Eventually, he sighted the River Rhine about sixty miles north of Cologne. From then on it was just a matter of following the river to the city where the machine landed after four hours eighteen minutes in the air. Due to the deviations caused by the weather, it had flown about 320 miles non-stop.

Just over a year later the nation was rocked by news of Hamel's death on, as it happened, a cross-Channel flight. On 22 May 1914 the aviator had travelled to Paris to collect a Morane-Saulnier monoplane which he intended to use in the following day's Aerial Derby at Hendon. At 04:40 hr he took off from Villacoublay despite warnings that the Morane's engine had previously been giving trouble.

TRIUMPH AND TRAGEDY

At 05:22 he landed at Crotoy for breakfast and arrived at Blériot's Hardelot airfield at 09:00. His machine was refuelled and he took off for Hendon at 12:15. Nothing further was seen or heard of him and it was assumed he had suffered engine failure in mid-Channel and crashed into the sea.

T.O.M. Sopwith

Thomas Octave Murdoch Sopwith was born in London in 1888, the only son of a well-to-do civil engineer and his wife. Initially interested in motorcycles, the young Sopwith entered the motor trade, selling cars from premises in London's Piccadilly. He made his first balloon ascent with Charles Rolls in June 1906 and subsequently bought his own balloon from the Short brothers.

In 1910 Sopwith won the £4,000 de Forest prize for making the longest flight from a point in England to anywhere on mainland Europe. He flew 169 miles (272km) in three hours forty minutes and used the prize money to establish a flying school at Brooklands in 1912. The following year he founded the Sopwith Aviation Company at Kingston-upon-Thames, although all its aircraft were flown at Brooklands.

In fact, Sopwith established three factories in Kingston, transforming a small town on the southern outskirts of London into the source of most of Britain's First World War fighters and the heart of the military aircraft industry for years afterwards. Over nine decades, Sopwith and its successor firm is thought to have employed 40,000 people in Kingston.

In addition to the Tabloid, a variant of which won the 1913 Schneider Trophy race, Sopwith turned out a variety of successful designs including the Pup, One-and-a-Half Strutter, Dolphin and Snipe. The company made a major contribution to the nation's war effort by producing over 18,000 machines and the 5,700 Camel fighters included in this total helped make the post-Armistice Royal Air Force the world's most powerful air arm.

But despite, or perhaps because of, its wartime success, the company was faced with punitive taxes. The decision was taken in 1920 to liquidate it and start a new company. In this enterprise

Sopwith was joined by close associates Harry Hawker, Fred Sigrist and Bill Eyre, each of whom contributed £5,000. To avoid any possibility of claims against the new company in respect of wartime contracts undertaken by the previous one, they chose to call it H.G. Hawker Engineering.

Later the company became Hawker Aircraft Limited and in 1935 it merged with Sir W.G. Armstrong Whitworth Aircraft and A.V. Roe & Company – Avro. Sopwith – he was knighted in 1953 – remained chairman of the Hawker-Siddeley Group until he retired in 1963 at the age of seventy-five.

In 1977 the group became part of the nationalised British Aerospace. Privatised in the 1980s, BAe Systems remains one of the world's leading defence companies. Thomas Sopwith died in 1989 at the age of 101.

Gustav Hamel

Good looking and highly accomplished as a pilot, it was hardly surprising that Gustav Hamel should have been an idol to the thousands of spectators who thronged to see him in action.

He was the only son of Dr Gustav Hugo Hamel, Royal Physician to King Edward VII, and his wife, Caroline Magdalena Elise. He was actually born in Hamburg, Germany, as his parents' first child, but the family moved to England at the end of the century to live at Kingston-upon-Thames. They became naturalised British citizens in 1910.

Hamel was educated at Westminster School and, like many others of his generation, became fascinated by aviation. In 1910 at the age of twenty-one he learned to fly at the Blériot school at Pau, France. He had gained his Aero Club pilot certificate in February 1911. His first flight of note was made the following month when he flew from Hendon to Brooklands in a record fifty-eight minutes.

In September Hamel flew a Blériot from Hendon to Windsor, covering the twenty-one miles (34km) in ten minutes to deliver the first official airmail to the Postmaster General. Included was a postcard Hamel had written en route.

His attempt to carry newspapers from Hendon to Southend a few weeks earlier had not been so successful as bad weather forced his machine down at Hammersmith in West London. In April 1913 he made the first non-stop flight from England to Germany and, in November, the fastest time in the London-Brighton-London race in which only four of the nine starters finished.

Following his disappearance over the Channel on 22 May the Admiralty sent out a flotilla of destroyers to search the Straits of Dover but nothing was found and the search was called off after two days and nights. In a rare tribute to a civilian from the armed forces, the Admiralty issued a statement praising Hamel's 'daring, skill, resource and modesty'.

A message of condolence to the Hamel family from Buckingham Palace also noted that the King and Queen, who had seen him fly at Windsor, 'were struck by the skill courage and mastery with which he controlled the aeroplane'.

Harriet Quimby

Journalist, film writer and professional display pilot: Harriet Quimby was all of these but her crowning achievement was becoming the first woman to fly an aeroplane across the English Channel. She was also the first woman to gain an aviator's certificate (number 37) in the USA.

Born in Michigan in 1875 to William and Ursula Quimby, Harriet was still a child when she and her family moved to San Francisco. At about the turn of the century, she joined the *San Francisco Dramatic Review* as a staff writer. Later she moved to New York in 1905 where she became drama critic on *Leslie's Illustrated Weekly*.

Quimby became fascinated by the technological developments of the age and wrote a piece about a 100-mph ride in a race car before turning her attention to flying. She covered several of the major flying meetings but soon realised she wanted to be part of this fast-moving new age.

She met John Moisant – first pilot to fly a passenger across the English Channel – who owned a flying school. Moisant persuaded

Quimby's editor to pay for her flying lessons so that she could write about her experiences. She also provided notes about suitable dress for flying as well as outlining some technical aspects. Moisant was killed in December 1910 but Quimby persisted with her flying lessons and, having gained her licence, set about joining the professional air show circuit. She was well aware that her good looks, charm and media savviness could be used to advance her career.

Indeed, success came quickly. Among her rewards was a $1,500 prize for being the first woman to fly at night. But her success wasn't confined to aviation. In 1911 she found the time to write a number of film scripts.

Had it not been for the unfortunate clash between her cross-Channel flight and the loss of the *Titanic*, Quimby would have been a lot better known in Britain. Undaunted, she returned to the USA where she intended to participate in the Boston-Harvard Meet on 1 July. With a passenger, event organizer William Willard, she set off in her Blériot two-seater for a flight round Boston Harbour. Nearing the lighthouse at 3,000 feet, the machine was seen to pitch unexpectedly forward. Both occupants were thrown out and fell to their deaths.

The cause of the accident was never satisfactorily explained. One theory was that Quimby had fainted, another that neither occupant had been strapped in. But it seemed unlikely that the fearless conqueror of the English Channel would have fainted or that such a safety conscious professional aviator would have neglected basic safety precautions.

Chapter Six

Lunch in Paris, Tea in London

The English Channel sparkles in the bright summer sunlight as competitors in the first London to Paris Air Race set off from Dover on the second stage of the great contest.

Soon, the machines flown by pilots from Britain, France, Italy, Japan and the USA will be strung out over the sea and heading for Calais. No doubt the intrepid contestants have been inspired by Louis Blériot's flight the previous July as much as the £10,000 prize on offer from a newspaper magnate.....

Actually, the makers of the 1965 movie *Those Magnificent Men in Their Flying Machines* were a little bit out in their timing. Reality was again lagging behind art. There was indeed a cross-Channel air race but not in 1910 as the film envisaged.

Air racing would become a popular spectator sport in the years leading up to the First World War and two events in particular caught the public imagination. The 1911 Circuit of Europe and the 1914 London-Paris-London race both involved not one but two Channel crossings.

Besides highlighting the frailty of contemporary aircraft, to say nothing of the courage and determination of pioneer aviators, it had become clear that London and Paris were now much closer.

The Circuit of Europe – it actually involved visits to four countries – was the biggest and most ambitious air race organized so far. A total purse of £18,300 was offered. It was planned to run it in twelve stages – Paris (Vincennes) to Liège via Reims, Liège-Spa-Liège, Liège-Utrecht via Verloo, Utrecht-Brussels via Breda, Brussels-Roubaix, Roubaix-Calais, Calais-London via Dover, London-Calais (via Shoreham and Dover) and finally Calais-Paris via Amiens. Clearly the most hazardous stages would be the two Channel crossings.

A total of forty-three aircraft lined up in three rows at Vincennes for the start scheduled for 06:00hr on 18 June 1911. A huge crowd, estimated at more than 500,000 million, had assembled in driving rain from midnight to watch the start of the race. A force of 6,000 soldiers and police was there to keep control.

The field comprised a wide range of aircraft types, some well-known, others obscure: eight Moranes, seven Deperdussins, six Blériots, three Sommers, three Caudrons, three Henri Farmans, two Maurice Farmans, two Bristols, two Voisins, two Astras, and single examples of Nieuport, Tellier, Antoinette, Train, Bonnet-Lab, Danton, Barillon, Vinet, Pischoff, REP and van Meel. Not all the entrants would make the start, however.

There were just two British machines, a pair of Bristol Boxkite biplanes flown by French pilots, and a single British pilot, James Valentine, who was flying a Deperdussin monoplane. First away was Maurice Tabuteau (Bristol) with Tetard flying the second Bristol following in fourth place but they were soon overtaken by the faster French monoplanes so that the leaders at Liège were Vidart (Deperdussin), Vedrines (Morane), Weyman (Nieuport), and Lieutenant de Vaisseau Conneau (Blériot) competing under the name 'Beaumont'.

Only eight of the forty-three contestants reached Liège. Three pilots had been killed and another badly injured in crashes before reaching the control point at Reims. The short stage from Liège to Spa and back had to be postponed because of bad weather. On the 21st eighteen contestants started the next stage and the fifteen finishers were headed by Vedrines, Vidart, and 'Beaumont'. By the time they reached Utrecht, Gilbert (REP), Garros (Blériot) and Vidart were the leaders.

Bad weather imposed a further delay and it was not until the 26th that the contestants were flagged away on the leg to Brussels. When they reached the Belgian capital, 'Beaumont' was three hours ahead of Garros who led Vedrines by seventeen hours. The journey to Roubaix whittled the number of runners down to ten with Vedrines, Vidart (flying a replacement Deperdussin) and 'Beaumont' forming the top three.

Now came the first cross-Channel stage. It had been postponed until 2 July, which allowed some of the slower machines to catch up. As a result, eleven pilots left Calais and all reached Dover safely, led by Vedrines, Vidart and Gilbert. After an hour's rest the contestants took off to fly along the coast to Shoreham. Two of the runners were delayed and another dropped out during this stage.

Vedrines took just under three hours to reach Hendon, thirty minutes ahead of Vidart. After a day's rest the surviving contestants left on their next stage of the journey which had been shortened so that the return flight across the Channel might form a separate stage.

LUNCH IN PARIS, TEA IN LONDON

Ten contestants started for Shoreham and only Valentine failed to arrive on the Sussex coast. He landed instead at Brooklands with a misfiring engine. Vedrines in his speedy Morane monoplane was leading at Shoreham and stopped there for just two minutes before taking off for Dover, where he arrived well ahead of the rest of the field. Vidart and 'Beaumont' followed him.

On the 6th nine pilots crossed from Dover to Calais without incident. Vedrines made the crossing in just over thirty minutes with Gibert (REP) and Kimmerling (Sommer) taking thirty-three and thirty-four minutes respectively. Tabuteau crossed in forty-three minutes but Valentine had retired from the contest at Brooklands.

It was nineteen days after the start when the nine remaining pilots started the final stage of the contest. Vidart was the first to reach Amiens, followed by Gibert, Garros and Vedrines. The latter crashed on landing and had to use another machine to complete the course. There was nothing in the rules to prevent such a substitution and, as it happened, most of the competitors took advantage of this concession.

Vidart was first to land at Vincennes, followed by Gibert, Garros and 'Beaumont'. Gibert was the only monoplane pilot to finish in the same machine with which he started. When the overall times were added up 'Beaumont' was declared the winner, followed by Garros and Vidart. Vedrines was fourth and Gibert fifth. Of the pilots of British machines, Tabuteau with the Bristol Boxkite managed to reach Paris but officials ruled that he hadn't completed the whole course.

The Channel had been crossed twice in four days and all the pilots who attempted the overwater flights were able to complete them successfully, eleven the first time and nine the second.

Even more testing was the London-Paris-London race of July 1914, run just a few weeks before the outbreak of the First World War. The contest was even more difficult and dangerous than the Circuit of Europe. The rules were tougher and the timescale far less leisurely with more than 500 miles to be flown, including nearly sixty over water and all in one day. It turned out to be a gruelling test of man and machine with only two classified as finishers.

The course was Hendon to Buc near Versailles and back. To avoid the risks involved in overflying London itself and of making long sea crossings, turning points were established at Harrow, Epsom, Folkestone and Boulogne. Despite the romance and challenge of participating in the first race between the British and French capitals only fourteen entries were received from pilots representing Britain, France, Germany, the USA and Switzerland.

CROSS-CHANNEL AVIATION PIONEERS

The field was further depleted even before the race started due to what aviation historian Dallas Brett called an 'epidemic of engine trouble' which prevented them from even reaching Hendon to start the race. Of the seven machines able to start all but two were monoplanes, mostly Morane-Saulniers. Lord Carbery had a fast Bristol Scout and other notable runners were the American William L. Brock, fresh from his victory in the London-Manchester race and the Aerial Derby and the French ace Roland Garros. In this handicap race only the Bristol was on scratch. Most of the contestants were wearing bulky life-jackets, which *Flight*'s reporter thought made them look like 'skippers of flying lifeboats'. Only Renaux and Garros weren't wearing them.

The field prepared to take off from Hendon at 06:30 hr on 11 July but cloud cover limited visibility to just 100 feet above the aerodrome and it was decided to delay the start for half an hour. By that time visibility at Hendon had not improved although reports from Dover indicated good weather over the Channel. As a result, the field was despatched at five-minute intervals.

T. Elder Hearn was first to go in his 80 hp Gnome-powered Blériot monoplane with Mrs Hearn as passenger. They took off at 07:30 hr, followed five minutes later by Eugene Renaux of France in his 120 hp Maurice Shorthorn pusher biplane, the most powerful machine in the race. He was accompanied by a passenger, Miss Unwin.

The Hearns didn't get far. Alarmingly, their engine stopped almost as soon as their machine had cleared the aerodrome fence. Hearn managed to land it safely but after working on the engine he decided it was not safe to continued and retired from the contest.

Renaux returned a few minutes after taking off saying conditions were too bad to continue but changed his mind later. The three Moranes flown by Louis Noel, Brock and R.H. Carr, which had been built at Grahame-White's factory at Hendon, all left on schedule, followed by Garros. Last to leave was Carbery and he only just managed to get away in a machine loaded down with fuel and oil.

There were two non-starters, Helmuth Hirth flying a Morane powered by an 80 hp Le Rhone engine, and R.L. Skene, piloting a 120 hp Martinsyde monoplane.

Carr soon lost his way in the mist and landed five miles from the start to await clearer weather. After an hour he took off again and headed for Dymchurch on the Kent coast where he retired from the race. Meanwhile, Noel led at the Epsom turn, followed by Brock and Garros. Carbery was next, going like the wind, but Renaux was reported to be near Gravesend and many miles off his course.

LUNCH IN PARIS, TEA IN LONDON

Noel was the next to retire just after crossing the English coast. A petrol pipe had fractured and he quickly turned back and glided to a landing at Camber near Rye. He had, however, missed the Folkestone control and would probably have been disqualified had he continued.

Even at this early stage the race seemed to have developed into a three-way contest between Garros, Brock and Carbery. By the time they reached Boulogne, Brock had a fifteen-minute lead over Garros and was thirty-nine minutes up on Carbery on actual flying time. But the American was short of fuel and had to land at Hardelot to top up his tanks. This didn't prevent him from extending his lead and he arrived at Buc forty-six minutes ahead of Carbery who had passed Garros on the run from Boulogne. Garros landed six minutes after the Bristol.

There was a two-hour stop at Buc and Garros used the time to work on the Gnome engine of his machine. The French mechanics feverishly dismantled it and finished by fitting a new magneto and propeller. The result was that Garros was twenty-five minutes late in starting his return leg. There was still a chance that Carbery could make up the forty-six minutes he had lost to Brock as his Bristol biplane was at least 20 mph faster than the American's Morane.

But despite another refuelling stop, at Hardelot, which took him just twelve minutes, Brock was well on his way. He reached Folkestone at 15:45hr and Epsom at 16:28. He swept around the Harrow turn and landed at Hendon at 16:48.

Brock had averaged 71 mph for the whole trip. 'Needless to say,' *Flight* reported,

> the reception he got was tremendous and the scene after his landing was one to be remembered. Long before the machine came to rest it was surrounded by an enthusiastic crowd that overwhelmed him with greetings and questions.

His first act on climbing out of his machine was to shed the bulky life-jacket before handing over some letters he had been given to deliver. Fifteen minutes after he landed Brock was hailed as the winner as Garros was still some way behind. Accordingly, Brock was presented with his trophy by Lady Reid, wife of Sir George Reid, the High Commissioner for Australia.

Carbery, meanwhile, had also landed to refuel but his stop was more leisurely and he didn't leave Hardelot until Brock had returned to Hendon.

By the time he set out across the Channel he was ten minutes behind Garros. But in mid-crossing his Le Rhone engine spluttered to a stop, landing him in the water. As it happened, he ditched near a steamer and was able to avoid getting his feet wet. The ship picked up both pilot and aircraft. A little later, Carbery was transferred to HMS *St Vincent* and taken to Folkestone pier.

At 18:20 hr Garros was sighted by spectators on the ground at Hendon approaching the airfield from the direction of the Welsh Harp pub which suggested he had not passed Harrow. When he landed he was asked if he had missed the Harrow turn but as he wasn't sure he immediately took off again, flew around the control point and returned to Hendon where he was credited with a time of eight hours twenty-eight minutes. Renaux had continued doggedly and reached Buc three and a half hours behind Brock. He started his return journey from there at 16:49 hr but it was too late for him to complete the course before darkness fell. He spent the night at Boulogne and reached Hendon at 12:25hr the following day. He had taken twenty-six hours fifty-five minutes to complete the course but was awarded third place in the race and a £50 prize.

Brock was the winner on handicap as well as on time and he won the £300 prize presented by the Royal Aero Club, a handsome trophy and the £500 awarded by the race organizers, the International Correspondence Schools. Garros won the second prize of £150.

The results of the contest were as follows:

	Total flying time (hr, min, sec)			**Average speed (mph)**
1 W.L. Brock	7	3	6	71.5
2 R. Garros	8	28	47	58.8
3 E. Renaux	24	34	0	-

Brock's time for the outward leg to Paris was three hours thirty-three minutes and twenty-four seconds and for the return flight it was three hours twenty-nine minutes and forty-two seconds. His altitude did not exceed 2,000 feet.

The result meant that Brock had won a total of £1,750 in three races within five weeks. He was victorious in the Aerial Derby around London and the London-Manchester-London race. In each case he had relied upon superior navigation and determination to beat faster machines.

After the race *Flight* reflected on its implications. It had shown the enormous potential of international communications by air, eliminated the artificial barriers of national borders and demonstrated the aeroplane's 'enormous' superiority in speed over other modes of transport. Brock had completed the course with its two-way crossing of the Channel in little more than seven hours. That was just twenty minutes more than a single journey by surface transport could be expected to take.

To *Flight* it meant that 'the aeroplane is destined to play a far greater part in the future of rapid communications than is imagined by most people.'

Claude Grahame-White, manufacturer of the winning aircraft, predicted that cross-Channel flying would soon become commonplace. This would enable pilots and their passengers to have lunch in Paris and be back in London in time for tea.

The Morane-Saulnier Type G

Morane-Saulnier monoplanes dominated the major competitive aviation events in the months before August 1914, being the first two finishers in the gruelling London-Paris-London race of July 1914.

Such machines were used to make two of the most outstanding flights of 1913. Robert Stack collected his example from the factory in Paris and flew it to Hendon in heavy rain and low cloud, spending six hours thirty-six minutes in the air to cover 260 miles. Claude Grahame-White was also collecting a G Type fitted with floats for delivery to London when he took off from the River Seine and landed on the Thames at Putney. He went via Le Havre, crossed the Channel from Boulogne to Dover where he landed for lunch, then followed the Kent coast to the Thames estuary. That day Grahame-White covered 500 miles.

The company had been formed by Raymond Saulnier and the brothers Léon and Robert Morane in 1911. The Model G, a wire-braced shoulder-wing monoplane was the company's first commercial-successful design, favoured by, among other pilots, Gustav Hamel, Roland Garros and William Brock.

It was constructed mainly of ash and pine with fabric-covered wing and fuselage. Ash was also employed for the wing spars with pine ribs. Wire provided internal bracing. Both front and rear wing spars were bolted to the fuselage structure by hinges to permit roll control by wing warping. The tail comprised an all-moving horizontal surface acting as elevators and a vertical rudder.

V-sparred tubular steel structures braced the wings from the top of the fuselage, anchored to the top of the fuselage just forward of the cockpit. Underneath a similar stricture was used for the landing chassis. The axle was free to move upwards in a smaller inverted V with rubber bands used to provide shock absorbers. There were two seats in the cockpit with the passenger seated behind the pilot. The engine was hung from a nose-mounted bearer and drove an eight-feet diameter propeller.

The type was also built under licence at Claude Grahame-White's factory at Hendon. Brock's machine differed in detail from French-constructed aircraft. It was claimed to have flown over 1,000 miles without major repair.

The Morane Type G was not considered suitable for war service, however, but it was developed into the Type L, which was to become the first fighter aircraft to be used during the First World War. Roland Garros fitted a machine gun to the nose his aircraft to fire forward through the propeller arc. Steel plates were fitted to the propeller to deflect the bullets striking the propeller.

When Garros had to make a forced landing behind German lines, the Germans, by now thoroughly alarmed, asked Anthony Fokker to come up with something better. The Dutch designer devised a synchronising mechanism that avoided machine-gun bullets having to pass through the propeller arc.

In the 1930s the company built the MS 406 which was the most numerous French fighter on the outbreak of the Second World War. After the war the company specialised in building light training and touring aircraft.

Specification
Accommodation pilot and passenger
Length 20 ft 8 in.
Wingspan 30 ft 2 in.
Wing area 172 sq. ft
Empty weight 208lb
Gross weight 815lb
Powerplant one Gnome Lambda 7-cylinder air-cooled rotary engine developing 80 hp
Maximum speed 76 mph
Rate of climb 345 ft/min.

Chapter Seven

Exploiting the Practical Possibilities

The outbreak of war on 4 August 1914 brought civil flying in Britain to an end for the duration. From then until 1919 the only aircraft that would be crossing the English Channel would be military machines.

The Home Office imposed an immediate ban on civil flying. This meant that only naval or army machines or those flying under naval or military orders were permitted to fly. The only exceptions were those operating within three miles of a recognised aerodrome. This meant that the work of civilian flying schools could continue, which they did until the Admiralty and War Office put in place their own pilot-training arrangements. In the meantime, the activities of flying schools were strictly regulated by the authorities and confined to tuition.

A veil of secrecy was clamped down over all aeronautical activities immediately after the declaration of war. Notices were posted at naval air stations to discourage unwanted interest in aviation. The public was warned that sentries had orders to challenge and, if not instantly obeyed, to open fire.

The ban on non-military flying was lifted on 1 May 1919, six months after the Armistice brought the fighting to an end. Yet on 8 February 1919, a Farman Goliath flew twelve passengers from Toussus-le-Noble to RAF Kenley. Since non-military flying was banned, Lucien Bossoutrot and his passengers were all ex-military pilots who wore uniforms and carried mission orders to cover their flight. It took two hours and thirty minutes. The return flight, made the following day, took two hours and ten minutes.

On 14 July the first international commercial flight arrived in the form of a Caudron aircraft piloted by Étienne Poulet, carrying photographs from Paris-Le Bourget airport in accordance with inter-governmental agreements marking the Treaty of Versailles. At that time, Hounslow Heath was the only approved aerodrome in the London area with customs facilities.

Following the Armistice of November 1918, the need for speedy communications between London and Paris increased. As a result, the RAF formed a special unit to transport mail, documents and government ministers between the two cities. No. 2 (Communications) Squadron, 86 Wing operated between Kenley in Surrey and Buc near Paris. Major J.R. McCrindle was the CO and the unit operated de Havilland DH 4 and Handley Page O/400 bombers.

Three silver-painted O/400s were put into service as HM Air Liners *Silver Queen, Silver Star* and *Great Britain* to provide rapid transport to Versailles. They were fitted with six to eight seats but passengers had to put up with engine noise and vibration.

The Versailles Peace Conference opened in January 1919 and the main business was concluded by June with the signing of the peace treaty. *Silver Star* flew the chief British delegates to the conference and was also the first aircraft to undertake a night passenger service to France.

While the conference was in session the RAF operated a daily cross-Channel courier and mail service using DH 4s. Many cabinet ministers took advantage of the rapid communication this service offered, including Chancellor of the Exchequer Bonar Law, Winston Churchill, Lord Milner, Major General Sir Frederick Sykes, and Australian Prime Minister William Hughes.

At the chancellor's request, several DH 4s were modified with covered cabins to accommodate a pair of face-to-face seats. This would enable a minister and his private secretary to travel in relative comfort and be able to work and converse during the flight.

Now under the command of Wing Commander W. Harold Primrose, the unit made history on 28 June 1919, the day the main peace treaty was signed. Four of its DH 4As flew in line astern over the Palace of Versailles during the signing of the peace treaty. One of them later carried Bonar Law from Buc to Kenley with a copy of Prime Minister Lloyd George's letter to the King advising him that the treaty had been signed.

The unit was disbanded in September 1919 and its DH 4As, like hundreds of other war surplus machines, were put on the market. Meanwhile, in July, four new DH 4s straight off the production line had been converted into DH 4As for use by Air Transport and Travel (AT&T), operating subsidiary of Airco, the company which had built them and of which Geoffrey de Havilland was the chief designer.

It was one of these machines which achieved everlasting fame by flying the first post-war commercial service. But the DH 4 was soon succeeded by the bigger DH 16 which was used to operate the early scheduled services between London and Paris.

EXPLOITING THE PRACTICAL POSSIBILITIES

The service had been anticipated by AT&T almost as soon as the Armistice brought the war to an end. On 15 November 1918 the airline announced that tickets for the London-Paris service would be available from the Ritz Hotel for £15 guineas (£15.75). Seats would be allocated according to the number on the ticket. At 10:00hr each day passengers would be transported from the Ritz in London to the airport for a 10:30hr departure, subject to weather. Traffic was clearly not the consideration it is today. The aircraft was scheduled to arrive at Le Bourget at 13:00hr and passengers would be at the Ritz in Paris half an hour later.

On Monday 25 August 1919 AT&T DH 4A G-EAJC piloted by Lieutenant E.H. 'Bill' Lawford, left Hounslow Heath aerodrome for Paris at 09:10hr. The aircraft carried one passenger, George Stevenson-Reece of the London *Evening Standard*. Also on board, according to *Flight* was

> a full load, including a number of daily newspapers, a consignment of leather from a London firm to Paris, several brace of grouse and a considerable number of jars of Devonshire cream. It arrived at Le Bourget, the Paris terminus, at 11:40.

By all accounts, the weather that day was 'grim with heavy rain'. Yet it was a busy one with several flights criss-crossing the Channel on routes between the two capitals. The first daily international service departed from Hounslow at 12:45hr for Paris later in the day piloted by Major Cyril Patterson. The aircraft was an Airco DH 16 (K-130) of AT&T.

If there is some ambiguity about which was actually the first scheduled service this is explained by the fact that Lawford's flight departed ahead of its intended time and was not, strictly speaking, *scheduled*.

In the event it hardly mattered: both aircraft were operated by the same airline. One of the journalists on Patterson's flight was Bruce Ingham, editor of the *Illustrated London News*. He was so impressed by the speed and convenience of air travel that he wrote

> What would have been thought some 50 years ago if anyone had seriously made the announcement that our businessmen would, in a few years, be able to have lunch in London and tea in Paris and return to London in time for dinner? And yet all this has now become possible. One cannot hope to describe adequately the interest, the sense of security and the comfort which such a journey gives, to say nothing of the time saved,

the avoidance of inconvenience caused by change from train to boat to train again, with the usual scramble for places, and the irritating delays at Customs in the journey between London and Paris.

The *Evening Standard* was also full of praise for the level of comfort offered by the DH 4As and DH 16s. The paper noted

> These are both comfortable and reliable machines with cabins through the side of which passengers can see easily. The old war cockpit has been superseded in favour of an enclosed transparent area. The machine will have a cruising speed of 100 mph so that winds of 30 to 40 mph will not delay us to any appreciable extent. The journey to Le Bourget should take about two hours and a quarter.

Lieutenant J. McMullin piloted the return AT&T DH4A service later that day. He took off from Le Bourget at 12:40 hr with two passengers, Bill Lawford and V.M. Console of the *Daily Mail*. They arrived at Hounslow at 2:45hr.

Also, on 25 August, an outbound proving flight was operated by Handley Page Transport, which had been created in June 1919 by the Cricklewood-based aircraft manufacturer, typically using passenger conversions of the Handley Page O/400 twin-engined bomber. The pilot was Major Foot and on board were a number of Fleet Street journalists. *Flight* reported:

> The machine started from Cricklewood at 08:20hr, called at Hounslow for Customs formalities, was away at 09:20 and landed at Le Bourget at 13:15hr. Owing to difficulty in obtaining petrol, the return journey was postponed to the following day. Handley Page brought a new level of comfort to cross-Channel flying.

The company began regular cross-Channel operations a week after its initial proving flights. Handley Page was AT&T's main rival but it had access to bigger machines through its parent company's production of twin-engined types like the O/400 bomber converted to carry passengers. George Woods Humphery was the company's manager.

EXPLOITING THE PRACTICAL POSSIBILITIES

In September Handley Page launched scheduled services between Cricklewood and Brussels and Paris. Fares were £10 10s (£10.50) for a single trip to Brussels and £15 15s (£15.75) for a single to Paris.

By November the airline had carried 554 passengers and 9,600 lb of freight. It had also introduced some enhancements that improved on the basic service offered by AT&T. From early October a limousine service provided transport between city centres and aerodromes. Wicker armchair seating was introduced and there were curtained windows which could be opened in flight, gilded mirrors and, as an added touch of luxury, vases for holding fresh flowers. Passengers were also offered lunch boxes containing sandwiches, chocolate and fruit. Toilets, though, were still in the future. Handley Page made much of the fact that its aircraft had two engines for added safety.

In December 1919 a new machine appeared. The first purpose-designed British airliner, the Handley Page W8 was the winner of a government competition and, although it went into service on the London-Paris route in October 1921, the single prototype was later re-built as the lower-powered but more economical W8b, of which Handley Page Transport was to operate three. The W8b evolved into a family of two- and three-engined airliners which included W8e, W9 and W10.

By September 1919 AT&T was announcing that it had made fifty-four flights in its first month of operation. One service had been cancelled due to bad weather and a second because of a mechanical defect with the aircraft. Depending on the weather, flights took two hours thirty minutes but if the winds were against them the time would be inflated by fifteen minutes.

Between 25 August and 18 September AT&T's aircraft flew a combined total of 24,750 miles. During its first seven weeks of operation AT&T completed ninety-nine flights from a schedule of 102; after fifteen weeks it had flown 200 services out of 227 timetabled. This was an impressive achievement considering the weather experienced.

In addition to carrying passengers AT&T reported that there was an increasing demand for air cargo. A 25lb parcel containing furs went at the premium rate of £9 7s 6d (£9.35.5p). The airline was contracted by the GPO to provide the world's first scheduled international airmail service between London and Paris on 10 November 1919, using DH 4A G-EAHF piloted by Lieutenant J. McMullin.

His attempt to begin the service the day before was frustrated by bad weather. Low clouds forced McMullin to turn back after reaching Epsom. The first airmail had to go by train and ferry. Things were just as bad in France. The French Post Office had awarded a similar contract to *Compagnie générale transaérienne* which used a Breguet aircraft. But it, too, encountered bad weather and the mail had to go by surface transport that day.

Once the service did start mail posted at several central London post offices was collected by motorcycle and taken to Hounslow to meet the 12:30h r flight. This reached Paris by 14:45 hr and the mail was then taken to the city centre for sorting and delivery by 16:00 hr the same day. The service improved the delivery times of onward mail to other European capitals by almost twenty-four hours. Consignments bound for places like Madrid and Rome continued on express trains leaving Paris during the evenings.

AT&T was paid 2s 0d (10p) out of the charge of 2s 6d (12.5p) per ounce that customers paid to send a letter by air. But loads were erratic and during the winter months the weather inevitably affected schedules. The pilots were still exposed to the elements in open and unheated cockpits and required to fly visually using unreliable compasses. They lacked any kind of radio aid.

Crossing the Channel was still a hazardous enterprise, as Captain Jerry Shaw and his passenger discovered on 29 October 1919. They left Le Bourget in poor weather and with a non-functioning compass. Shaw planned to follow another aircraft but they became separated in the poor visibility. He became lost and was forced down in the sea. He did, though, come down near a ship which enabled his passenger, bowler hat in hand, to walk along the aircraft's wing and step aboard the rescue vessel. After landing at Weymouth, Shaw and his passenger continued their journey to London by train.

Even though some of AT&T's aircraft had enclosed cabins, they were still draughty and unheated as well as noisy. As a result, passengers often had to wear bulky flying gear to have any hope of keeping warm.

But it was still heavy going for the British airlines. AT&T, part of Airco run by George Holt Thomas, was absorbed by the BSA Group, which was mainly concerned with the manufacture of cars, motorcycles and guns. AT&T therefore flew its last service in December 1920.

By that time there were several airlines, British and foreign, operating cross-Channel services. *Compagnie des messageries aériennes* (CMA) had alternated with Handley Page on the Paris route using Breguet 14s. As CMA was establishing relations with Handley Page, *Compagnie générale transaérienne* had been appointed AT&T's Paris agent but later introduced its own aircraft to compete on the route. In September *Lignes aérienne farman* joined the already over-subscribed London-Paris operations.

EXPLOITING THE PRACTICAL POSSIBILITIES

Another new operator was *Koninklijke Luchvaart Maatschappij voor Nederland en Kolonien,* or in English, Royal Dutch Airlines for the Netherlands and its Colonies. Usually, though, it would be known just as KLM. The operation was formally established on 7 October 1919 and a fortnight later moved into its first office on Heerengracht in The Hague. But it would not be until the following year that it would operate its first service.

The deed of incorporation was signed in March 1920, enabling operations to begin but first the airline had to acquire aircraft and pilots. KLM's management established contact with UK-based Air Transport and Travel (AT&T) to discuss ways of launching the airline. The idea of joint operations was explored but it was decided to lease aircraft and crews from AT&T.

So it was that on 17 May 1920 DH16 G-EALU landed at Schiphol airport, Amsterdam, captained by Jerry Shaw. He had flown from London's Croydon airport with two passengers and a selection of London newspapers. The passengers were two British journalists and by all accounts their 135-minute flight across the North Sea had been somewhat rough. At times bad weather forced the aircraft down to just 300 feet above the waves.

In June 1920, a Brussels-London service was launched by the Belgian company *Syndicat National pour L'etude des Transports Aériens* (SNETA) using DH 4 aircraft. Handley Page had dropped this route in February in favour of Amsterdam, although it was resumed in July. The Amsterdam service began in conjunction with KLM. On 26 July Lieutenant E. Halliwell began an experimental service carrying British, Belgian and Dutch mail on the London-Brussels-Rotterdam-Amsterdam route. It was discontinued in October 1920 due to insufficient loads. Handley Page ceased flying the Paris route the following month.

The airline suffered another blow in December when one of its O/400s crashed on take-off in fog at the company's Cricklewood base. The pilot and flight engineer were killed, as were two passengers, but four others escaped.

Meanwhile a new British cross-Channel airline had entered the market. in October 1919 S. Instone and Company, a shipping line and coal exporter, began operating its own small airline, initially to ferry staff and internal mail from Cardiff to Hounslow and then on to Paris. The company had become involved in aviation in 1910 when it sponsored Ernest Willows' airship *City of Cardiff* on its flight from South Wales to London and France. It was the first crossing of the English Channel by airship.

In May 1920 the company became Instone Air Line when it opened the Paris sector of its route to the public. Its first aircraft was DH 4 G-EAMU which had an enclosed cabin for two passengers. The airline lost little time in ordering something bigger and better.

Advertisements in *The Times* featured the airline's new Vickers Vimy Commercial, a bulbous-nosed machine based on the Vimy bomber which had gained fame by becoming the first aeroplane to fly the Atlantic non-stop. The Commercial could accommodate ten passengers and featured a lavatory, which may have made it the first airliner to boast such a feature.

Instone was offering single fares to Paris at £12 but the aircraft, christened *City of London*, its fuselage painted royal blue and its wings silver, also flew to Brussels and Cologne. The airline was highly innovative and claimed to be the first to provide uniforms for its crew, which were similar to those worn by the crews of its ships.

Fares were cut to £10 in a bid to deal with the competition. But by the end of 1920 all British airlines had ceased operations. The chief bone of contention was the level of subsidy offered to the continental carriers by their governments. By the winter the newly opened airport at Croydon, which had superseded Hounslow in March 1920, was providing facilities only to foreign airlines and their passengers.

At first the British government seemed determined to ignore the benefits of civil aviation. It was certainly against any form of direct subsidy for the struggling airlines, arguing that it already provided indirect help by making ground facilities available to them. The airlines began a vigorous lobbying campaign in favour of subsidies, supported by most sections of the press.

Winston Churchill, Secretary of State for Air, responded to this criticism by establishing a high-powered committee to consider the matter and make recommendations. The committee, chaired by Lord Weir of Eastwood, former Secretary of State for Air, produced a report that was tabled to the cabinet in May 1920. It was clear from the outset that its members were divided on the issue and some expressed reservations about its key recommendations.

A majority of members, however, agreed that a measure of financial subsidy was justified to see the airlines through the immediate crisis. Its report noted that the lead in aviation gained by Britain during the war could be lost and that national prestige would suffer 'in a new and potentially important sphere of commercial activity'.

The cross-Channel services, it said, could be regarded as 'a nucleus' from which greater development would follow. The committee recommended that direct assistance, limited to £250,000 should be offered to companies operating on 'approved routes' but only for the 1920-21 and 1921-22 financial years. The approved routes were London-Paris and

The moment that history was made. This engraving shows the balloon flown by Jean-Pierre Blanchard and Dr John Jeffries landing at Calais, having taken off from Dover, on 7 January 1785. (Library of Congress)

The first two men to cross the Channel by air – Jean-Pierre Blanchard on the left, and Dr John Jeffries on the right. (Library of Congress)

On 19 July 1909, Hubert Latham became the first airman in history to make a forced landing on water when the engine of his Antoinette monoplane (in which Latham is pictured here) failed while he was attempting a crossing of the Channel. (Library of Congress)

Hubert Latham's Antoinette monoplane. Six days after his ditching on 19 July 1909, Hubert had planned to make a second attempt, only to be woken in the morning and told that one of his competitors, a certain Louis Blériot, had just taken off. (Library of Congress)

The engine of Louis Blériot's aircraft is prepared for starting on the morning of 25 July 1909. Shortly after this picture was taken, Blériot would set off on his ground-breaking flight across the English Channel. (Library of Congress)

With the end of his flight in sight, Louis Blériot is pictured here during the final stretch, the cliffs at Dover visible in the distance, on 25 July 1909. (Library of Congress)

Some 36 minutes and 30 seconds after he had taken off, Blériot made a very heavy landing, damaging his aircraft, on an area of gently sloping land called Northfall Meadow close to Dover Castle – where this picture was taken. (Library of Congress)

Charles Stewart Rolls and Mrs. Assheton Harbord pictured in the basket of a balloon. On 2 June 1910, Rolls become the first person to complete a double crossing of the Channel in a heavier-than-air aircraft. For her part, Mrs. Assheton Harbord was also a dedicated aeronaut, crossing the Channel a number of times.

On 23 August 1910, the American John B. Moisant made the first flight across the Channel with passengers – a mechanic, Albert Fileux, and his cat, Mademoiselle Fifi (seen here on Moisant's shoulder). The flight, from Calais to Deal, was made in a Blériot XI. (Library of Congress)

Harriet Quimby became the first woman to fly across the English Channel on 16 April 1912. The 59-minute-long flight was made between Dover and a beach near Neufchâtel-Hardelot, south of Boulogne. (Library of Congress)

On 6 September 1945, a captured German Focke-Achgelis Fa-223 Drache made the first crossing of the Channel by helicopter. (San Diego Air & Space Museum)

This Bristol 170 Superfreighter, G-ANWJ, was operated by Silver City Airways, this being the company that developed air ferry flights for cars and their passengers across the English Channel. (Dutch National Archives)

Saunders Roe's SR-N1, seen here during trails undertaken by the Royal Navy, made the first crossing of the Channel by a hovercraft on 24 July 1959. (The National Archives)

The first purpose-built hoverport opened at Pegwell Bay, near Ramsgate in Kent, on 2 May 1969. This is Hoverlloyd's SR.N4 *The Prince of Wales* pictured at Pegwell Bay. (Courtesy of Philip Halling; www.geograph.org.uk)

Bryan Allen piloted and pedalled the first human-powered Channel crossing in the *Gossamer Albatross* on 12 June 1979 – the cabin of which is pictured here a few weeks before the flight. (NASA)

Flying an Airbus E-Fan, the aircraft seen here, Didier Esteyne completed the first crossing of the Channel by a battery-powered aircraft which took off under its own power on 9 July 2015. (Courtesy of Pete Webber)

EXPLOITING THE PRACTICAL POSSIBILITIES

London-Brussels. Payments would be calculated on the basis of 25 per cent of the total certified gross revenue of each company earned by the carriage of passengers, mail or goods.

A minority report was filed by Air Marshal Sir Hugh Trenchard, Chief of Staff of the RAF, who strongly opposed direct subsidies on both military and commercial grounds. In any case, he doubted they would be effective.

The cabinet decided to postpone a decision and did so again when the matter re-appeared on the agenda at the end of July. But criticism of the government intensified and at a three-day air conference in October Churchill felt obliged to re-state the government's policy on the issue.

The government, he insisted, intended to help the airlines by every means in its power but its resources were limited. He trusted, however, that the day had come when it would be possible for the government to increase to some extent the resources which were available for the development of civil aviation.

It was at this point that he made a remark which has been widely quoted over the years. 'In the main,' he said, 'civil aviation must fly by itself and the function of the government is to facilitate, stimulate and encourage its action.' It was clear that Churchill was assuming that any financial aid to the industry would be offered on a temporary basis, to tide it over a difficult period.

It was also clear that Churchill's remarks had done little to blunt press hostility. The *Pall Mall Gazette* criticised the government for its 'grudging and gingery' attitude towards civil aviation. 'Commercial aviation,' it declared, 'cannot be expected to show any remarkable enterprise at the present unremunerative stage of its development if it is given to understand that the State does not care whether it survives or not.'

The *Morning Post* said that some form of government assistance was essential because the industry was in a 'topsy turvey state' and would not be able to secure the necessary financial support to start and continue new air services 'unless the public realises that the government means seeing this thing through the initial stages'.

C.G. Grey, editor of *The Aeroplane,* declared that 'British civil aviation died with the cessation of Handley Page cross-Channel service, killed by the forward policy of the French government and the apathy of our own'.

Churchill's response was to appoint the Cross-Channel Committee within the Air Ministry, and chaired by his junior minister Lord Londonderry, to consider the question of subsidies. When the issue came up before the cabinet for a third time, in November 1920, it had before it a memorandum prepared by Lord Weir who said he had considered the matter further. In essence, it was a plea to the government to provide financial subsidies to the airlines without further delay.

Weir argued that while the cross-Channel routes might not be commercially remunerative, they were 'of very great immediate value to the community and to British aviation progress'. They were, he said

> showing what is needed in technical development and in the commercial and traffic problems. Today they are the best air services which exist in the world. Accordingly, I hold that they should be financially encouraged.

Before they made a decision Weir urged members of the cabinet to go to Croydon and watch civil aviation in operation at the sharp end for a couple of hours. They should, he said,

> See the machines with their passengers, goods and mails arriving and departing to Paris, Brussels, Amsterdam. Speak to the passengers, go into the customs-house, examine the character of the goods. The whole thing is full of romance and of practical possibilities. The service may be irregular, many of the arrangements very crude, but quite definitely the work is started and is being done. The possibilities are being disclosed and a new era in communication is being opened up. This has all been done in 18 months. Think what might be done with some help in the next two years!

General Sykes, now Controller-General of Civil Aviation, saw it in rather less lyrical terms. In a memorandum tabled at the same cabinet meeting he argued that the number of letters and passengers and the weight of goods carried by aircraft during the first fifteen months of airline operations had shown

> a steady though slow progress and there is every reason to assume that, with continued improvement in the regularity of services, this number will increase in geometric progression because speed saves time, time saves money, and business firms using air transport will enter into successful competition with those who do not ... .

EXPLOITING THE PRACTICAL POSSIBILITIES

Sykes was also looking at a wider picture when he added: 'Unless these services are ultimately successful, Imperial commercial aviation will suffer a serious setback.'

The matter came to a head in March 1921 when the French government increased the level of subsidy for its airlines and British companies were finding it almost impossible to compete successfully on a commercial basis. As a result, another committee was set up to find a solution as quickly as possible that would enable the cross-Channel service to be maintained.

What emerged was a scheme to enable Handley Page and Instone, which were the only two British airlines still operating the services, to continue doing so. At this stage, however, the assistance was provided only until mid-October. By that time the British airlines carried a total of 4,496 passengers on the London-Paris route compared with the 3,942 flown by the French companies.

In June 1921 the government announced a programme of assistance for civil aviation for the next three years. Aviation minister Lord Gorell, who had succeeded Lord Londonderry, explained how it would work. There were, he said, two main points:

> first, that the Air Ministry should order machines of proved types, which will be hired out to firms to augment their existing fleet; and secondly, the Air Ministry will pay subsidies on a basis of 25 per cent to approved firms on gross receipts from carriage of passengers, goods and mails taken on any of three routes – London to Paris, Brussels and Amsterdam. The machines are to be insured by the companies. They would be hired out to the company at a monthly rental of 21 per cent of the cost of the machine and after the 30th payment they would become the property of the company – that is to say at 75 per cent of their costs. Other conditions are that personnel are to be of British nationality and the aircraft and engines of British manufacture and design. In order to qualify for the subsidy any company approved would be required to make a minimum of 45 complete single journeys in each direction during each period of three months.

Machines acquired by the Air Council and leased to the airlines in the way foreshadowed by the government's announcement included the de Havilland DH 18 and the DH 34. Both were single-engine types.

Four DH 18s and two of the improved DH 18As were built, five of them being operated by Instone on the Croydon-Paris and Croydon-Brussels route. Three were lost in accidents but one, G-EARO, flew 90,000 miles without mishap.

Two of the ten-passenger DH 34s were ordered by a new entrant in the cross-Channel business, Daimler Hire, later renamed Daimler Airline. In February 1920 the BSA group acquired the failing Airco group which included Aircraft Transport and Travel (AT&T) which had flown the first scheduled services after the war. The assets were later placed under the control of Daimler Hire, a subsidiary of the BSA Group in 1921. Major George E. Woods Humphery, a former RFC pilot and general manager of Handley Page, was appointed manager of Daimler Airway.

The company ordered two DH 34s which were painted in its all-red livery. G-EBBQ made the inaugural flight from Croydon to Paris on 2 April 1922 with Captain W.G.R. Hinchcliffe in command.

Instone's G-EBBR *City of Glasgow* went into service the same day on the same route with Captain F.L. Barnard in command. He reached Paris with a full load in two hours forty minutes. Daimler's policy was to work its aircraft hard and its DH 34 G-EBBS became the first aircraft to make two return trips between Croydon and Le Bourget in one day. Scheduled services were flown on 122 days out of a possible 165 and double return journeys were made on forty-five occasions. By early December 100,393 miles had been flown in nearly 8,000 hours without incident or overhaul, to provide a foretaste of the enormous mileages that DH 34s were to cover successfully over the next four years.

Instone's *City of New York*, again piloted by Barnard, inaugurated a new Croydon-Brussels service on 2 May 1922 but in view of the small amount of traffic the Director of Civil Aviation decided later in the year to prevent undesirable competition by means of a route allocation system. Services to Brussels and Cologne were to be flown only by Instone; those to Paris by Handley Page and a new route to Berlin by Daimler. The Berlin route was opened in September by G-EBBS, piloted by Hinchcliffe.

Steady increases in traffic resulted in the delivery of one additional Air Council DH 34, named *City of Chicago*, to Instone in August 1922 and another to Daimler to replace one written off in an accident. A total of eleven DH 34s is known to have been produced. The aircraft were eventually withdrawn from service in March 1926.

By that time they were being operated by another new airline. The Imperial Airways era had just opened.

EXPLOITING THE PRACTICAL POSSIBILITIES

The RFC Heads for France

In the days following the outbreak of war on 4 August 1914 the programme of mobilisation for the Royal Flying Corps was, in the main, successfully carried out. From then on, the Channel pioneers would be wearing military uniforms.

As part of this movement, some of the first elements of the RFC to head across the Channel were headquarters personnel. Having left Farnborough for Southampton on the night of 11 August 1914, they embarked on the morning of the 13th. As their troopship prepared to sail for France, a number of RFC squadrons took off to make a similar journey.

Of the squadrons that flew to France, 2 Squadron, which had been based at Montrose, had the hardest task. Its pilots started on their southward flight to Farnborough as early as 3 August; after some accidents they all reached Dover. No. 3 Squadron was at Netheravon when war broke out; on 12 August its pilots flew to Dover, though the squadron suffered a loss at Netheravon when Second Lieutenant R.R. Skene, with Air Mechanic R.K. Barlow as passenger, crashed soon after taking off. Both pilot and passenger were killed.

For its part, No. 4 Squadron had been sent to Eastchurch on 31 July 1914 to assist the Royal Navy in its preparations for home defence and to be ready for mobilisation. It was from Eastchurch that 4 Squadron flew to Dover, where, by the evening 12 August, the aircraft of Nos. 2, 3, and 4 squadrons had been concentrated. Just before midnight, the final orders arrived: 'All machines to be ready to fly over at 06:00hrs the following morning, 13 August.'

The first aircraft of 2 Squadron to take off departed from Dover at 06.25hr that morning; the first to arrive landed at Amiens at 08:20hr. This machine was flown by Lieutenant H.D. Harvey-Kelly. He landed his Royal Aircraft Factory B.E.2c at Amiens. Major Hubert Dunsterville Harvey-Kelly DSO, Royal Irish Regiment, attached to the RFC, was killed on 29 April 1917, the twenty-fifth victim of the German ace *Leutnant* Kurt Wolff of *Jasta 11*.

The aircraft of 3 Squadron also arrived safely at Amiens, with the exception of one piloted by Second Lieutenant E.N. Fuller who, along with his mechanic, did not re-join his squadron at Maubeuge until five days later.

While one flight of 4 Squadron remained at Dover to carry out patrol duties, some of the remainder were damaged on the way over by following their leader, Captain F.J.L. Cogan, who was forced by engine failure to land in a ploughed field in France.

No. 5 Squadron moved a little later than the other three, having been delayed by a shortage of shipping and a series of accidents to its aircraft. On 14 August, when starting out for Dover, Captain G.I. Carmichael wrecked his machine at Gosport. On the same day Lieutenant R.O. Abercromby and Lieutenant H.F. Glanville damaged their machines at Shoreham, and Lieutenant H. leM. Brock damaged his at Falmer. Such incidents aside, the squadron finally took off from Dover for France on 15 August. Even then, the journey was not without further incident when Lieutenant R.M. Vaughan made a forced landing near Boulogne. He was promptly arrested by the French and was imprisoned for nearly a week.

In due course, all four of the initial RFC squadrons deployed to France were ready for operations. The RFC's official historian noted that the flight represented the 'first organized national [air] force to fly to a war overseas'.

A memorial to commemorate the departure of the RFC's first four squadrons for France as part of the British Expeditionary Force was subsequently erected near Cliff Road between Dover and St Margaret's at Cliffe. Today, this memorial stands in the shadow of two remaining truncated masts from the Swingate Chain Home radar station, legacies of another, more recent war.

The First Cross-Channel Airliners

The first cross-Channel commercial services were operated by converted bombers. They were all that was available.

The DH 4 was designed by Geoffrey de Havilland as a day bomber and it became one of the war's most outstanding aircraft. Its fabric-covered, wire-braced, spruce and ash structure were typical of the day but the front fuselage, housing the pilot's and gunner's cockpits and main fuel tanks, was strengthened with plywood covering.

EXPLOITING THE PRACTICAL POSSIBILITIES

By 1918 over 3,200 had been constructed including nearly 1,900 built under licence in the USA. After the war many were converted for civilian use in countries like Australia and Canada. In the USA they formed the backbone of the first airmail operations.

Nine aircraft were modified by Airco and Handley Page to carry two passengers in an enclosed cabin behind the pilot. This was a light fabric-covered wooden structure fitted with sliding Triplex windows. The starboard side and roof were hinged to fold upwards for entry and exit. Curved decking faired the cabin into the rear fuselage and tail.

Normal DH 4 fuel tanks were retained behind the pilot and the two wind-driven fuel pumps were mounted above them. But to compensate for the weight of the additional passenger, the aircraft was re-rigged with the upper mainplane twelve inches aft of its original position. This represented a major variant to which the designation DH 4A was applied.

The DH 16 was a development of the DH 4/DH 4A. It was enlarged and, although powered by the same 320 hp Rolls-Royce Eagle VIII engine, faster. It also carried four passengers, making it considerably more economical and commercially attractive to operate than the DH 4As. Nine DH 16s were eventually built.

SPECIFICATION
de Havilland DH 4A
Accommodation pilot and two passengers
Length 30 ft 8 in.
Wingspan 42 ft 5 in.
All-up weight 3,750lb
Power Plant one 20-litre 350 hp liquid-cooled Rolls-Royce Eagle VIII V12
Max speed 121 mph

Chapter Eight

On Silver Wings

The programme of assistance for British airlines unveiled by the government in June 1921 did not provide the hoped-for solution to the problems they had been facing.

The operating environment was now more stable but competition from generously subsidised Continental operators was as intense as ever and the British airline industry had yet to break out of its post-war straitjacket. Between them, the four companies still operating on cross-Channel routes, Daimler, Handley Page and Instone, employed just 117 staff, of whom only eighteen were pilots.

In the five years to 1923 the airlines had received a total of £313,000 in subsidies but a change of government in October 1922 signalled a new approach. In January 1923 the incoming Conservative administration appointed yet another committee to study the issue and try to resolve the matter for the long term.

The committee, under the chairmanship of banker Sir Herbert Hambling, worked with commendable briskness so that a month after its formation it was ready to announce its recommendations. It called for the four leading British independent airlines to be merged into one to produce a company that would be strong enough to hold its own in the marketplace. Its name indicated the direction the government was plotting for the new entity: Imperial Air Transport Company.

The government subsidies it was offered totalled £137,000 in the first year, tapering off to £32,000 in the tenth. Minimum mileages to be achieved and penalties to be applied if they were not were also laid down by the government. All equipment and crews were to be British and in the event of a future war the government would acquire the company's assets for war service. Crews would be required to become members of the RAF Reserve.

Clearly this was a blueprint for nationalisation but Churchill's successor as Secretary of State for Air, Sir Samuel Hoare, preferred to talk in terms of 'a single national company'. Hoare told his cabinet colleagues in November 1923 that it would be strengthened by the addition of government directors and by 'city men of standing'. This, he believed, would bring 'a real chance of big future developments and the possibility of civil air transport becoming a national asset'.

But Hoare warned that there was no time to be lost in forming the new company if a promised investment of £500,000 of private capital was to be realised. Accordingly, Imperial Airways Limited was formally established on 31 March 1924 with Sir Eric Geddes as chairman. The irony of this appointment was that Geddes had earlier led the Committee on National Expenditure and wielded what became notorious as 'Geddes' Axe' to slash public expenditure and delay resolution of the subsidies question.

Directors from each of the merged companies joined government appointees – one of whom was Hambling – on the board. The airline's equipment was drawn from the constituent airlines. British Marine Air Navigation contributed two Supermarine Sea Eagle flying boats, Daimler Airway three DH 34s, Handley Page Transport three W8bs, *Princess Mary*, *Prince Henry* and *Prince George*, and the Instone Air Line Vickers Vimy Commercial *City of London* plus four DH 34s.

British Marine Air Navigation had been formed in 1923 as a joint venture between Supermarine Aviation Works and Southern Railway, owners of Southampton Docks. It had operated flying boats across the Channel, and in August 1923 had launched the world's first scheduled flying-boat service with flights to Cherbourg, Le Havre and the Channel Islands. It operated from Woolston which, as a result, became Britain's first commercial flying-boat base with its own customs and immigration facilities. The Sea Eagle amphibians used for these operations were designed by Reginald Mitchell who would later create the legendary Spitfire fighter.

Most of Imperial Airways' new fleet were obsolete types and five of them were unserviceable. Its first new airliner, Handley Page W8f *City of Washington*, was not to arrive until 3 November 1924. The W8f was an enlarged version of the original W8 with three engines instead of two.

The new airline also inherited 1,760 miles of cross-Channel routes. Landplane operations were based at Croydon and services to points north of London offered by Imperial's predecessors were immediately discontinued to match the focus now being placed on international and imperial routes rather than on domestic flights.

It did not get off to an auspicious start. The new airline was due to begin operations on 1 April 1924 but an industrial dispute with pilots delayed the start of services for over three weeks. Technically, the pilots had become unemployed on 31 March, the intention being that Imperial would re-employ the majority. But the pilots claimed the remuneration they were being offered was less than they had received from the constituent companies: some pilots had received annual salaries of around £1,000. The new management's proposals would have meant an average of up to £850.

The Aeroplane's C.G. Grey was unsympathetic. He regarded the disgruntled employees as 'silly, inexperienced, unbusiness-like, temperamental young pilots'. He may have had a point. The pilots were certainly caught in a trap as there were no other British airlines to employ the dissidents.

A complicating factor was that the pilots lacked confidence in Imperial's general manager, George Woods Humphery. This stemmed from his claim to have been an experienced pilot when he was no such thing. The dispute led to the formation of a pilots' union, the Federation of Airline Pilots, but as it dragged on through April the new Secretary of State for Air, Lord Thomson, was becoming impatient, especially when he learned that Woods Humphery was planning to hire RAF pilots to fly Imperial's passenger services.

Thomson intervened and brought the dispute to an end with a face-saving formula. On 26 April Imperial Airways finally began its operations with a daily London-Paris service using a DH 34. Thereafter the task of expanding the routes between England and the continent began, with Southampton-Guernsey on 1 May 1924, London-Brussels-Cologne on 3 May, London-Amsterdam on 2 June 1924, and a summer service from London-Paris-Basel-Zürich on 17 June 1924. Despite its problems, the new airline flew 853,042 miles and carried 11,395 passengers and 212,380 letters in its first year of operation.

More competition arrived when Belgian and German airlines joined their French and British counterparts on cross-Channel routes. SABENA (*Societé Anonyme Belge d'Exploitation de la Navigation Aérienne*) opened its Brussels-London service in 1926 using a Farman Goliath. *Deutsche Aero Lloyd* had operated initially in collaboration with Daimler Airway and had launched a London-Berlin service in April 1923 but by 1926 it had become part of *Deutsche Luft Hansa* with a network of routes radiating from Berlin.

Much of the infrastructure used by Imperial Airways had to be provided from scratch. Croydon had been a military airfield operated by the RAF until it opened as a civilian facility in 1920. When they moved in the airlines had to use the old hangar buildings that had been vacated by the service a month earlier. There was no office accommodation and no terminal buildings for passenger processing. As a temporary expedient old wooden army huts were erected along the edge of the airfield.

Aerial navigation was in its infancy too. In the very early days pilots found their way – on a clear day – by following key landmarks. Particularly helpful were railway lines. Those between Guildford and Ashford were relatively straight and individual stations could be identified by the names conveniently painted on their roofs: Redhill, Penshurst, Tonbridge. In poor visibility compasses similar to those used by the cross-Channel pioneers were still in use and proving no more reliable. Under these circumstances it was surprising that so many of the cross-Channel passenger services reached their destinations safely.

Radio seemed to offer an answer. In 1920 the Marconi Company established a wireless station at Croydon to enable simple communications to be established between aircraft and the ground. This meant that pilots had to use a trailing aerial which had to be wound inboard before landing. Pilots seldom placed great trust in these arrangements and still preferred to find their way to Croydon by following landmarks like the twin towers of the Crystal Palace.

Clearly none of these arrangements could be considered good enough for what would become Britain's premier airport and the country's premier airline. It was a difficult and complex task to establish reliable air schedules. This meant that establishing a reliable system of air traffic control was essential. Croydon was the major innovator in this area. It employed Civil Aviation Traffic Officers and Radio Officers and pioneered some of the first procedures and concepts which are still used for ATC today.

Radio Position Fixing was a Croydon-based procedure approved by the Air Ministry in 1922. This was a new system using aircraft radio transmissions to fix an aircraft's position – an essential first step in establishing a radio-based global air navigation network. Pilots were able to fix their position by calling up Croydon and then obtaining cross-bearings from stations at Pulham in Norfolk and Lympne in Kent.

G.J.H. 'Jimmy' Jeffs, civilian air traffic control officer at Croydon, was one of the great innovators in developing the new discipline. Issued with Air Traffic Control Licence No. 1 in 1922, Jeffs developed many of the systems and procedures that were approved by the Air Ministry.

The need to find a way of avoiding collisions between aircraft in flight had been graphically demonstrated in April 1922. In poor visibility a Farman Goliath of *Grandes Express Aériennes*, flying from Le Bourget, collided head-on with a DH 18 of Daimler Airways on its way from Croydon to Paris. There were no survivors. The accident highlighted an urgent need for proper international air navigation laws and hastened the international negotiations then in progress. The collision also led to the establishment of 'rules of the road' for what was becoming a busy route.

Jeffs invented a rudimentary form of control using a large map showing the main cross-Channel routes flown by airlines operating from Croydon. This he pasted onto the back of an old cork bathmat. Through regular position reports radioed by pilots, Jeffs was able to keep track of the aircraft on their way to and from the airport.

The step from the use of radio telegraphy (Morse code) to radio telephony (speech transmissions) saw the need for a new way to use language to ensure clearly understood messages. F.S. 'Stanley' Mockford, Croydon's senior radio officer, conceived the distress phrase 'Mayday, Mayday, Mayday' in 1923. The British Government embodied the Mayday distress call as part of the required radio procedures to be used in an emergency, promulgating its use in *The Air Pilot: Great Britain*, published in 1924. Adopted by the International Radiotelegraphy Convention of Washington in 1927, 'Mayday' (from the French *M'aidez*) became the international standard distress phrase.

In 1920 the Air Ministry formulated a specification for the construction of the world's first technical building to control air traffic. The specification called for the 'platform of the tower to be 15 ft above ground level', with 'large windows placed in all four walls'. A wind-vane was to be fitted to the roof with a geared-down indicator placed inside 'enabling the control officer to read changes of wind'. The world's first Air Traffic Control Tower was on its way.

When completed in 1928, the new control tower replaced the temporary timber structure that had been in use since 1920. It also represented a significant advance in airport infrastructure design with each level providing a dedicated air traffic control support function that became standard. Its square shape was unusual but was considered striking in its restrained classical design. Its sheer scale was impressive: it was the world's biggest control tower with three of its four floors dedicated to supporting ATC functions.

A key innovation was the 360-degree field of vision which gave controllers a panoramic view of the airfield. The tall central mast had a dual purpose. It incorporated a wind anemometer feeding data down through the centre of the building to an anemograph machine located on the first floor

Meteorological Office. The mast also facilitated two-way communications between the radio officers, controllers and aircraft.

As time is a key element in navigation and safe inflight aircraft separation, the tower featured three clocks located on the airfield sides of the balcony and visible to the pilots to ensure synchronisation to the correct time. The three clocks were linked into the administration buildings' electronic master clock system and accurate to a minimum of two seconds per week.

The top floor was accessed by a spiral staircase which led into a room divided into two sections – the control room and the radio room. The radio officers were licensed to operate and communicate with the airliners by radio telephony (speech) and wireless telegraphy (Morse code) with custom-built equipment built by Marconi's Wireless Telegraph Company. Speech radio transmission represented cutting edge technology in the 1920s.

Marconi's equipment was vital in facilitating ATC. The controllers, supported by assistants, managed the departing and arriving air traffic to and from the UK. The area of coverage extended across the English Channel to the French coast to the south and the Dutch coast to the north.

An element of the advanced design of the control tower was the facility to control airfield facilities remotely. The radio transmitting station, located three miles from the airport for safety reasons, featured four 3-kilowatt custom-built transmitters and four 103-feet steel radio masts. Inset runway lighting was another important feature as it facilitated take offs and landings in poor visibility. Specialised runway markings helped pilots maintain orientation especially in poor visibility.

Passenger numbers grew significantly after the airport was opened in 1920. The first year of operations saw 2,000 passengers, rising to 26,000 a year when the new terminal building was opened in 1928. The early 1930s saw a sharp jump in passenger numbers, rising to over 120,000 in 1935.

As aeronautical technology advanced the equipment used by the airlines was also developing with bigger and more comfortable aircraft. An example was the Farman F60 Goliath, which had originally been designed as a bomber. Converted into an airliner, it could accommodate up to fourteen passengers and represented a popular choice for French airlines.

Unlike many of the types initially operated by Imperial Airways, it was a twin-engined machine. But when the airline issued its specification for new airliner equipment, it declared that all its aircraft would be multi-engine designs to enhance safety.

This need had been tragically brought home by the loss on Christmas Eve 1924 of DH 34 G-EBBX soon after taking off from Croydon for Paris.

The pilot, Captain D.A. Stewart, and seven passengers all died. The crash was followed by an explosion and fire. *Flight* reported that the aircraft was 'observed seen to be in difficulties and dived to earth'. The journal described the accident as 'the worst that happened in the history of civil aviation in this country'.

It was the first fatal accident suffered by Imperial Airways and led to the first public inquiry into a civil aviation accident in the United Kingdom. The inquiry found that the aircraft had crashed due to an unknown mechanical defect and subsequent stall while an emergency landing was being attempted. Unofficially, the cause was widely thought to have been fuel starvation. As a result of issues brought up during the inquiry, Croydon Airport was expanded.

Possibly influenced by this accident, Imperial Airways declared that henceforth all its aircraft would be multi-engine designs. The Armstrong Whitworth AW 154 Argosy stemmed from this. The first example (G-EBLF) flew in March 1926, following an initial order for three aircraft. An improved Mk II version was introduced in 1929.

The Argosy was initially used on European routes but later operated on services to South Africa. The first passenger flight left Croydon on 16 July 1926 bound for Paris. The Argosy could carry twenty passengers in wicker seats. Despite the three Jupiter engines, the operating economics of the Argosy were soon found to be superior to those of the DH 34. In April 1931 Edward, Prince of Wales, and his brother Prince George flew home from Paris in *City of Glasgow* (G-EBLF), which set them down in Windsor Great Park.

Three Argosies were lost during service with Imperial Airways, one being written off in a forced landing near Aswan and one during a training accident, both in 1931, with no injuries sustained in either accident. On 28 March 1933, however, the *City of Liverpool* caught fire over Belgium, causing a crash in which all three crew and twelve passengers were killed.

The French airlines were also introducing new aircraft. *Lignes Farman* introduced the Farman F180, an elegant, twin-engined biplane whose blue-painted fuselage earned it the nickname of *Oiseau Bleu*. The two engines were mounted back-to-back on the top wing above the fuselage to minimise engine noise inside the cabin.

It was far roomier than its predecessors and could accommodate twenty-four passengers in a light and airy cabin with seven windows on each side. There was a bar at the rear. On night flights up to seventeen passengers could be carried in *couchettes*. The aircraft went into service on the Paris-London route in February 1928 where it was in competition with *Air Union*'s Loiré et Olivier series of biplanes which had been introduced in 1923.

Air Union introduced the Loiré et Olivier 213 on its luxury lunchtime Paris-London service. Painted in red, gold and white, it was named *Rayon d'Or (The Golden Ray)*. The cabin design was influenced by the *Wagon-Lits* company, which is probably why it strongly resembled a railway dining car. Tables, each with four comfortable chairs, lined one side of the cabin. Luggage was carried in railway-style overhead racks with cord netting.

Although Imperial had invented in-flight meals, the French were able to bring their own standards and culinary flair to bear so that by 1927 a typical cross-Channel repast would comprise hors d'oeuvres, crayfish a la Parisienne, chicken chasseur, York ham in gelatine, salade Niçoise, ice cream, cheese and fruit. This could be complemented by Champagne, red and white Bordeaux, spirits, soft drinks and coffee.

As the flying time between the two capitals was around two hours, there was ample time to serve and savour such meals but, as these early airliners flew through rather than above the weather, there might have been some indigestion on gusty days.

Other competitive inducements introduced during the 1920s included in-flight entertainment. On Friday 13 November 1925 the BBC broadcast an orchestral concert from an Imperial Airways Vickers Vanguard. Despite fog and a broken engine oil pipe the broadcast was judged successful despite the intrusion of engine noise.

The following year a space was cleared in the cabin of an Argosy operating a *Silver Wing* flight to permit leading exponents of the Charleston to give an in-flight dancing lesson. But a taste of what future passengers might expect came aboard Handley Page W8b G-EBBI on 7 April 1925. A silent film adaptation of Sir Arthur Conan Doyle's book *The Lost World* starring Wallace Beery was projected during a flight from Croydon.

In the year to 31 March 1926 Imperial Airways had carried over 14,600 passengers, over 1,100 more than during the previous corresponding period. It had flown 865,000 miles on a route network which featured services between London and Paris; London-Paris-Basle-Zurich; London-Brussels-Cologne; London-Ostend and London-Amsterdam. These services were operated daily or, in some cases, twice daily during the summer, although not all continued during the winter season. A Southampton-Channel Islands service operated weekly between October and April.

Imperial Airways sought to capitalise on its success by introducing the world's first named air service. At noon on 1 May 1927, Argosy G-EBLO *City of Birmingham* (G-EBLO) left Croydon for Paris with Captain Gordon Olley in command to launch the luxury *Silver Wing* service. Two seats had been removed from the cabin and replaced by a bar with a white-jacketed steward in attendance. The *Silver Wing* service offered a luxury lunchtime service in the most comfortable aircraft that Imperial Airways could offer at the time.

Compared with the standard Argosy the *City of Birmingham* featured an improved interior. There were eighteen cushioned seats with armrests, curtains and a toilet located at the rear of the cabin. During the two hours and thirty minutes flight passengers were treated to a full cabin service that included a light lunch served by a steward from a buffet located at the rear. This first-class service was included in the single fare of 6 guineas (£6.30p) which was £1 more than the normal price.

Air Union responded with the introduction three months later of its *Golden Ray* service with its white linen covered tables. The LeO 21 twin-engined biplanes could accommodate twelve passengers. Additional seating for six more was available in a nose cabin if required. But the French service was no match for the Argosy which proved so popular that by the following year Imperial Airways was carrying almost 70 per cent of all traffic on the London-Paris route.

By the summer of 1930 Imperial Airways was advising its passengers 'always to fly across the English Channel'. Its publicity material declared

> The journey will be one of uncrowded calm from hotel to hotel. There is no crush at Customs, no hectic change from train to boat and back again to train; just an effortless speeding through the air at twice the speed of an express train, sunk in the embrace of an easy chair, while the panorama of Europe's countries slides gently away below.

And it was all-British. It was during this time that Imperial Airways was exploring ways of building on the early cross-Channel services by extending its operations eastwards to British-administered territories and dominions in Africa, Asia and Australasia. Survey flights to South Australia in 1925 and 1926 foreshadowed passenger services to Cape Town, Cairo, Baghdad, Karachi, Delhi, Calcutta, Singapore, Hong Kong, Darwin, Sydney and Melbourne. These would be developed during the 1930s.

More new aircraft would clearly be required and during Imperial's second decade two of the machines that would forever be linked with the airline made their appearance. Both were four-engined types: the Handley Page HP 42 and the Short C Class Empire flying boat.

The giant Handley Page biplane set new standards of comfort and reliability when it began a series of proving flights on the London-Paris route in June 1931. It was built in two versions, one for European or western operations and the other – which offered twice the baggage space – for eastern operations.

Eight machines, four of each variant, were delivered to Imperial Airways by February 1932. The HP 42Ws were named *Hannibal*, *Horsa*, *Hanno* and *Hadrian*, while the HP 42Es were *Heracles*, *Horatius*, *Hengist* and *Helena*. By the standards of the day these were big machines. Each mainwheel of the fixed undercarriage dwarfed the average family car. The wings were carried above the fuselage and supported by a system of diagonal struts. The uncowled engines were mounted two on each wing. The pilots' cabin was enclosed and there were dual control columns dominated by a giant steering wheel that would not have looked out of place on a double-decker bus.

But they quickly established a reputation for efficiency and safety, flying millions of miles and carrying hundreds of thousands of passengers. By September 1938 *Heracles* had covered a million miles on European routes and carried 95,000 passengers.

In a demonstration of the aircraft's robust construction, *Hannibal* had to make an emergency landing with a full load of passengers on a flight from Croydon in August 1931. A propeller came loose and, in falling from the aircraft, damaged those on two other engines. Captain F. Dismore was able to set *Hannibal*, now flying on one engine, safely down in a Kentish field. Afterwards, the aircraft was taken back to Croydon by road, repaired and returned to service.

If the HP 42 had a fault it was its low speed. Droning along at a stately 100 mph was all very well if passengers valued the opportunity to study the countryside as it gently slipped by. But other airlines, notably KLM, were introducing more modern equipment with double the cruising speed.

The HP 24's cabin re-created the elegance of an English country house drawing room with comfortable chairs and chintz curtains. High quality meals prepared in flight were served to passengers on bone china with silver cutlery. It was all fresh food; Imperial Airways boasted that no tinned food was ever used on any of its services.

But the new American types like the Boeing 247 and Douglas DC-2 were monoplanes with innovative features like retractable undercarriages and cowled engines. They could cruise considerably faster than the old biplanes. When a KLM DC-2 arrived in Britain for the Mildenhall to Melbourne air race of 1934 it acted as a much-needed wake-up call to the British aviation industry.

Consequently, Imperial Airways was obliged to re-equip with more modern equipment. Out went the stately biplanes and in came monoplanes like the Armstrong Whitworth Atalanta and Ensign. But it was the Short C Class which formed the backbone of the airline's long-range services for the rest of the decade.

Later came the sleek and elegant de Havilland Albatross which was of all-wood construction. Its monocoque fuselage built of cedar ply laminated around balsa wood foreshadowed the Second World War Mosquito multi-role combat aircraft. The Albatross could cruise at 210 mph and carry twenty-two passengers. It entered service on the Croydon-Brussels and Zurich routes in November 1938.

But within the year the outbreak of another world war would bring civil flying across the Channel to an end.

The DH 34

The DH 34 which appeared in 1922 was a single-engine biplane which could accommodate twenty passengers.

It had a wooden, plywood-clad fuselage with a cockpit for two pilots positioned ahead of the wings and the passenger cabin. Its Napier Lion engine featured inertia starting which avoided the need for hand swinging of the propeller.

Unusually, the design allowed an entire spare engine to be carried on board across the rear of the passenger cabin. The cabin door was shaped to permit the engine to pass through and a 'porthole' on the other side of the cabin could be removed to allow the propeller boss to protrude through it. Spare engines were not carried routinely but this facility was used by operators to rush spare units to aircraft that had suffered breakdown.

Ten DH 34s and the bigger-winged DH 34bs were built and operated by Instone Air Line and Daimler Airway before being acquired by Imperial Airways which operated them on its routes to Brussels and Zurich.

SPECIFICATION
DE HAVILLAND DH 34
Accommodation 2 pilots and 12 passengers
Length 39 ft
Wingspan 51 ft 4 in. (DH34B – 54 ft 4 in.)
All-up weight 7,200lb
Power plant 1 450hp Napier Lion 12-cylinder broad arrow liquid-cooled engine
Cruising speed 105 mph

The Handley Page HP 42/45

The HP 42/45 was a large unequal-span biplane of all-metal construction except for the fabric covering the wings, tail surfaces and rear fuselage. The wings were braced by a Warren truss. The tail plane was a biplane incorporating three fins. Two engines were mounted on the upper wing and one on each side of the fuselage on the lower wing.

The prototype (registered G-AAGX and later named *Hannibal*) made its first flight on 14 November 1930, just over a month after the loss of the R101 which ended Britain's hopes that the airship would provide long-range passenger transport. Squadron Leader Thomas England was at the controls. The certificate of airworthiness, permitting the start of commercial services, was granted in May 1931.

The HP 42's crew compartment was enclosed, a new development for the time, and there were two passenger cabins, one forward and one aft of the wings. The HP 42W (W for western) seated eighteen forward and twenty aft, with reduced baggage capacity.

The HP 42E (Eastern) carried six (later twelve) in the forward compartment and twelve in the after cabin with more room for baggage.

The aircraft was economical as well as reliable. It was certainly not fast. One regular passenger commented: 'I had quite often been landed in a '42' at Lympne to take on sufficient fuel to complete the flight from Paris to London against a headwind. Ninety mph was its normal cruising speed.'

Three of the surviving aircraft were pressed into RAF service on the outbreak of the Second World War.

SPECIFICATION
HANDLEY PAGE HP 42
Accommodation 2 pilots, 2 stewards and 24 passengers
Length 92 ft 2 in.
Wingspan 130 ft
Max take-off weight 28,000lb
Power plant 4 x 490hp Bristol Jupiter XIF 9-cylinder radial engines (HP42W)
Cruising speed 100 mph.

Britain's First Cross-Channel Air Terminal

Croydon Airport's new passenger terminal was part of the redevelopment of the airport provided for by act of parliament, the Croydon Aerodrome Extension Act 1925. Work was completed in 1928 and the building became fully operational on 2 May. With an accompanying tenfold increase in the flying field the expanded airport with its new buildings covered thirty-four acres to make it the world's biggest airport.

The terminal building, also known as the administration building, was located alongside the Purley Way (one of the UK's first by-passes built in 1925) to improve rapid distribution of goods and traffic arriving by air. The building was designed by the Air Ministry's Department of Buildings and Works and constructed by Wilson Lovatt and Son at a cost of £267,000.

It was built around a steel frame, which allowed for future extension, and walled with 50,000 concrete blocks. These blocks were finished in a special aggregate mix to give the appearance of Portland Stone.

The aerodrome hotel and terminal building, including its grand booking hall, were built in the neo-classical geometrical design that was fashionable in the early twentieth century. An eye-catching feature was the time zone tower in the booking hall with dials showing the time in different parts of the world.

Central to the administration building was the check-in area, also known as the booking hall. There were six check-in desks as well as administration facilities for the international airlines. The building featured a high-speed pneumatic vacuum tube communication system connecting the air traffic controllers in the control tower to the meteorological office and commandant's office.

A further notable feature was the large two-storey atrium surrounded by a first-floor balustrade with geometric patterned railings. On top of the atrium was an impressive steel-framed glass dome which flooded the area with light.

From the booking hall passengers passed through emigration, security and customs checks before exiting through the world's first departure gate to the south side of the control tower. The arrivals gate was on the north side of the tower.

Chapter Nine

The Flight of the Dragon

The dream of creating a flying machine able to take off and land vertically is almost as old as that of flight itself. Yet it was to be thirty-six years after Blériot's flight that the first helicopter crossed the English Channel.

Centuries before the Wright brothers made their first sustained and powered flight with an aeroplane, engineers and scientists had been sketching ideas for what we would now call helicopters. Perhaps the most celebrated was Leonardo da Vinci whose design for an 'air screw' was created between 1483 and 1485. It is believed that Leonardo might even have flown such a machine in model form, probably powered by clockwork.

In 1784 French inventors Launoy and Bienvenu demonstrated a toy with a rotary-wing that could lift and fly which proved the principle of helicopter flight. The first piloted helicopter was invented by French engineer Paul Cornu in 1907 but it wasn't until the middle of the twentieth century that aeronautical technology had advanced to the stage where the rotary-winged aircraft could progress from the theoretical to the practical.

Two of the key pioneers of rotary-winged flight were Juan de la Cierva and Heinrich Focke. On the face of it, the chubby Spanish aristocrat with the toothy grin and the studious German professor branded as 'politically unreliable' by the Nazis would appear to have had little in common.

But Cierva is credited with the invention of the autogyro and it was his accomplishments which inspired Heinrich Focke a decade later to produce the first practical helicopter. As it happened, the era of rotary-wing aircraft development dominated by Cierva and Focke was book-ended by an achievement which attracted considerable attention: cross-Channel flight.

Cierva came from a wealthy and influential family. He trained as a civil engineer and gained a degree but his most famous accomplishment was the invention in 1920 of the autogyro in which the rotor was drawn through the air by a conventional propeller with the result that the rotor generated lift to sustain level flight, climb and descent.

THE FLIGHT OF THE DRAGON

Before this could be satisfactorily achieved, de la Cierva experienced several failures. These were mainly associated with the unbalanced rolling movement generated when attempting take-off, due to dissymmetry of lift between the advancing and retreating blades. This major difficulty was resolved by the introduction of the flapping hinge. In 1923, Cierva's first successful autogyro made its maiden flight from Getafe airfield, Madrid by former cavalry officer and flying instructor Lieutenant Alejandro Gómez Spencer.

Two years later, Cierva brought his latest C.6 machine to Britain and demonstrated it to Air Ministry officials at Farnborough. The machine had a four-bladed rotor with flapping hinges but relied upon conventional aeroplane controls for pitch, roll and yaw. It was based on the fuselage of an Avro 504K trainer and rotation of the rotor was initiated by the rapid uncoiling of a rope passed around stops on the undersides of the blades. The aircraft resembled contemporary fixed-wing machine with a front-mounted engine and propeller. At that stage of its development the ailerons were carried on booms either side of the fuselage where the wings would have been on a conventional aircraft.

The Farnborough demonstration was a great success, so much so that it resulted in an invitation to Cierva to continue his work in Britain. As a direct result, and with the assistance of the Scottish industrialist James Weir, the Cierva Autogiro Company was formed the following year. From the outset Cierva concentrated on the design and manufacture of rotor systems, relying on other established aircraft manufacturers to produce the airframes, predominantly the A.V. Roe company.

The Avro-built C.8 was a refinement of the C.6 but with a more powerful 180hp Armstrong-Siddeley Lynx radial engine. Several C.8s were built. The C.8R incorporated drag hinges to eliminate high blade root stresses in the rotor plane of rotation caused by blade flapping motion. But this modification led to other problems such as ground resonance and hinge dampers were installed to correct this.

Resolution of these fundamental problems opened the way to progress and confidence in Cierva's machine rapidly built up. After several notable cross-country flights, a C.8L4 (G-EBYY) was entered for the 1928 King's Cup Air Race piloted by Flight Lieutenant Arthur Rawson, Cierva's test pilot. A headwind combined with an oil leak made a forced landing in a field at Nuneaton necessary. Although forced to withdraw, the machine subsequently completed a 3,000-mile tour of Britain visiting many civil and service aerodromes. Rawson was again at the controls.

The event which undoubtedly signalled the autogiro's coming of age came on 18 September when Cierva took G-EBYY from Croydon to Paris Le Bourget carrying a passenger, Henri Bouche, editor of the French journal *L'Aéronautique*.

Contemporary photographs show the moon-faced Spanish aristocrat and his wary-looking passenger preparing for the flight at Croydon surrounded by a group of ladies in cloche hats. Both aviators are dressed in smart double-breasted suits and are wearing collars and ties topped by leather flying helmets and goggles.

The crossing was accomplished in sixty-six minutes at a height of 4,000 feet and marked the first international flight by autogiro as well as the first crossing of the Channel by such a machine. The onward flight to Paris was accomplished with stops at Saint-Inglevert and Abbeville.

It was hailed as a triumph by the French who, rather as Britain had heralded Blériot not two decades earlier, feted Cierva. In fact, as author and autogiro historian Arthur Orde-Hume noted, the reception Cierva received at Le Bourget 'was little short of ecstatic and almost mirrored that which greeted a certain Frenchman at Dover two decades earlier'.

Cierva was awarded the *Grand Prix d'Académie des Sports* and the Lahm Prize presented by the Aéro Club de France. These awards were accompanied by a purse of 45,000 francs and a further recognition from the *Union pour la Sécurité en Aéroplane* was worth an additional 20,000 francs, a total not far short of £20,000 in today's money. The international publicity, however, was priceless.

The London-Paris flight was actually the first stage of a continental visit which was to take what the journal *Flight* called the 'Windmill Plane' on a 1,450-mile ten-day demonstration tour of four countries. In Paris Rawson took over the controls from Cierva and flew the machine for the rest of the tour with H. Blake, company secretary of the Cierva Autogiro Company, as passenger.

Apart from routine maintenance, the machine required minimal attention during the tour. A new set of interbracing rubbers was fitted at Berlin as one of them was showing signs of wear. The large extent of tarmac at Berlin took its toll and a damaged tail-skid shoe had to be replaced. A new set of sparking plugs was also fitted to the Lynx engine at Berlin as the engine was not giving full revs.

On the flight from Rotterdam to Brussels the engine started to splutter but this did not prevent the aircraft from reaching the Belgian capital safely. There the trouble was traced to the quality of petrol in use and the fuel filter and two of the plugs were cleaned. The trouble did not recur.

THE FLIGHT OF THE DRAGON

According to *Flight*

> the machine was extremely successful in every way and the receptions accorded to it in France, Belgium, Germany and Holland were very gratifying and enthusiastic. The programme was carried out absolutely according to plan except where weather conditions made it necessary to change the route at Leipzig and delay at Valenciennes.

The tour was hailed as a success and appeared to confirm the soundness of Cierva's concept. As he continued to refine the basic design, manufacturing licences were sold to France, Germany and the USA. During a visit to the USA, Cierva was interviewed by the magazine *Popular Mechanix*. The inventor predicted a bright future for his brainchild. He said, 'To fly the autogyro without risk only a few hours' training are necessary.' The magazine quoted him as saying, 'In addition, the autogyro will make possible the utilisation of very small fields as landing ground.'

The German company *Focke-Wulf Flugzeubau AG* also acquired a manufacturing licence from Cierva the same year. This enabled it to incorporate some of Cierva's ideas in the helicopter the company intended to design and build in collaboration with well-known aerobatic pilot Gerd Achgelis.

It is accepted that the first practical helicopter was the Breguet-Dorand created by Rene Dorand in association with the well-known French aircraft manufacturing company and first flown in the summer of 1935 by Maurice Claisse. Despite its complexity the machine established a number of internationally-recognised records by flying at 67 mph and reaching an altitude of 518 feet. It was also the first helicopter to be properly certificated by a responsible airworthiness authority.

Its achievements were, however, eclipsed by Heinrich Focke's first helicopter design, the Fw 61. Like the early Cierva autogyros, the Fw 61 was based on a successful trainer, in this case the Fw 44 Stieglitz biplane. In 1936 Focke was ousted from his company, apparently by shareholder pressure but possibly to enable its production capacity to be used to build the new Messerschmitt Bf 109 fighter.

But the success of the Fw 61 had caused a change of attitude within the air ministry. It encouraged Focke to start a new company with aerobatic pilot Gerd Achgelis to build on what had been achieved with the Fw 61 and develop a larger, commercially viable machine. This eventually emerged as the Focke-Achgelis Fa 223 *Drache* (Kite).

The Fa 223's story is an amazing one. The *Drache* was the first practical transport helicopter and the first helicopter to be placed in quantity production. But the highlight of its career was to come as a glorious finale in a flight of just a few miles.

But the success did not come easily. Over 100 hours of ground and tethered testing of the *Drache* prototype revealed numerous problems but these were progressively resolved, enabling the machine to make its first flight in August 1940. In October it was flown to the *Luftwaffe* test centre at Rechlin where it reached a top speed of 113 mph and a maximum altitude of 23,000 feet. This far eclipsed the performance of any other helicopter in the world.

It was still, however, far from ready for service. Focke-Achgelis was instructed to accelerate the development programme amid talk of an initial order for 100 machines. The first prototype was destroyed in an accident in 1941 and the second by Allied bombing soon afterwards. In fact, subsequent raids delayed progress at the company's Delmenhorst factory. Production was moved to another factory near Ulm, where the eleventh prototype was able to demonstrate its load-carrying ability by winching a Bf 109 fuselage and a complete Fieseler Storch aircraft on to vehicles.

When a Dornier Do 217 crashed in an inaccessible location in Lower Saxony in 1944 Fa 223 V11 was sent to recover it. However, it too crashed before it could attempt to lift the Do 217 and V14 was then sent to recover both. Karl Bode and *Luftwaffe* helicopter pilot *Leutnant* Helmut Gerstenhauer made ten recovery flights to lift the remains of both crashed aircraft to locations where they could be loaded on to lorries.

The Fa 223 V16 was assigned to the Mountain Warfare School near Innsbruck with V14 as back-up to evaluate its potential as a transport aircraft in mountainous regions. When the trial had ended in October 1944 the machine had made numerous landings over 5,000 feet above sea level and carried artillery pieces to mountain troops. Over eighty flights were made.

After further bombing raids, the Laupheim factory was closed and production halted. Plans were, however, made for a move to Berlin-Tempelhof airport where a production line was to be established to produce 400 helicopters per month. Like many of the ideas dreamed up in the Third Reich at this stage of the war, it was pure fantasy but the *Drache* was not finished yet.

Early in 1945 the company was ordered to prepare a machine to fly to Danzig on what was described as a special mission the details of which remain obscure to this day. It was required to fly to Gdansk, then known as Danzig, on the express orders of Adolf Hitler. Flown by *Leutnant* Helmut Gerstenhauer, possibly the Luftwaffe's premier helicopter pilot, the Fa 223 took off from Tempelhof airport on 26 February. Two other pilots accompanied Gerstenhauer.

Plagued by bad winter weather, lack of fuel, and the need to skirt enemy-occupied territory, Gerstenhauer and his colleagues found Gdansk was falling to the enemy when they finally arrived. They had flown the perilous last leg of the journey directly over the Russians' heads but on reporting the situation they were ordered to return. They arrived back at their starting point on 11 March after an aerial odyssey covering more than 900 miles and logging sixteen hours and twenty-five minutes of flight time.

Three of the surviving Fa 223s were assigned to *Transportstaffel 40*, a special transport unit in Bavaria. This was the Luftwaffe's only operational helicopter squadron. When the war ended one of the aircraft was destroyed by its pilot to avoid capture but the two remaining examples were seized by the US 80th Infantry Division. Three further complete examples together with fifteen more in various stages of completion fell into the hands of Soviet forces at Tempelhof.

The two machines captured by US forces were the V14 and *Werk-Nummer* 00051 which had undertaken the Danzig flight. The intention was to ship both aircraft to the USA for examination and evaluation. But a shortage of space on the US-bound ship meant that only one *Drache* could be accommodated.

The surplus machine was therefore offered to the British authorities who gratefully received it. The victorious western allies were all anxious to uncover the secrets of the Nazis' advanced aeronautical engineering, particularly their work on helicopters.

At the time of its transfer, the *Drache* had logged 170 flying hours since its first fight in 1943, more than any other helicopter in the world. As V14 was airworthy the most obvious way of getting it to Britain was to fly it there. Accordingly, on 25 July 1945 the aircraft became the first helicopter to fly the English Channel.

The captured German machine was repainted in British markings with RAF roundels. On board were *Leutnant* Gerstenhauer, probably the world's most experienced helicopter pilot although officially a prisoner or war, Squadron Leader Cable, RAF, and Lieutenant Buvide, USNR. They flew the machine in stages from Germany to the French coast. It crossed the Channel from Le Havre and landed at RAF Beaulieu near Lymington, Hampshire.

CROSS-CHANNEL AVIATION PIONEERS

This was the location of the Airborne Forces Experimental Establishment, a branch of the Air Ministry which had the task of researching and developing non-traditional airborne applications such as gliders, rotary-wing aircraft and the dropping of personnel and equipment by parachute between 1942 and 1950.

Among the aircraft that passed through AFEE were such weird and wonderful creations as the Hafner Rotachute, a strap-on rotor kite designed to replace a conventional parachute in delivering a soldier accurately to a battlefield. Another was the Hafner Rotorbuggy, which was essentially a Jeep converted into an autogiro to produce an air-droppable vehicle. Other captured helicopter types tested at Beaulieu included a Flettner Fl 282.

Drache V14 was not to remain at Beaulieu for long. During its third test flight in the UK on 3 October the helicopter suffered a failure of its auxiliary drive, causing the rotors to change automatically to the autorotation condition. But as this happened just sixty feet above the ground the pilot was unable to attain the forward speed necessary for an autorotative landing. In the ensuing crash the machine was completely wrecked. The occupants, Helmut Gerstenhauer, O.L.L. Fitzwilliam and two specialists from the Ministry of Aircraft Production, escaped without serious injury.

The fate of the other aircraft captured by the Americans is not recorded. However, development of the *Drache* continued elsewhere. During the final stages of the war plans had been made to transfer production to Czechoslovakia and two partially assembled machines were completed in the autumn of 1947.

Such was the progress made during the war that the leading German helicopter engineers were in great demand by the victorious Allies. Many were offered the opportunity to continue their work in the UK, USA and France. It was to the latter country that Heinrich Focke and twelve of his principal technicians had been persuaded to go. There they were employed by aircraft manufacturer SNCASE, which continued development of the *Drache* under the designation SE 3000.

The experience gained helped the company develop a highly successful rotorcraft family but it also showed that Focke's concept of a transverse rotor layout was too fraught with difficulties to be worth pursuing.

There were to be some interesting echoes of the Cierva C.8's 1928 Continental tour three decades later in a European sales trip organized by Westland Aircraft of Yeovil for its S.51 Dragonfly helicopter G-ANLV. The Dragonfly was a licence-built Sikorsky design powered by a British-made Alvis Leonides engine. In command was Westland test pilot John Fay and he was accompanied by assistant sales manager Bill Hinks, and service engineer John Coombs.

THE FLIGHT OF THE DRAGON

In October 1954 'LV left Yeovil and crossed the Channel from Ferryfield airport, Lydd, to Le Touquet. The aircraft flew in stages from there to Madrid and Lisbon where it was to make a series of demonstration flights. At Madrid's Barajas airport the Dragonfly was met by representatives of Helicopteros SA, a company formed specially to sell Westland helicopters in Spain. Among them was a director of the company, General de la Cierva, a cousin of the autogiro pioneer himself.

In an article in *The Aeroplane* describing the trip, John Fay wrote: 'The general had a ride in the aircraft some days later, his first trip in a rotating wing aircraft since he flew in one of Cierva's early autogiros some 25 years ago.'

By early November the Dragonfly was on its way to Portugal and a series of demonstrations, the highlight of which was an air-sea-rescue exercise for the coast guard. This created considerable interest locally. 'It was watched with interest by many hundreds of people who crowded Lisbon harbour and who created quite a traffic problem,' John Fay wrote later.

When the helicopter returned to Yeovil it had covered 3,000 miles and logged a total of forty-two hours. 'She behaved like a thoroughbred all the way and arrived back as smooth as when we had set out three weeks earlier,' was John Fay's verdict.

The early 1950s saw airlines in North America and Europe starting helicopter services between city centres or between city centres and major hub airports. But at that stage of their development helicopters were neither big enough nor fast enough to make such services viable.

The Belgian airline SABENA, which had launched services between Brussels and Rotterdam, Brussels and Bonn and Brussels and Liège, predicted a profit-making helicopter would not be available before the mid-1960s.

British European Airways formed a helicopter experimental unit at Gatwick in 1951 led by Wing Commander Reggie Brie. A Heathrow-Birmingham service was launched later that year using S.51s. But BEA wanted something bigger and it called for the industry to produce a 'BEALine Bus'. Its chief executive, Peter Masefield, predicted that a such a machine, able to carry forty-eight passengers over 250-mile sectors and cruising at 160 mph, could replace fixed-wing aircraft on all but the longest domestic trunk routes.

The challenge seemed to about to be met by the Fairey Rotodyne. This machine featured a rotor driven by tip-jets with forward propulsion provided by a pair of turboprop engines. It appeared to combine the best features of the helicopter and a medium-sized airliner. In June 1959 the prototype Rotodyne flew from London to Paris for the air show via Brussels.

Fairey claimed that the aircraft had completed the flight between London and Brussels in fifty-eight minutes, compared with a scheduled service time of three hours fifteen minutes. The aircraft had cruised at 200 mph.

Military and civil variants were proposed but the intriguing Rotodyne was cancelled in 1962, due to its excessive development costs, the noise made by its tip-jets and inter-service rivalry.

Juan de la Cierva's dream of roof landings by rotary-winged craft in the middle of cities had not materialised. But nothing could rob him of the honour of making the first flight across the English Channel by a rotary-winged aircraft.

Definitions

'Autogyro' is the generic name for a flying machine supported by a free-spinning rotor and propelled forwards by a normal arrangement of engine and propeller. The term 'Autogiro' was registered in Spain as a trade name by Juan de la Cierva in 1923.

'Helicopter' is the generic term for a rotary-winged aircraft in which the lifting rotor is wholly powered by one or more engines in flight. This rotor may be moved in such a manner as to create vertical lift, hover and, by tilting the angle of the rotor disc in any direction, forward, lateral or even reverse motion. Unlike the free-spinning rotor of the autogyro, a helicopter generates torque, necessitating the use of a sideways-thrusting tail rotor to compensate for the effects of this torque.

That is the basic configuration which has dominated helicopter design since 1940 when Russian-American aviation pioneer Igor Sikorsky first flew his VS-300, which is considered the first really successful design. As a result, Sikorsky is seen as the 'father' of the helicopter, although there have been other layouts, such as twin rotors in tandem.

It was, however, the French writer Gustave de Ponton d'Amécourt who is credited with coining the term 'helicopter' from the Greek words *helix* for spiral and *pter* for wings.

Autogyros and helicopters have often been confused, such as when newspapers headlined the story of Reggie Brie's 1931 cross-Channel flight in an autogyro as 'British Airman's Helicopter Flight to France'.

The Autogiro Man

Born in Murcia, Spain, in 1895, Juan de la Cierva was prompted while still a teenager to start an aircraft manufacturing company with two friends. They built the first aircraft to be manufactured in Spain, the BCD-1 *Cangrejo* (Crab). It was not a success and after a crash caused by flying too slowly Cierva decided to build an aircraft that could fly at low speed without stalling.

By 1919 he was considering a machine whose main feature was a horizontally-mounted rotor that would generate lift at low airspeed and eliminate the risk of stalling. The following year Cierva had produced what he called the Autogiro. But it wasn't until 1923, after four years of experimentation, that he developed the articulated rotor which achieved the world's first successful flight of a stable rotary-wing aircraft with his C.4.

By the time the C.8 appeared, in 1928, Cierva had moved to Britain and started the Cierva Autogiro Company. The Avro-built C.8 was, like most of its predecessors, a derivative of the Avro 504N, the latest variant of the long-lived RAF trainer.

The C.8 did, however, dispense with the characteristic finless comma-shaped rudder in favour of a semi-circular rudder with a large fixed fin. A tandem two-seater, the machine featured dual controls. A noteworthy feature was the provision of removable balance weights at the aft end of the fuselage to allow the machine to be flown as a single-seater from the front cockpit: normal single-seat flying was from the rear cockpit, the front cockpit being more or less on the centre of gravity. It was important before attempting flight to check the balance weights.

The four rotor blades had a single steel tubular spar, spruce ribs that were closely spaced. They were covered with plywood. Small adjustable weights were provided at the tips for balancing. The wire-braced blades featured adjustable pitch and the central hub ran on four ball races – two radial and two thrust.

The C.8 led to the first production Cierva Autogiro, the C.19, which featured stub wings and twin fins and rudders. One example, C.19 Mk III G-AAYP, was flown to Paris by Reggie Brie for demonstrations on 17 December 1931.

As Cierva's machines gained acceptance other constructors followed and there was further innovation. Direct rotor control through cyclic pitch variation was a major development and led to the C.30 which was produced in quantity in Britain, France and Germany.

Cierva's initial motivation had been to produce an aircraft that wouldn't stall but towards the end of his life he accepted the advantages offered by the helicopter and began to switch the focus of his work accordingly. He died in December 1936 when the KLM DC-2 aircraft on which he was planning to travel to Amsterdam crashed soon after take-off at Croydon Airport.

It was, Wing Commander Reggie Brie wrote in 1947, Cierva's foresight and tenacity which 'well and truly laid the foundations upon which the helicopter now so surely stands'.

CIERVA C.8 SPECIFICATIONS
Accommodation 2 seated in tandem with dual controls
Length 36 ft
Rotor diameter 39 ft 8in.
Power Plant 1 x 180hp Armstrong Siddeley Lynx IV seven-cylinder air-cooled radial engine
Maximum speed at sea level 100 mph
Cruising speed 85 mph
Endurance 3 hours

Meet the Fockes

Heinrich Focke was born in Bremen on 8 October 1890. He studied at the University of Hanover, where he befriended Georg Wulf. In 1914 both reported for military service but Focke's was deferred due to heart trouble, although he was eventually drafted into an infantry regiment. After serving on the Eastern Front, he was transferred to the Imperial German Army Air Service. After the war Focke returned to his studies and graduated in 1920 with distinction as an engineer.

Three years later, Focke co-founded *Focke-Wulf-Flugzeugbau GmbH* with Wulf and Dr Werner Naumann. In 1927 Wulf died while test flying the Focke Wulf Fw 19 canard monoplane. Although Focke declined the offer of a chair at Danzig Institute of Technology, the city of Bremen awarded him the title of professor.

In 1931 Focke Wulf was merged with the *Albatros Flugzeugweke*. Two years later the company acquired a licence to build Juan de la Cierva's C.19 and C.30 autogiros. This inspired Focke to design and build what was to become the world's first practical helicopter, the Fw 61.

A modified Fw 44 fuselage was used featuring a nose-mounted 160 hp Bramo Sh 14a radial engine but instead of driving a conventional propeller it was attached to a small-diameter cooling fan. Extending from each side of the forward fuselage were pyramidal outriggers of chrome-molybdenum steel tubing attached to the main structure at three points.

These outriggers terminated in rotor heads each carrying three double-articulated blades built up from plywood screwed to a tubular steel spar and then fabric covered. Power to the contra-rotating rotors – and this is the clever bit – was transmitted through a friction clutch to a gearbox from which two shafts ran parallel to the front strut of each supporting pyramid. Cyclic blade pitch provided longitudinal and directional control, differential operation of the cyclic pitch giving lateral control.

Two examples of the Fw 61 were built and, after a series of tethered flights, D-EBVU made the first free flight in June 1936. A year later the machine had pulverised all existing internationally-recognised world records for rotorcraft and by some margin. Ing Ewald Rohlfs achieved a speed of over 76 mph.

In February 1938 the celebrated German aviatrix Hanna Reitsch made a remarkable demonstration of the Fw 61's controllability and reliability by flying it *inside* the *Deutschlandhalle* in Berlin.

In the meantime, as was not uncommon in Nazi Germany, politics intervened. The air ministry had decided to integrate the Focke-Wulf company into the Messerschmitt Bf 109 production programme and reorganized it as a limited liability company. Wulf had been killed in an accident and Focke, now considered 'politically unreliable', lost control of the company to AEG.

But with encouragement from the air ministry, Focke formed the Focke-Achgelis company to develop his helicopter designs.

He was, therefore, no longer associated with his old company when it produced such noteworthy designs as the Fw 200 airliner and the Fw 190, arguably the best German piston-engined fighter of the Second World War.

Meanwhile, Focke's next helicopter design had emerged. The Fa 223 featured a twin-rotor layout similar to the Fw 61 but with a fully-enclosed cabin for six occupants, load bay and single Bramo engine and gearbox mounted in the middle of the fabric-covered tubular steel fuselage.

After the war Focke went to work for the French company SNCASE to assist in developing its SE-3000 based on the Fa 223. In 1952 Focke and some of his former design team moved to Brazil to develop a convertiplane which relied heavily on Focke's wartime work. He also developed a light helicopter.

He returned to Germany in 1956 to work on further helicopter designs. He died in 1979. Today his achievements are remembered in a museum in Bremen.

FOCKE-ACHGELIS FA223 *DRACHE* SPECIFICATIONS
Accommodation flight crew of 2 plus up to 4 passengers
Length 40 ft 2 in
Span (over rotors) 80 ft 5 in
Max take-off weight 9,513 lb
Fuel capacity 108 gal plus external tank containing 66 gal
Powerplant 1 BMW Bramo 323D-2 nine-cylinder radial developing up to 1,000 hp
Maximum speed 116 mph (cruise, 83 mph) at 6,600 ft
Range on internal fuel 272 miles (ferry range, 435 miles)
Endurance 2 hr 20 min.

Chapter Ten

Air Bridge

We're just crossing the English coast as Ramsgate slides past the big square windows of Royal Mail Airliner *Vortex*. We've travelled eighty miles since taking off from London's Northolt airport.

In sixteen minutes' time we should be able to see Dunkirk on the right. According to the in-flight bulletin circulated to passengers by Captain T.M. Griffith, we're cruising at 190 mph and expect to land at Brussels, our destination, in two hours.

It's 1953, seven years since commercial airline services resumed after the Second World War. Air travel is still for the well-to-do, but things are very different from the so-called 'golden age' of the 1930s. Times are changing. The aviation industry is developing new ways to fly faster, go further and carry more. The whole character of air travel is on the verge of change.

British European Airways, the newly-formed state-owned short-haul airline, began cross-Channel operations in the summer of 1946. Its services to Marseille, Rome and Athens used the ubiquitous Douglas DC-3 that had been in use since before the war. Further route launches, to Amsterdam, Brussels and Lisbon, followed.

Initially, BEA's ex-RAF Transport Command Dakotas were supplemented by six eight-seat de Havilland Dragon Rapide biplanes and seven-seat Avro Nineteens developed from the Anson military trainer. But between August and October 1946, the airline took delivery of the first eleven of an eventual eighty-three Vickers Vikings. *Vortex* was one of them. They were BEA's first new aircraft and it leased them from the government.

The first Viking revenue service left Northolt for Copenhagen on 1 September 1946. Compared with the Dakota, the new type cut thirty-five minutes from the journey time. From then on Vikings progressively replaced Dakotas on BEA's services to Amsterdam, Oslo, Stockholm, Gibraltar and Prague.

Croydon was no longer London's aerial gateway. Most short-haul services used the RAF airfield at Northolt in west London pending the completion of what would become known as Heathrow Airport. The last BEA service before it was handed back to the RAF left Northolt on 30 October 1954 for Jersey. 'Pionair'- class DC-3 *Charles Samson* was commanded by Captain T. Froggatt. One of the passengers on board had made 200 return crossings since 1946.

Gatwick, in the meantime, was in the process of being transformed from a requisitioned wartime airfield to London's second airport. But it would be a while before it was able to offer regular scheduled flights. The first passenger service to leave the redeveloped airport with its new concrete runway following its official opening by the Queen was a BEA DC-3 chartered by Surrey County Council and bound for Jersey and Guernsey with messages of goodwill.

Its first operations as a civil airport had been flown by charter companies, which included Ciro's Aviation operated by Ciro's Club in London which had three de Havilland Dragon Rapides and three DC-3s. For a while the Dragon Rapides were used to fly clients to a casino at Le Touquet. Another was the Windmill Theatre Transport Company named after and operating on behalf of London's Windmill Theatre. Its chief pilot was ex-ATA pilot Mrs Zita Irwin.

Among the entrepreneurs who were about to change the face of commercial aviation was the rather unlikely figure of a retired RAF senor officer. Yet what he came up with would later be described as one of the brightest ideas in air transport.

Taffy Powell liked nothing better than popping across to France with his Lancaster. Car, that is. Even former air commodores couldn't expect the air force to provide them with their own private heavy bomber to swan around in.

What Griffith Powell could expect, though, was that his experience of running trans-Atlantic aircraft ferrying operations would be in demand after the war. And within a few years he had combined his fondness for Continental motoring trips with his aviation expertise to establish unique and increasingly popular cross-Channel car ferry services.

The operation was launched in 1948 at a former wartime airfield on the Kent coast and later, as business expanded, moved to its own purpose-built facility near Dungeness. Within ten years it had shifted a total of 215,000 cars and 790,000 passengers on 125,000 cross-Channel flights.

Stocky and round-faced, Powell had joined the RAF in 1926 and learned to fly. Four years later he moved to Imperial Airways and was appointed to command a Short C Class Empire flying boat. In 1937 Powell whisked *Cambria* from Newfoundland to Eire in the record time of ten hours thirty-three minutes. This feat earned him a novel form of immortality: his own cigarette card in a series called 'Kings of Speed'.

Powell was to make many more crossings, ferrying aircraft from North America to Britain, finishing the war as an air commodore in what had become RAF Transport Command.

Powell had initially been based in Montreal as operations controller of the Atlantic Ferry Organization which had been formed to ferry aircraft built in the USA and Canada across the Atlantic. In 1941 it was transferred to the RAF as Ferry Command but renamed Transport Command two years later. Powell was appointed senior air officer to the commander in chief which placed him in charge of operations.

During the war the Command's chief responsibility was transporting aircraft across the Atlantic to the United Kingdom and from the UK to the Middle East and beyond. Passenger and freight services were developed initially between Canada and Britain and later throughout Europe, the Middle East, the Mediterranean and India. Aircraft from Transport Command also towed gliders and dropped paratroopers during the Normandy and Arnhem landings.

After the war the Command became increasingly engaged in providing tactical and strategic mobility for the services. Transport Command was renamed Air Support Command in 1967 but five years later was absorbed by Strike Command.

During his wartime service Powell had also flown Winston Churchill in the converted Consolidated Liberator bomber *Commando* which was the prime minister's favoured wartime transport. This association was to continue.

Another wartime contact was Captain A.G. Lamplugh, head of the British Aviation Insurance Group. He offered Powell a job as chief technical officer, a role that led to his discovery that many airlines were finding it difficult to get the aircraft they needed. Powell and Lamplugh persuaded some of their company's shareholders to set up British Aviation Services to ferry US-built aircraft to European operators like Air France and KLM.

But then Powell met W.S. Robinson, chairman of the Zinc Corporation, a London-based mining company with interests in Australia, South Africa and Burma. Robinson asked Powell to act as a company adviser. Among the places he visited was Broken Hill, Australia, a town also known as Silver City because of the silver lode discovered there in 1883.

'It was in the company guest house in Broken Hill that the idea of a new air company to service the mining industry was born,' Powell wrote later.

'That it should be called Silver City was a foregone conclusion.' Silver City Airways was incorporated on 25 November 1946 with Powell as one of its three directors. Four Dakotas were acquired, together with two new Lancastrians, airliners based on the Lancaster bomber, which had also been ordered by British South American Airways. Another was acquired soon afterwards.

The Lancastrians were configured with thirteen seats and although they lacked passenger appeal they were ideal for a company with worldwide operations. Silver City's shares were subsequently acquired by British Air Services, which had initially owned 10 per cent, and under the name Britavia was now intending to operate trooping flights.

As it happened, Silver City's first major operation had little to do with trooping or mining. In October 1947 India received its independence from Britain and there was an urgent need to transport people who suddenly found themselves on the wrong side of the border between India and the newly-formed state of Pakistan.

British Overseas Airways Corporation was actually running the operation and chartered aircraft from Silver City. But when one of its Dakotas became unserviceable, a Bristol Freighter was leased from the manufacturer. That, recalled Powell

> unwittingly started a love affair with an aircraft type that could win nothing if judged by its good looks but as a large boxcar with wings was a striking success on the repatriation airlift. It got an immediate dispensation to exceed its normal passenger capacity of 32 and the limit became simply the total that could get in.

On occasions, as many as 111 passengers were crammed into the Freighter which in nine days carried 1,050 people and their belongings. The airlift ended at the end of November but a seed had been sown. In considering what to do with the ungainly but capable Freighter, which Bristol was trying to persuade Silver City to buy, Powell's thoughts turned to its use as a car ferry. Using specially-made ramps to elevate cars up to the aircraft's clamshell nose doors, a series of experiments was carried out over the winter of 1947/48 to test the theories.

Powell was now convinced that the Freighters could be used to take cars across the Channel quickly and conveniently. The first route would be from Lympne near Folkestone to Le Touquet, a forty-seven-mile hop that would take just twenty minutes. The airports offered good connections with London and Paris, although Powell thought that 'airport' was rather a grand name for Lympne, a grass aerodrome just big enough for Freighter operations.

At the back of Powell's mind was the thought that the world was changing. The war had been over for two and a half years and continental holidays were showing signs of being an attractive proposition in spite of the £50 foreign travel allowance restriction. 'In retrospect,' Powell reflected,

> I suppose we should have foreseen the Continental travel explosion after the drab years of war. Of course, it was a mini explosion compared to what was to happen 25 years later but it quickly became a feature of the travel trade with the sea ferries by no means ready for it. The shipping companies had been left at the end of the war in the same state as the airlines – very short of equipment and substantial additions to the cross-Channel fleet were years away.

The paperwork involved in taking cars across the Channel could also be daunting. Customs officers on both sides of the water were extremely diligent in checking that chassis and engine numbers matched the accompanying paperwork.

Powell reasoned that some of these difficulties would be minimised on a short twenty-minute hop with just two cars which at this stage was the capacity of a Bristol Freighter. Despite its deficiencies, Lympne did have a control tower together with its own customs and immigration facilities. There was even a country club available.

Le Touquet had been a popular destination before the war with its casino and golf course. It now had a new airport, courtesy of the Luftwaffe, which was owned by a municipality anxious to restore its tourist traffic.

The next hurdle for Silver City to clear was a regulatory one. At first, the Air Registration Board was uncomfortable with the idea of the cars being carried ahead of the passenger cabin. 'After one or two rather depressing meetings,' Powell recalled in his autobiography, 'we finally demonstrated that our cross-over chains on each car wheel really bit into the tyres and made the car virtually immovable.'

The ARB also had to be persuaded that the bulkhead between the passenger cabin and the car deck was strong enough to avoid cars ending up in passengers' laps. It insisted on a door being provided in this bulkhead in addition to the normal entry door in the side of the fuselage.

There were other regulatory issues. Because of the monopoly on scheduled services enjoyed in the immediate post-war years by the two state-owned airlines, Silver City's services had to be launched as charter operations, a concept that, not for the first time, had to be interpreted creatively to stay within the law. Help, though, did come from the motoring organisations as both the AA and the RAC offered to act as agents for the proposed operation.

A second Freighter was acquired and brochures were printed to advertise an all-inclusive car-freighting service to the continent with car, luggage and four passengers transported by an air charter service from Lympne to Le Touquet for an inclusive price of £32.

A proving flight was made on 7 July with a party of journalists, a spare pair of loading ramps and Taffy Powell's imposing Armstrong Siddeley Lancaster saloon. The return flight brought home its first charter load in the shape of another up-market car, a Bentley Mk VI. 'There was just half an inch to spare when the doors were closed,' recalled Keith Dagwell, a former instrument engineer who, many years later, would chair the Silver City Association.

But that half inch was enough. 'That return flight,' Powell recalled, 'persuaded all on board that we could carry two above-average size cars and eleven passengers without any problems and there were favourable items written by the journalists before the regular operation started a week later.'

It also removed some of the scepticism of Silver City's shareholders and insurers who were worried about the prospect of an expensive car falling out of the front of a Freighter in mid-Channel. They needn't have worried. The securing of the cars had been well-thought-out before services started. The journal *Flight* explained:

> Cars are held firm in flight by a chain which forms a loop around the top half of each wheel; the chain, in turn, is attached to a toggle device which picks up on attachment points in the hold and enables the chain to be tightened in a single moment of a lever.

The world's first regular car ferry service began on 14 July 1948 when Freighter G-AGVC took off from Lympne for Le Touquet with Captain

Storm Clark in command. By the end of September 178 cars and their passengers plus a significant number of motorcycles and push-bikes had been carried. This was a just a small fraction of the total that would be transported across the Channel before the use of Lympne became untenable.

The following year, the regulatory straitjacket was to be loosened just a little. Britain's independent airlines secured what was known as an Associated Agreement with BEA which enabled them to run scheduled services on routes not in competition with the state-owned carrier. Yet there would be continuing opposition from British European Airways – eventually overcome – to carry passengers travelling without vehicles.

There was also a new fare structure: £32 for large cars and £27 for smaller ones. Although the first year's results had been 'insignificant', Powell felt that the operation's feasibility had been proved. Silver City started 1949 with an expanded fleet of four Bristol Freighters but by the end of the year had acquired a fifth. That year the airline carried 2,700 cars and 10,000 passengers. It was still a small proportion of the total cross-Channel market but still good enough to keep the operation going through the winter with two aircraft. At the same time, the airline started delivering new cars to France and returning with loads like textiles and cheese.

In 1950, 5,000 cars and 24,000 passengers were carried. This figure included the Alfa Romeo racing team which dominated the British Grand Prix at Silverstone, the first-ever Formula One event counting towards the newly-established world championship of drivers. BRM and Jaguar were among the British teams which would regularly use Silver City services.

The 1950 season had started with the aircraft being overhauled by the manufacturers. Collection of the aircraft, said aviation historian Dave Thaxter, was a simple matter: 'Silver City's crews drove to Filton, popped their vans in the Freighters and flew them back to Lympne.'

Yet even as the operation expanded there were doubts about the adequacy of Lympne. Adam Thomson, later to become Sir Adam and chairman of British Caledonian Airways, was a Silver City pilot flying from Lympne. When it rained, Thomson wrote in his autobiography *High Risk*, the aircraft skidded on the mud.

The answer was both simple and effective: the gate to an adjoining field was left open. 'If an aircraft skidded and needed more room to come to a halt than the runway length allowed we would simply steer though the gate into the next field,' Thomson recalled.

When necessary, air traffic controllers radioed a warning to inbound pilots that also contained the reassuring message 'gate open!' And this was the airport that was now Britain's third busiest for the volume of freight handled after Heathrow and Northolt.

By 1953 Silver City was offering the following single fares: cycles, 5 shillings (25p), motorcycles £1-15s (£1-75p), cars £7-10s (£7.50p) and passengers £2. On 1 June 1954 a new service between Lympne and Calais was launched.

That year Silver City started looking for another site. Winter operations had to be transferred to other airports but Lympne's owner, the Ministry of Transport and Civil Aviation, was disinclined to spend money on it. 'Another disadvantage,' Powell recalled, 'was that it was perched on a ridge over 300 ft above the coast at Hythe, which put it much nearer the cloud base and sometimes in it.'

Powell spent many hours in a light aircraft scouring the Kent coastal area for a suitable site. The new base would have to be no further from Le Touquet than Lympne and closer to sea level. These requirements suggested the Romney Marshes, an area best known for the quality of sheep reared there. The most suitable site was described by Powell as 'an area of scrubby grazing land on the edge of the shingle desert of Dungeness'. So it was that there, near the village of Lydd, that Britain's first privately-owned, fully operational airport was to be constructed.

The new airport, to be called Ferryfield, was to have two runways, a control tower, passenger terminal with a restaurant, a maintenance area and petrol station. It was also to have a link with the airways system including a radar service controlled by its own staff. The contract price was £400,000. 'Remarkably cheap,' according to Powell. The terminal building itself, 300-feet wide by 100-feet long, was a simple functional structure of steel clad in white concrete blocks. As the first terminal designed to handle both vehicles and passengers simultaneously, it was divided into three main sections by covered 'carways'.

There was a spacious concourse with a glazed wall that looked out over a sun terrace with the loading apron beyond it. To the left of the main entrance hall was the ticket office and on the right RAC, AA and Lloyds Bank offices. After checking in passengers could pass through to the shop, lounge, buffet and restaurant. *Flight* was impressed. 'The light effect given by the glazed wall and roof windows is coupled with excellent contemporary interior decoration,' the journal reported. 'Signposting is especially clear and effective and well in advance of anything previously seen at British airports.'

When their flight number was called, passengers walked across the outgoing carway, where vehicles were brought for customs inspection, into the centre building, location of both arrival and final departure rooms.

AIR BRIDGE

Ferryfield was the first airport used by Silver City to be equipped with radar, a Decca 424 system which provided both en route and approach coverage. It had a range of sixteen miles and a similar installation was planned for Le Touquet..

Facing the terminal was a loading apron with space for six Superfrieghters parked wingtip to wingtip. After taxying to its loading station, the nose doors of incoming aircraft were opened as the brakes were applied. The car ramp was moved forward to the sill of the aircraft's freight hold. Scheduled time for a complete turn-round was twenty minutes.

Securing the cars was completed before specially-designed tractors towed departing aircraft tail first from their loading bays. They were then turned through 90 degrees ready for engine start and taxying to the runway threshold. After take off the aircraft made a left-hand turn that put them on track for Le Touquet. Cruising at 1,000 feet, the aircraft reached their destination in about twenty minutes. A check call was made in mid-Channel. Return flights cruised at 2,000 feet and were brought in for straight-in approaches at minimum intervals of five miles. 'Stacking' was virtually unknown.

As a general rule, each aircraft operating between Ferryfield and Le Touquet refuelled every second round-trip. A blue flag was flown from the cockpit when an aircraft taxied in to indicate refuelling was required. Reserves consisted of fuel for one hour's holding and diversion to an alternate airport.

By the time of the move to Ferryfield, Silver City employed forty-eight pilots of whom forty-two were based at Ferryfield with six at Southampton. The twenty-four captains had logged an average of 6,000 flying hours. They made up to twelve Channel crossings a day at peak times. Captain Jerry Rosser held the record with 5,500 since 1948.

A typical crew comprised a captain, first officer and a car marshal, who occupied a small tip-up seat in the nose. The car marshal's duties included supervising the load during flights, enforcement of seatbelt and no smoking rules on take off and landing and later the sale of duty-free goods to the occupants of the fifteen passenger seats.

On 3 October 1954 Freighter G-AGVC commanded by Captain Rosser, who had been co-pilot on the first flight, brought six years of car ferry operations at Lympne to an end. A total of 54,600 cars, 18,372 motorcycles, 11,025 pedal cycles and 208,457 passengers had been carried.

The same year saw Silver City take delivery of the first of six enlarged Bristol Freighter Mk 32s that were to join a fleet now comprising nine Mk 21s. With its longer nose the new aircraft could carry three cars.

Further car ferry services had been launched in 1952: Southampton-Cherbourg and Southend-Ostend. A DC-3 passenger service between Gatwick and Le Touquet followed in 1953.

Meanwhile there was stiff competition from British Rail's big new ferry *The Lord Warden*, which could carry 120 cars and 700 passengers. Most independent airlines faced opposition from the state-owned airlines but Silver City had to contend with the state-owned rail operator as well and now it was aggressively promoting its new purpose-built facility at Dover. Silver City, which had 20 per cent of the market, responded by offering services from Lympne to Calais and Ostend and with a further reduction in fares, something that would become virtually an annual event.

In 1954 control of Britavia passed to the P&O shipping company and a Gatwick-Le Touquet car ferry service was started although the year's major event was the opening on 14 July of Ferryfield.

It was better than Lympne but it was still far from perfect. When he arrived in 1956 Freighter pilot Ken Honey thought it 'a bit Spartan'. 'You were on limits on many occasions,' he recalled.

> The runway was lengthened several times but at that stage it was relatively short. It always seemed to be a bit of a challenge but I don't remember too many anxious moments. Perhaps we had a different approach in those days. You were quite busy, but it was marvellous for gaining experience if not for building flying hours.

The expansion continued. In 1955 there were more new services including Stranraer-Belfast, Southampton-Deauville and Birmingham-Le Touquet. The following year the airline was able to launch its London-Paris Silver Arrow passenger service, which initially involved a coach journey to Ferryfield and another from Le Touquet to Étables where passengers boarded the train for Paris. At the end of the decade it was being advertised as a daily service at a return fare of £8.90.

But times were changing. A re-organization had split the airline into two divisions, one looking after Silver Arrow and car ferry services and the other handling cargo. By now Taffy Powell had retired. He admitted, 'I suppose I drove my personal machinery too hard and too long.' In November 1957 he received a letter on Chartwell-headed notepaper expressing the hope that he would 'have a speedy return to good health'. It was signed by Winston Churchill, for whom Powell had provided transport on several occasions when he was out of office.

Powell was missed and not just because he was an astute businessman. 'He didn't suffer fools gladly,' recalled Keith Dagwell. 'He was very impatient and most of the managers were threatened with the sack two or three times a day.' Ken Honey remembered: 'If he got a bit wound up he'd throw the `phone at people. It reached a point where the GPO were reluctant to put a new telephone in for him!'

It was inevitable that rival carriers would be looking for a share in Silver City's success. Air Charter had been a struggling charter company until it was acquired by aviation entrepreneur Freddie (later Sir Freddie) Laker in 1951 and added to his growing air freight and trooping operations. In 1953 Air Charter acquired its first brand-new aircraft, a Bristol Freighter, and by the end of the decade was operating a fleet of nine, which included six of the long-nosed Mk 32s.

At first they were used for ad hoc charter operations including the carriage of racehorses. But the success of Silver City's cross-channel car ferry operation prompted it to enter that market. Accordingly, in 1954, Air Charter applied for a licence to fly car ferry services between Southend and Calais. It was launched on 1 September with a fleet of three Mk 31 Freighters.

By the end of its first year it had carried nearly 20,000 passengers and 7,000 cars. This prompted Air Charter to order two Mk 32 Bristol Freighters, the first of which arrived in March 1955. 'From a small beginning,' observed *The Aeroplane*, 'Air Charter has become, together with its associated companies, a considerable undertaking.'

The airline applied for a second route and was able to start operations on Southend-Ostend in October. By that time the name Channel Air Bridge had been applied to the car ferry operation and during the second year 31,000 passengers and 10,000 cars were carried. Over August Bank Holiday 1956 there were 500 flights carrying 1,000 vehicles and 3,500 passengers.

That October a third route was opened with a twice daily service between Southend and Rotterdam. By mid-1957 Air Charter's cross-channel services were carrying over 13,000 cars and 46,000 passengers, double the volume of traffic recorded in the first year. Douglas Whybrow, a former army major who'd masterminded trooping flights, was now in charge of the Channel Air Bridge operation.

But the mercurial Laker had decided to sell the operation, much to the surprise and consternation of its staff. So it was that in January 1959

Air Charter became a subsidiary of Airwork. Channel Air Bridge continued as an independent entity with its Bristol Freighters. Eighteen months later Air Charter was subsumed within British United Airways which had resulted from the merger of Airwork and Hunting Clan. Channel Air Bridge also became part of BUA.

As did Silver City. By the early 1960s competition from sea ferry operators with their roll-on-roll-off ships designed to carry road vehicles was growing fast. In 1962 Silver City's principal shareholders decided to sell the operation to BUA. Channel Air Bridge and Silver City were merged into an operation called British United Air Ferries. In 1967 BUA decided to operate the air ferries as a separate company named British Air Ferries.

But the days of the car ferry business were numbered. Traffic peaked in 1962 at 137,000 cars; three years later it was down to 110,000. The fleet of Bristol Freighters declined from twenty-two to five and BUA's share of cross-Channel traffic was down to 5 per cent from 27 per cent at its peak.

By 1958 Lydd was doing better than Gatwick and handling around 200,000 passengers a year. A decade later that figure had dropped to 160,000 but the operation was still carrying 50,000 cars a year. 'There used to be up to 200 Freighter flights a year,' recalled Ian Maskins, Lydd's manager of air traffic control. 'They were literally in and out every few minutes, but it was killed off by roll-on, roll-off ferries and hovercraft.'

Indeed, the start of hovercraft services caused a further diversion of traffic and the Ferryfield-Le Touquet operation was finally terminated on 31 October 1970. *Motor* magazine reported on the last flight that 'as we disembarked at Ferryfield and the Silver City flag was hauled down more than one gentleman with a lot of gold braid had tears in his eyes'.

The Admirable Freighter

It was slow, noisy, ugly and perhaps, because it appeared at the beginning of the jet age, rather boring. No wonder the Bristol Freighter was so underrated.

Yet it not only flew better than it looked but, with 214 built, it was one of Britain's more successful commercial aircraft. And because it was both affordable and sturdy this unpretentious workhorse proved to be the right aircraft at the right time. As a result, Freighters were so hard used that they were worked into the scrapyard but not before they had shown they could be overloaded when the need arose, pioneer a new concept in travel and even star in a film.

In the 1940s Freighters flew refugees who found themselves in the wrong place when India was partitioned; in the '50s they flew cars across the English Channel and in the '60s they flew military supplies and equipment into Vietnam. In fact, some Freighters flew on into the '80s carrying livestock.

The Bristol Type 170 Freighter was inspired, it was said, by the demands of Orde Wingate for a transport aircraft capable of using short jungle strips to keep his Chindits supplied as they operated behind Japanese lines. Two military prototypes were ordered to Specifications 22/44 and C.9/45 but the end of the war changed the emphasis of the design.

The team led by Bristol's chief designer Archibald Russell, later to play a key role in the development of Concorde, adapted it to perform a primarily civilian role and to be to be available in two basic forms. The Freighter (Series 1) was to feature a pair of clamshell doors in its bulbous nose and a floor able to accept vehicles and cargo up to 4.5 tons, while the fixed-nose Wayfarer would have seats for thirty-two passengers.

The basic design featured a high wing as well as a fixed wide-track undercarriage to save weight, avoid complexity and appeal to operators using small rough airfields. In line with the underlying philosophy of making the machine easy to maintain, both engines could be changed in just ninety minutes.

Because it was simpler to construct, the Wayfarer was the first to fly and on 30 April 1945 G-AGVB took to the air commanded by chief test pilot Cyril Uwins. It was followed on 2 December by the first Freighter (G-AGPV) which was later to demonstrate its load-carrying ability in India and Pakistan.

The first Wayfarer, meanwhile, was leased to Channel Islands Airways and by June 1946 had carried 10,000 passengers between Croydon and Jersey. But the best-known operator was probably Silver City Airways which between 1948 and 1956 operated thirty-two examples on its Lympne-Le Touquet route.

The Series 1 Freighters could carry two cars while the long-nosed Mk 32 could carry three plus twenty-three passengers. Silver City operated fourteen Mk 32s. The last plus those of one-time rival Air Charter were consigned to the scrapyard in 1970.

The Carvair Story

The Bristol Freighter Mk 32 brought increased capacity to the cross-Channel car ferry operation but only by one car. It was clear that the economics of the operation would be improved with bigger aircraft.

Silver City considered the Blackburn Universal Freighter, later to become the RAF's Beverley heavy transport. The thinking boy's comic *Eagle* published a cutaway drawing of a Universal modified to carry five cars. The cost ruled it out, however.

During the 1950s the length of the average British car increased by ten inches, making it even more of a squeeze to get three into a Mk 32 Freighter. Repeated landings and short flights at low altitude were taking a toll of the Bristols' structure and the regulatory authorities were insisting on costly modification programmes.

But they were all that was available despite a search for something bigger and faster within a £200,000 budget. It needed a genius to come up with something suitable. And like Archimedes, Freddie Laker, so the story goes, came up with a solution while taking a bath.

He scrambled out and, still dripping, telephoned the chief engineer of Southend-based Aviation Traders – which he still controlled despite also being managing director of British United Airways – and instructed him to measure the fuselage of a DC-4 at certain points. His big idea had been the conversion of the DC-4 to carry cars.

Before the end of the day Laker had made a cardboard model of the DC-4 with doors in the nose and the flight deck perched on top of the fuselage. It would be able to carry five cars and around twenty-five passengers. DC-4s were then available for as little as £50,000, and could be converted for £80,000. A hundred hours of wind tunnel testing established the best shape for the conversion which became known as the ATL 98 Carvair.

'It was a complete rebuild,' Laker recalled. 'We kept the wings and tail section of the DC-4 and built a new nose on it and put the crew above the fuselage.' There were more powerful brakes and new tail control surfaces.

Re-routing the controls, nearly all of them mechanical, from the cockpit proved one of the trickiest jobs. In the end, with the use of nearly 600 additional pulleys, many hundreds of cast brackets and over six changes of direction, the work was completed.

The prototype conversion first flew in June 1961. Twenty-one Carvairs were produced in the UK, with aircraft 1, 11 and 21 built at Southend and the remainder at Stansted.

The Carvair conversion was granted a full certificate of airworthiness in 1962 at the same time as the Silver City-BUA merger. The new operation had ten examples. The aircraft's greater range compared with the Bristol Freighter enabled them to operate longer routes, to places like Lyon, Strasbourg, Dusseldorf, Bremen, Basel and Geneva.

Yet, recalled Griffith Taffy Powell, Silver City's managing director,

> It was not really a success. The conversion costs were high so the economics were at fault. Compared with the Bristol Freighter they were very short on reliability but it was an early example of Freddie Laker's will to push an idea to a conclusion. He was not easily put off.

It was inevitable that cross-Channel car-ferry services should find their way into popular culture. In the 1959 James Bond novel *Goldfinger*, the criminal master-mind's armour-plated Rolls-Royce is so heavy that it has to have an aircraft to itself. Having insinuated a tracking device on board, 007 follows on a later flight in his Aston Martin.

Chapter Eleven

A New Era in Air Travel

The passengers checking in for flight BE 329X2 at London's Northolt airport were in for a big surprise.

It was Saturday 29 July 1950 and they were about to make civil aviation history. Rubbing shoulders with senior government officials and titans of the British aviation industry, they were to be the first fare-paying passengers in the world to be wafted across the English Channel by a new type of aircraft that would change commercial aviation for ever.

Britain had emerged from the Second World War as the undisputed leader in jet propulsion. Until other nations, notably the USA, caught up, Britain's aircraft manufacturers had the field to themselves. It was to be another nine years before a foreign-built airliner incorporating the new technology – but using British engines – would be available for cross-Channel operations.

The first new airliners built in Britain after the war were thoroughly conventional types. The de Havilland Dove was a small feeder-liner of which more than 500 were eventually sold around the world, while the Vickers Viking could seat up to twenty-seven passengers and began supplementing the Douglas DC-3s in service with the nationalised British European Airways in 1947.

The Viking was powered by sleeve-valve Bristol Hercules engines developing up to 1,690 hp, yet little time was to pass before a jet-powered version appeared. As a result, the 107th Viking airframe on the Weybridge production line was to become one of the most significant aircraft in commercial aviation history.

Starting off as a standard Mk1B long-nose Viking, it was modified with completely new wing pods each housing a Rolls-Royce Nene jet engine. The Ministry of Supply-owned aircraft, which had the civilian registration G-AJPH as well as the military serial number VX856, was built to test the feasibility of jet power for passenger aircraft. It was also intended to investigate noise levels and the general effect of altitude and temperature on performance.

Compared with Hercules-powered aircraft, the Nene-Viking, designated Type 618, had metal-covered elevators with stronger hinges and thicker wing skinning. The trailing edge was extended at the rear to blend smoothly into the top of the nacelles. The main landing gears were of a totally new type with twin main-wheel units to absorb higher landing weights and speeds. These units retracted to lie on each side of the jet pipe inside the nacelle. The Viking's tailwheel undercarriage was, however, retained.

Vickers' chief test pilot, Joseph 'Mutt' Summers, took the Nene-Viking into the air for the first time on 6 April 1948. Although the maiden flight was made at Wisley, much of the test programme was undertaken at Chilbolton, the Hampshire airfield also used by Vickers' Supermarine division for testing jet prototypes. The test flying was shared between Summers and his deputy, Gabe R. 'Jock' Bryce, who would later succeed him.

In a flight test report dated 15 June 1948 it was stated that the maximum take-off weight was 34,000 lb and maximum landing weight 31,000 lb. Take off was described as pleasant and straightforward but the aircraft's tail-down attitude caused loose material like stones to be blown onto the tail and cause damage.

The best climb speed was found to be 200 knots. Engine handling was satisfactory except for resonance in the port unit on start up. Both engines could be successfully re-lit in flight but under conditions of high power and slow speed it was noted that engine fumes entered the cabin. The aircraft was stable longitudinally and up to 270 knots remained easy and pleasant to fly. No undue concentration was required to maintain stable flight.

Landing presented a problem compared with the standard Viking but a technique was quickly evolved to ensure it could be accomplished without difficulty. Approaches needed to be long and low. High approaches made it difficult to lose airspeed.

A wide circuit was made downwind at 130 knots IAS (indicated air speed) with the engines at 7,000-8,000 rpm, wheels down and flaps at 20 per cent. On finals, speed was reduced to 90 knots until the aircraft was some distance before the runway. The throttles were then closed to enable the aircraft to 'glide in'. During level speed tests VX856 achieved 320 knots in smooth air.

The Nene-Viking's place in aviation history was ensured by its status as the world's first pure jet transport aircraft. The highlight of its career came on 25 July 1948 when Summers flew it from London Airport (today's Heathrow) to Villacoublay, Paris, and back at an average speed of 394 mph. The outward leg took thirty-four minutes seven seconds, less than half the time of the regular scheduled flight by a propeller-driven Viking. The aircraft reached a speed of 415 mph.

Vickers' chief designer, George (later Sir George) Edwards spent some time on the flight deck sitting next to Summers. Later he said that the flight had been 'a bit of baloney but a lot of fun'. He told his biographer about being met in Paris by Blériot's widow.

The only incident of note during the flight was that a passenger window blew in but, as the cabin wasn't pressurised, there was no damage. Edwards also remembered upsetting the airport manager at Heathrow when the aircraft wrecked his flower beds with its jet efflux.

Edwards hadn't seen the flight as a serious exercise. 'I never thought it would cut much ice,' he shrugged. But he did adopt a more positive attitude when he and Summers appeared on the BBC radio programme *In Town Tonight*. 'We both went suitably over the edge,' he recalled.

Yet Edwards was impressed by the aircraft's performance. He told his biographer, Robert Gardner:

> A couple of Nenes were two pretty big engines in a relatively light aeroplane. It was bound to scoot along. I suppose the value was the exposure of what happens when you put a jet in an airframe previously powered by two old thumpers.

The Nene-Viking programme continued until 1954 when Vickers bought the aircraft back from the ministry and converted it to Hercules power. It was then sold to British Eagle and added to the fleet of Vikings the airline used for inclusive tour operations.

Meanwhile, Vickers and the Ministry of Supply had been applying the new technology to commercial aircraft in a rather different way to the Nene-Viking. The result would be one of civil air transport's milestones: the first gas-turbine powered aircraft to operate a revenue passenger service.

This would reveal the potential of the revolutionary powerplant at a time when pure-jet transports were experiencing setbacks in their operational development. It was the first British airliner to be sold in quantity in North America and it went into service with airlines all over the world in many varying climates and differing operating environments.

And the Viscount was the first turbine-powered aircraft to operate a cross-Channel service carrying fare-paying passengers.

A NEW ERA IN AIR TRAVEL

But it could have been very different. The Viscount came close to being stifled at birth by a combination of the troubled development of its Rolls-Royce Dart engines and nervousness about the novel form of propulsion.

In November 1944 the second of the two Brabazon committees appointed by the government to consider the equipment Britain's airlines would need in the post-war world formulated the specification for a DC-3 replacement. This called for not one but two aircraft; one to be powered by conventional piston engines, the other by turbo-jets.

Rex Pierson, then Vickers' chief designer, didn't like either proposal. In December 1944 he appeared before the committee to argue that the second specification should be for an aircraft powered by propeller turbines. He thought that such a powerplant would offer better fuel economy than jets on short-haul routes. After some debate, the committee agreed and the specification was changed accordingly as the Type IIB.

Pierson's next move was to draw up a proposal for an aircraft with a double-bubble fuselage, a pressurised cabin and four unspecified turboprop engines. But Pierson died in 1948 and Edwards became chief designer.

Edwards was always reluctant to credit the Brabazon Committee with originating the Viscount design. He maintained that he and Pierson had not seen the Viscount as merely a DC-3 or Viking replacement but as a more sophisticated design with a pressurised passenger cabin. 'We took a poor view of it being labelled a committee sponsored aeroplane, which it wasn't,' Edwards insisted.

Although he was always happy for Pierson to be known as the father of the new aeroplane, it was Edwards who turned the VC.2 into the Viscount. He supervised the required design changes and drove all the later developments. He also selected the Dart engine, despite the evidence against it, and maintained his unshakeable faith in the aircraft when most around him were turning against it.

The MoS favoured the Armstrong-Siddeley Mamba whose development it was funding. But Edwards steadfastly championed the Dart despite its poor initial performance. In private, though, Edwards could be scathing about the Dart. He called it 'little short of disastrous' but he stuck to his view that its centrifugal compressor offered superior reliability compared with the Mamba's axial-flow compressor. 'You cannot take chances with engines when doing something fairly special with the aeroplane,' he insisted.

Edwards' attitude brought him into conflict with senior ministry officials and he pulled no punches in his dealings with Rolls-Royce. He told its chairman Lord Hives: 'We need a major effort from you.'

Impressed by Edwards' frankness, Hives promised a renewed effort. Before long the Dart was generating 1,000 shaft horsepower. In December 1946 Vickers began construction of the two Viscount prototypes funded by the MoS. By now the aircraft had grown in size and was intended to accommodate thirty-two passengers. In 1947 the Ministry finally agreed with the selection of the Dart to power what was now known as the V. 630.

But BEA had announced plans to order the rival Airspeed Ambassador. It was larger than the V. 630 but, with two Centaurus piston engines, its operating economics were similar to the Viscount.

Vickers and BEA had been working closely together on the Viscount and Edwards and his team were well aware that the airline had been lobbied vigorously by Airspeed, a company owned by de Havilland. But the BEA order still came as a body blow.

In fact, to many at Vickers it signalled the end of the Viscount programme. But Edwards kept his nerve. The Ambassador might be an impressive aircraft but he was convinced it represented a step backwards. His faith was infectious and he was able to convince the Ministry to continue funding the V. 630.

The first prototype Viscount, registered G-AHRF, flew for the first time on 16 July 1948 from the grass runway at Wisley. The day before, Summers insisted that Edwards accompany him to the local golf club to practise his swing. Many years later, Jock Bryce, who accompanied Summers on that maiden flight, recalled that it was a short one but long enough to act as a morale booster for the whole company.

When they landed Summers praised the aircraft as 'the smoothest I've ever flown'. When asked if anything needed to be done to it, he replied: 'No, don't touch a thing.' More than a decade earlier he'd said the same thing about the prototype Spitfire.

In September the aircraft was demonstrated to the press at Brooklands before appearing at the Farnborough Air Show. Later in the month the Viscount made its first cross-Channel flight when it was demonstrated at the French military airfield of Villacoublay near Paris. Press flights were arranged for December. When a journalist asked Edwards if the bugs had been ironed out of the aircraft he replied: 'That's what's worrying us. We can't find any.'

After he'd flown the Viscount, Peter Masefield, senior civil servant, qualified pilot and soon to be appointed chief executive of BEA, joined the band of Viscount enthusiasts. His influence was to be crucial in the airline's subsequent decision to order the aircraft.

A NEW ERA IN AIR TRAVEL

It wasn't that he didn't believe in the Ambassador because he regarded it as a fine aircraft. But, as he recalled in his autobiography, 'it vibrated through the sky at 240 mph' while the Viscount promised to give its passengers 'a ride almost 100 mph faster and so smooth that they could stand coins on their edges on the seat-back tables'.

But Masefield was well aware that the turboprop was still a high-risk engine and, as insurance against its failure, he agreed with the decision to order twenty Ambassadors in September 1948. But the Ambassador also had its problems, not so much with the complex Centaurus engines, but with electrical and structural issues. It didn't therefore enter operational service (as the 'Elizabethan' Class) until 1952.

Meanwhile, Rolls-Royce was able to offer a more powerful Dart with 1,250 shp. This made a stretched Viscount a practical proposition. As a result, the V.630 was put on hold and the type V.700 Viscount emerged. With a wingspan increased by further five feet six inches and a fuselage lengthened by seven feet six inches, it had a gross weight of 45,000 pounds and could accommodate forty-three passengers. Cruising speed increased to 335 mph.

The MoS ordered one prototype in February 1949, largely inspired by two senior officials, Sir Alec Coryton, Controller of Supplies (Air) and Sir Cyril Musgrave, Under Secretary (Air). This aircraft, G-AMAV, made its maiden flight on 28 August 1950 from Brooklands with Bryce in command. BEA signed up for twenty examples (later increased to twenty-six) of the improved V.701 with five-abreast seating for forty-seven passengers.

Meanwhile, the V.630 had been despatched on several tours of Europe and East Africa. In March and April 1950 it visited Amsterdam, Brussels, Zurich, Rome and Paris, then Copenhagen, Stockholm, Oslo and Amsterdam. On board, Edwards and Summers were joined by Sir Hew Kilner, aviation managing director of Vickers-Armstrong. In command was BEA's Captain Wylie Wakelin. In June tropical trials were flown in Kenya and Sudan where the Viscount was accompanied by a Vickers Valetta transport lent by the MoS.. Both aircraft returned in early July

The Viscount was in the air for a total of sixty-one hours and made seventy flights totalling 4,400 miles. *Flight* reported that 'the manufacturers have subsequently expressed extreme satisfaction at the high degree of serviceability and the negligible amount of daily maintenance required'.

But BEA was anxious to find out how the Viscount would perform in actual passenger operations. On 20 July, following its return from Khartoum, the airline asked Vickers and the MoS for the loan of the prototype to enable it to gain more experience of the aircraft in operational conditions and to gauge passenger reaction.

On 27 July 1950 the aircraft was granted a special Certificate of Airworthiness and delivered from Wisley to BEA at Northolt the following day. That same evening the aircraft made a proving flight to Le Bourget with seventeen Vickers, BEA and Rolls-Royce representatives on board. This also enabled the airline to set up approach procedures with ATC at Le Bourget.

The aircraft left Northolt later than planned due to a lack of engine power experienced during trials at Wisley which had delayed the handover. It was also delayed in Paris. The airline's report observed: 'It was found difficult to conform to the planned turnaround at Paris because of the delays experienced through press and publicity agents awaiting the arrival of this aircraft at Le Bourget.'

The following day BEA operated the first commercial service by turbine-powered aircraft, from Northolt to Le Bourget. Because of heavy seasonal demand, fourteen of BEA's Paris-bound travellers found they had been booked on a supplementary flight. They'd expected to be flying on a Viking. The first passenger to buy a ticket to travel on a turbine-powered airliner was Miss J. Allison from Australia. Others included Captain A.G. Lamplugh of the British Aviation Insurance company, Normand Hill of Redifon and D. Murarji of rival carrier Pan American.

Before boarding the aircraft, the passengers were handed a letter informing them that they were about to make aviation history and invited their comments on the aircraft. Signed by Peter Masefield, the letter predicted that 'in due course' BEA's network of continental and British services would be operated as 'an everyday procedure by developments of the Vickers Viscount with its Rolls-Royce Dart propeller turbine engines'.

Masefield promised passengers a new standard of passenger comfort 'with the reduction in vibration and noise which you are now experiencing despite the fact that the engines are making 14,000 revolutions per minute'.

On board G-AHRF the passengers joined jet-propulsion pioneer Sir Frank Whittle, Peter Masefield and Viscount designer George Edwards together with the two MoS officials who had supervised the aircraft's development from Whitehall, Coryton and Musgrave.

The aircraft was commanded by Captain 'Dickie' Rymer who was the first pilot to be licensed to command a turbine-powered aircraft. He would later join Vickers as a test pilot and lose his life in 1963 in the crash of the prototype BAC One-Eleven jet airliner. His co-pilot was Captain Wylie J. Wakelin, I.A. Dalgleish was radio officer and C. Dodds and M. Gunn steward and stewardess.

The aircraft left Northolt at 12:48 hr and reached Le Bourget at 13:58, a journey time of one hour ten minutes, twenty minutes less than the scheduled time by Viking. An altitude of 18,000 feet was reached and the aircraft cruised at 273 mph. Masefield recalled: 'Passenger reaction was all we hoped it would be. Together with BOAC with the jet-engined Comet, BEA was starting a totally new era in air travel.'

On Thursday 3 August the airline began scheduled services with the Viscount, flying two services a day (BE 327/332 and BE 337/344) between London and Paris until 14 Monday August.

A *Flight* reporter who sampled the service noted there were twenty-five passengers on board and that, while the aircraft had been flown at varying heights on the proving flights, it had been found that '15 min cruising at 14,500 ft is a satisfactory compromise on this comparatively short haul'. He added, 'It means, in effect, a fairly fast climb from Northolt and a let-down beginning at Dieppe. A cabin height of 2,000 ft is maintained.' On this flight Captain Wakelin was in command with Captain Mitchell as second pilot and Captain Rymer as navigator.

The journalist also quizzed some of his fellow passengers on their impressions of the aircraft, given that they'd been told at BEA's Kensington terminal that they'd be flying in a 'jet aircraft'. One woman thought the Viscount flight had been 'by far the quietest and most comfortable' she'd ever made. She was also impressed by the roominess of the cabin and the width of the aisles. An American passenger was more succinct. 'Brother,' he declared, 'it's just swell.'

The thirty-six round trips from London to Paris were followed by eight more to Edinburgh. By the time the aircraft was returned to Vickers on 23 August, it had flown a total of 137 hours and 57 minutes, equivalent to a total annual utilisation of 1,940 hours. A total of 1,815 fare-paying passengers was carried.

'In general,' Masefield noted,

> the series of operations provided encouraging evidence of the technical quality of the design, the probable low maintenance cost of the Rolls-Royce Dart engines and the potential attractiveness of the turbine aircraft from a passenger and crew viewpoint.

But it was also clear that the V.630 was 'not an economic aeroplane and confirmed the correctness of BEA and Vickers-Armstrongs decision to proceed only with the larger, developed V.701'.

BEA launched services with its V.701s in April 1953 on the London-Rome-Athens-Nicosia service. 'By this time,' Masefield recalled, 'the aircraft and its revolutionary engines were already mature and reliable.'" The Paris flights had not only been historically significant but crucial in ensuring the aircraft's success. By the time production ended 445 examples of all variants had been produced.

On 29 July 1990 a group of enthusiasts was able to commemorate the fiftieth anniversary of the first-ever Viscount service with the help of British World Airlines' G-AOYN. Flying from Northolt, the aircraft parked on the same spot at Le Bourget as the first Viscount half a century earlier.

In August 1992 another of British World's Viscounts (G-APEY) made a special flight to raise money for the restoration of the Brooklands Museum's example, G-APIM. Flying from the airline's Southend airport base, the aircraft overflew Heathrow before moving on to Brooklands where Captain Towle demonstrated the manoeuvrability of this thirty-four-year-old aircraft.

On 18 April 1996 – exactly forty-three years after BEA had launched its first services with the V.701 Viscount – a similar aircraft participated in a special event at Heathrow to mark the withdrawal from passenger service. On board were some of those who had been on the first commercial service in July 1950, including Sir George Edwards, Sir Peter Masefield and Jock Bryce.

British World planned to convert its remaining Viscounts into freighters but G-APEY was sold in 1997 and probably scrapped in 2008. As Jock Bryce – who accumulated 2,100 hours on the type – said: 'Who would have thought that it would still be in service in 2000?'

The Viscount's successor was the Vanguard. It was faster, more capacious and more economical to operate but it was the wrong aircraft at the wrong time. Aesthetically, the Vanguard was a big brute which lacked the delicate grace of the Viscount, its powerful Tyne engines driving propellers like giant scimitars. For all its superior operating economics, sales of Vanguard reached one tenth of the Viscount's. The reason was simple: jets were on the way.

BEA had originally contemplated operating turboprops well into the 1960s because it assumed that, for short-haul work, pure jets wouldn't approach their operating economics for some time. But for other

A NEW ERA IN AIR TRAVEL

operators the passenger appeal of jets would trump the turboprops' lower seat-mile costs.

The Vanguard was a private venture project which represented Vickers' response to Masefield's request for a Viscount successor with 10 per cent lower seat-mile costs. That implied a bigger aircraft and Vickers produced sixty different design studies before settling on a straight-winged aircraft with a double-bubble fuselage to accommodate a large amount of freight.

Jet-power was considered but at that stage Edwards was keen on the new Rolls-Royce Tyne which offered adequate power and would have enabled the aircraft to carry 100 passengers at over 400 mph. It was launched in 1955 as 'the first of the second-generation turboprops with all the desirable attributes associated with the Viscount of smooth quiet and comfort'. In short, it was claimed to be 'ahead of all known competition'. BEA's response was to order twenty for service from 1959.

As the jets were gaining airline orders rumours of difficulties with the Tyne were beginning to emerge from Rolls-Royce. It was more than just teething troubles; there had been a series of high-pressure compressor failures. The Vickers board was becoming jumpy about the programme's viability.

By then the aircraft was already in production at Weybridge. Cancelling it would involve substantial compensation payments and put the whole company at risk. Now BEA was getting worried too. But Edwards was adamant that only turboprops could deliver the operating economics it was demanding.

In its construction the Vanguard broke fresh ground. It used the advanced manufacturing techniques being developed at Weybridge like the sculptured milling process that provided lighter, stronger components.

The Vanguard made its maiden flight from the short runway at Brooklands to the test airfield at Wisley. Jock Bryce was in command and he was accompanied by his deputy, Brian Trubshaw. At the end of the eighteen-minute flight Bryce described the aircraft's performance as 'quite sprightly'.

Later, the Vickers staff concerned gathered at their favourite pub in Wisley for a celebratory drink. According to Robert Gardner's biography, when Edwards stepped outside for some fresh air during the evening he was asked by a local couple what was going on. He told them they'd just flown the Vanguard from Brooklands to Wisley. The wife was clearly unimpressed. 'That's not very far!' she said.

The Type 952 Vanguard entered service with Trans-Canada at the beginning of February 1961, followed a month later by BEA's first Type 951. It had actually been used on an ad hoc basis during the peak 1960 Christmas holiday period on the London-Paris route.

BEA soon found that the Vanguard offered great load flexibility, high speed and low seat-per-mile costs, particularly with high density all-economy seating. On shorter flights it matched the block times of the pure jets. The type was phased out of passenger service following the formation of British Airways in 1974 and the last BA passenger flight with the type was on 16 June.

For Vickers, though, the Vanguard turned out to be something of a disaster. The company lost £16 million on the programme. 'We lost our shirt on it,' Edwards admitted ruefully.

In 1953, when BEA was introducing the V. 701 Viscount into commercial service, Sud Aviation of Toulouse was building two prototypes of a brand-new airliner powered by a pair of jet engines. It was known by the company designation SE 210; it would later be called the Caravelle and it would be Europe's first commercial jet.

Design studies had actually started in 1946 and in 1951 the idea of a French jetliner was officially accepted by government and airline representatives. Pierre Satre and his team at Sud Aviation considered a number of different designs, including one with three rear-mounted engines. But by 1952 the most favoured concept emerged with a pair of Rolls-Royce Avons mounted either side of the tail. It could accommodate sixty-five passengers. The aircraft would later carry up to 100 in high-density configuration.

On 27 May 1955 the first Caravelle, F-WHHH, made its forty-one-minute maiden flight in the hands of the company's chief test pilot, Pierre Nadot, co-pilot Andre Moynet, navigator Jean Avril and flight engineer Roger Beteille. Over the next eleven months the aircraft made 173 flights totalling 411 hours. The second prototype flew in May 1956 and in April 1959 the aircraft received its type certificate.

Scandinavian Airlines System was the first airline to operate the Caravelle, launching it into commercial service on its Middle Eastern routes in April 1959. Air France followed in May with Paris-Istanbul services. The airline began operations to London from Nice via Paris on 27 July 1959. The aircraft, F-BHRE, had been christened *Lorraine* by Madame de Gaulle, wife of the French president. With the arrival of the Caravelle, Paris was now twenty minutes closer to London than it had been and Nice fifty minutes.

A NEW ERA IN AIR TRAVEL

According to *Flight*, the actual flying time between the two capitals had now been brought down to thirty-seven minutes. But a third of the total journey was spent on the ground.

By the mid-1960s Caravelles were dominating European short to medium haul routes with over 200 in service. United Airlines ordered twenty for use on US domestic routes. When production ended in 1972, 282 examples had been produced.

But it wasn't for its sales alone that the Caravelle has come to be regarded as one of the most significant aircraft ever produced in Europe. True, it was the world's first short-haul jet airliner and it introduced the much-copied rear-mounted engine layout, but the Caravelle represented an early step towards a pan-European aerospace industry.

The design and construction of the Caravelle involved collaboration with the British aerospace industry, notably Rolls-Royce and de Havilland. The latter company made available much data gained from its experience with the Comet. One result of this collaboration was that the Caravelle had an identical nose section and similar flight deck layout to the world's first jetliner. Compared with what was to follow this may seem minor stuff, but it was to be followed by further cross-border collaboration on aerospace projects such as Concorde and Airbus.

By the mid-1960s cross-Channel flyers could choose between five different types of jet. In April 1960 BEA put the first of eighteen Comet 4Bs into service on several routes including London-Paris-Nice. The high-capacity version of the heavily revised Comet 4B followed the catastrophic loss of several Comet 1s and an exhaustive inquiry into the disasters. BEA ordered eighteen of the 100-seaters.

They were, however, regarded as a stopgap pending the arrival of the de Havilland 121 which eventually went into service as the Hawker Siddeley Trident. The design of the three-engined aircraft was, however, influenced by the airline's changing demands and the Trident 1 was considerably smaller than the DH 121 as originally envisaged.

A major casualty of this downsizing was the promising Rolls-Royce Medway engine. This was to have far-reaching consequences. The Spey, originally designed for military use, was substituted for the now-cancelled Medway but lacked its development potential. The Trident 1 with its trio of rear-mounted engines went into service in April 1964 on the London-Nice route. The expanded Trident III came close to the capacity of the original DH121 – and also the best-selling Boeing 727 which was widely used by major European airlines on short- to medium-haul routes.

CROSS-CHANNEL AVIATION PIONEERS

A year after the Trident's introduction came the debut of the twin-engined BAC One-Eleven. This was the first product of the newly created British Aircraft Corporation which had resulted from the merger between Vickers, English Electric, Bristol and Hunting. Two of the constituents, Vickers and Hunting, had both been thinking about producing a short-haul jet but came at it from different directions. Hunting's H107 was envisaged as a thirty-seater, while the Vickers VC 11 was seen as a scaled-down version of the long-haul four-engined VC10 able to seat 140 passengers.

From this eventually emerged the One-Eleven, a seventy-nine-eighty-nine-seater, whose design was supervised by Sir George Edwards, now chairman of BAC. The launch customer was Britain's largest independent airline, British United Airways. According to legend, the details of the deal were settled over dinner in a London restaurant by Edwards and BUA's managing director, Freddie Laker. The discussion was said to have ended with Laker telling Edwards: 'If it's as good as you say it is, I'll have ten.' The price, it's said, was agreed between Laker and one of Edwards' senior colleagues at Sandown Park racecourse.

The prototype first flew in August 1963 with Jock Bryce in command. Two months later the aircraft was lost. It had entered a 'deep stall' from which there was no recovery. Aircraft with rear-mounted engines and T-tail were found to be susceptible to what was then a little-known condition. The entire test crew died in the accident, including Bryce's deputy Mike Lithgow, former holder of the world's air speed record, and Dickie Rymer who had commanded the first turbine commercial service in 1950.

The loss of the prototype might have threatened the One-Eleven's whole future. It probably cost it the early mass penetration of the short-haul market that it deserved. Despite orders from American Airlines, Braniff and Mohawk the resulting damage to its reputation inevitably played into the hands of Douglas with its DC-9 and Boeing with its best-selling 737.

The One-Eleven's first commercial service was flown in April 1965 from London-Gatwick to Genoa. From then on the type cemented its popularity with both passengers and crews. An expanded version, the Series 500 able to seat over 100 passengers, was operated by BEA, but further development was hampered by the limitations of the engine. 'The performance of the One-Eleven with the Spey engine just hadn't got the power that the American airlines really needed,' Edwards recalled.

British Aerospace even contemplated offering the One-Eleven with Pratt and Whitney JT8D engines. Detailed brochures were prepared for British Airways and British Caledonian Airways but it was too late and production stopped with 244 examples built.

A NEW ERA IN AIR TRAVEL

Nevertheless, many thousands of passengers flew on services between London-Gatwick and Paris and other cities on the One-Elevens operated into the 1980s by carriers like Dan Air and British Caledonian, successor to launch customer, British United.

Cross Channel Commercial Services by Turbine-Powered Aircraft

	First flight	First X-Channel Service	Airline	Route
Viscount Srs 630	16 Jul 48	29 Jul 50	BEA	Lon-Par
Viscount Srs 700	20 Aug 52	18 Apr 53	BEA	Lon-Nicosia
Sud Caravelle	27 Jun 55	27 Jul 59	Air France	Nice-Par-Lon
DH Comet 4B	26 Jun 59	01 Apr 60	BEA	Lon-Par-Nice
Vanguard	20 Jan 59	17 Dec 60*	BEA	Lon-Par
HS Trident 1	09 Jan 62	01 Apr 64	BEA	Lon-Nice
BAC 1-11	20 Aug 63	09 Apr 65	BUA	Lon-Genoa

*Temporary Christmas service

Sir George Edwards

From humble origins George Robert Freeman Edwards rose to become one of the most-respected figures in the British Aerospace industry. His design credits included Viscount, Vanguard, VC10 and BAC One-Eleven. He was also a key player in the development of the Concorde Anglo-French supersonic airliner.

Edwards was born above his father's toyshop near Chingford, Essex. His mother died two weeks after his birth and he was brought up by an aunt. He won a scholarship to South West Essex Technical College at Walthamstow, where he showed a talent for mathematics. Moving on to the West Ham Municipal College, Edwards learned to be a practical engineer, then gained a BSc in Engineering from London University.

Edwards worked as a junior structural engineer at London's docks before applying for a job in Vickers' drawing office at Weybridge, Surrey in 1935. He was offered the job at a weekly salary of £5.25, 25p more than he was expecting.

When war broke out in 1939 Edwards became experimental works manager. One of his first tasks was to design an aerial minesweeping system for Coastal Command Wellingtons. Edwards had been working with Vickers' chief designer Rex Pierson whom he succeeded in 1945. In his new post Edwards was responsible for the Viking airliner together with its military variants, the Valetta and the Varsity. Then came the jet-powered Valiant, the first of the RAF's three nuclear deterrent V-bomber types.

When it appeared in 1948 the Viscount was not only the world's first turboprop airliner to operate passenger services, it was also the first British airliner to make significant headway in the American domestic airline market.

As managing director of Vickers-Armstrongs (Aircraft) from 1953 Edwards remained responsible for overall technical direction of the Viscount's successor, the Vanguard. But this large, four-engined turboprop was being marketed just as jets were superseding propeller-driven types.

Even before that, however, Vickers was on the brink of pulling off a major success with the V. 1000 military transport jet and its civilian counterpart the VC7. Edwards described the project's cancellation in 1955 as 'the biggest blunder of all'. He was convinced it could have upstaged both the DC 8 and Boeing 707, which were not to appear until the end of the decade. Some compensation was his knighthood in 1957.

The VC10 with its four rear-mounted engines was designed in response to a challenging specification issued by BOAC which wanted an aircraft that could operate from short, hot and high airports in Africa and Asia. The aircraft proved popular with passengers but its operating economics were inferior to the 707 and only a relative handful were built.

Edwards played a key role in the creation of the British Aircraft Corporation. In 1961 he was appointed managing director of its operating arm and, in 1968, chairman of the company itself.

Without Edwards' patience and perseverance when dealing with politicians and with his counterparts across the Channel, it is doubtful if the supersonic Concorde project would have come to fruition, let alone survived. Edwards' appointment to the Order of Merit in 1971 not only acknowledged his overall contribution to British aviation but also his participation in the development of Concorde.

Edwards retired in 1975 after forty years devoted to the British aircraft industry. During that time, he was recognised not just as a talented engineer but also as a consummate salesman and businessman whose organisational skills helped ensure that the British aerospace industry continued to punch above its weight in world markets. Down-to-earth and lacking in pomposity, Edwards was also known for his pithy comments.

He was, said Sir Peter Masefield, who as chief executive of BEA was one of Edwards' customers, 'one of the most impressive people in the entire plane making industry, whom I had known and admired since I was up at Cambridge'.

George Edwards died in 2003 aged ninety-four.

London to Paris and Back in Half an Hour

The Nene-Viking's achievement was put into perspective by the man who would become Bryce's deputy at the British Aircraft Corporation. In July 1953 Lieutenant Commander Mike Lithgow, chief test pilot of Vickers' Supermarine division, whisked a Swift jet fighter from London to Paris and back in little more time than the Nene-Viking had taken to complete its outward journey.

On 5 July Lithgow flew the bullet-shaped fighter from London's Heathrow airport to Le Bourget in nineteen minutes five seconds. His average speed was 669.3 mph. He returned to London in nineteen minutes fourteen-point-three seconds at an average speed of 664.3 mph. Lithgow's total time for the return journey was thirty-eight minutes twenty seconds. The Nene-Viking took thirty-four minutes seven seconds.

A year earlier Lithgow's colleague, Dave Morgan, flew the Supermarine 541, prototype of the Swift from London to Brussels at the remarkably similar speed of 665.9 mph to cover the 200 miles in eighteen minutes three-point-three seconds.

Of his flight, Lithgow recalled in his autobiography: 'Over the Channel there was fog and I streaked over the French coast without recognising a thing.' Conditions were similar on the way back. He reckoned his speed would have been higher than on the outward journey but for a strong headwind. Even so, visibility improved towards the end of his flight. Lithgow wrote: 'I was able to use the reheat for a short spell, arriving over London airport at well over 700 mph.'

Chapter Twelve

The Great Race

It started, like many great aeronautical adventures before it, in the editor's office at *The Daily Mail*.

The sponsor of the contest which in 1909 resulted in the first crossing of the English Channel by aeroplane could hardly fail to mark its fiftieth anniversary. But the question before the newspaper executives in conference that day in the autumn of 1958 was: how?

Most of the barriers to progress in aviation had been surmounted and venturing into space travel didn't seem like a good idea. Then the paper's air correspondent, Stevenson Pugh, remembered a casual dinner-table conversation. An airline executive had argued that a top racing driver who drove from London to Dover, flew the Channel in Blériot's 1909 aircraft and then sped on by road to Paris would be there before a modern airline passenger.

Pugh also had at the back of his mind a 1948 demonstration sponsored by the journal *The Aeroplane* in which a relay of helicopters and a jet fighter carried a message between the two capitals (see box on page 165). The trip between a bomb-site near St Paul's to the Place des Invalides had been accomplished in the record time of forty-six minutes and forty-four seconds.

For what was billed as the Blériot Anniversary Race, the *Mail* decided to offer a total purse of £10,000 for the fastest time between London's Marble Arch and the Arc de Triomphe in the centre of Paris. This was ten times what Louis Blériot received for his Channel crossing in 1909.

The race would be run between 13 and 23 July 1959. Competitors could travel in either direction and were free to make as many attempts as they wished between those dates. It was open to contestants of any nationality and they could use any combination 'of any number and types of conveyance to make the journey'. The only stipulation was that competitors obeyed the laws of the country through which they were passing or flying over.

In the rock and roll age with the horrors of the Second World War beginning to fade the idea of the race caught the public imagination.

It didn't hurt that northern Europe was enjoying a prolonged period of fine and sunny weather. Even a national printing dispute which could have reduced the competition's impact failed to dent the enthusiasm.

For many, indeed, it was all a bit of a giggle. But it was taken very seriously in some quarters as a way of shedding the tedium of modern air travel which expanded forty minutes' flying time by scheduled Viscount flight to a total of three hours fifteen minutes to cover the 214 miles between the two capitals.

Despite improvements to roads and airports, and the introduction of faster aircraft, the total journey time by scheduled airline services between the two capitals had actually increased. An open contest, the *Daily Mail* executives reasoned, could actually tackle the problem at its roots. It would uncover the real obstacles to travel and show how they could be overcome.

But staging the race itself was something of an act of faith. Afterwards Stevenson Pugh wrote

> We had to take it on trust that there would be enough imaginative, adventurous entrants to make it a race. We believed there would be. But now we can humbly admit that we were amazed by the eventual response.

Indeed, they needn't have worried. Support came from the highest places in both Britain and France. In a message to the *Mail's* editor, Prime Minister Harold Macmillan wrote

> I am glad to hear that the *Daily Mail* propose to mark the anniversary in this imaginative way. Certainly, we shall get a great deal of interest out of it and perhaps, who knows, some new ideas for speedy travel between our two cities.

His cabinet colleague, Minister of Supply, Aubrey Jones, said that the race 'addresses itself to a crucial contemporary problem'.

Flight predicted it would be the most exciting race since the 1934 MacRobertson Trophy race in that it would stimulate air transport 'in the global sense'. 'Never since that memorable contest,' the journal declared,

> has there been quite such a quickening of beat in aviation circles, such as a healthy rash of schemes and notions, or such an animated buzzing at the bar. The game's afoot and

THE GREAT RACE

the midsummer days will be seeing some matchless deeds attempted dared and done.

The journal also speculated on the possibility that the Fairey Rotodyne, which combined the vertical take-off and landing capability of a helicopter with the speed of a conventional airliner, might be entered for the race. 'It was conceived for just such a task,' the journal added.

But on 2 July Fairey Aviation announced that the Rotodyne wouldn't be taking part. 'It is essential that an unbroken flight development programme be completed between now and the end of August,' the company said in a statement.

The Aeroplane's enthusiasm for faster cross-Channel flights seemed to have waned over the past decade. 'It is questionable,' a staff writer observed sourly in a pre-race analysis, 'whether what is learnt will be useful to serious students of transport.'

But it would soon be clear that the majority of contestants were not serious students of transport. According to *Flight*'s reporter covering the race, the 135 entrants included 'efficient and well-drilled service entries, a number of enthusiastic amateurs flying their own light aircraft and a sprinkling of one-off off beats'.

There was certainly plenty of variety in the methods of transport that would be employed during the ten days of the race. Among the first of the contestants to set off from Marble Arch on 13 July was racing driver Stirling Moss, who was at the wheel of a specially prepared Renault Dauphine, a naval officer on roller skates and a 23-year-old technical college student from Wembley driving a lawn mower.

But it was soon clear that, to stand any chance of putting up the fastest time, contestants needed access to jet aircraft and helicopters with powerful motorcycles to whisk them through the city traffic at either end of the journey. That pointed to members of the armed services since only they had access to the necessary technology plus the resources to provide a strong support organization. As a result, the race developed into a three-way contest between the Army, the Royal Navy and the Royal Air Force.

This was soon apparent from the exploits of a young army officer, Captain Roderick 'Red Rory' Bamford Walker. The twenty-nine-year-old veteran of fighting in Malaya and the Arabian Desert, boxing champion, all-round sportsman and regular adjutant of the Territorial Army's 23rd Special Air Service Regiment was the first competitor to set off from Marble Arch on 13 July.

Within two hours Walker would become a national hero. His time of fifty-seven minutes forty-seven seconds gave some idea of what would be achieved in the coming days. Walker's return journey, slowed by headwinds, was one hour fifteen seconds. Stevenson Pugh recalled

> The dashing captain with his unruly shock of red hair, his unbelievable nickname and the win or bust way in which he cannon-balled down the course – leaping from motor cycles to moving helicopters and clinging grimly outside the cockpit of his jet as it swept down the runway – literally fired the imagination of the world.

Walker had started his journey to Paris with a motorcycle dash to Chelsea Embankment where an Army Air Corps Skeeter helicopter was waited on a floating heliport anchored fifteen yards offshore.

The helicopter had previously been stripped of all unnecessary equipment to make it faster and polished to reduce wind resistance. 'It is supposed to do 95 knots top speed,' Walker told the *Daily Mail,* but

> we touched 125 knots. I didn't have time to talk much before we reached Biggin Hill. I leaped out with my passport in my teeth. The Customs boys were there but they said: 'Don't stop. We know you are a Briton.' I ran to the Hunting Jet Provost which stood 40 yards away with its engines running. As I threw myself in, Stanley Oliver, [Hunting's chief test pilot] opened the throttle. All I remember is the enormous wind and noise. Then we were at 1,700 ft. Ollie grinned at me and raised his thumbs.

When the Jet Provost landed at Villacoublay, Walker put his passport back between his teeth and climbed out on to the wing as Oliver taxied in. He jumped off and ran towards the Customs control. 'They shouted "Bravo!" and waved,' Walker recalled. 'One of them stamped my passport in a flash.'

On his return journey the helicopter took off from Issy before Walker was fully on-board. He fell out, the helicopter came down again, Walker clambered aboard and they were off. But that wasn't the reason Walker was wary of repeating the journey. 'The most terrifying part of the trip was the ride from Issy Heliport to the Arc de Triomphe,' he recalled. He told *The Daily Mail*

THE GREAT RACE

Georges Houel, former champion racing motor cyclist, did the 4.5 miles in 4 minutes flat. Will I do it all again? I don't think I could stand more motorcycle rides like that in one morning again.

Walker had set the ball rolling in fine style but by the time the race had closed on 23 July his record had been beaten no less than forty-four times. In eleven days of racing, forty-nine trips had been made between Marble Arch and the Arc de Triomphe in less than sixty minutes by twenty-one contestants.

Yet so close were the times that in the seven days between 15 and 22 July only three minutes fifty-three seconds were shaved away by the members of the British and French air forces, the Royal Navy, Royal Marines, Army and a civilian competitor backed by Britain's leading manufacturer of fighter aircraft. In the end eleven runs were recorded in times between forty-three and forty-four minutes. But even that wouldn't be enough to win the race.

The RAF relied on the two-seat 700-mph Hunter T7 supported by a combination of motorcycles and helicopters which whirled the RAF men between floating platforms in the Thames at Chelsea and Biggin Hill and between Villacoublay and Issy.

But even the Hunter wasn't the most powerful jet in the race. Its power and speed were trumped by the mighty Supermarine Scimitar of Commander Ian Martin, chief tactical instructor at the Naval Air Fighter School at Lossiemouth. The only trouble was that the supersonic Scimitar was a single-seater. Martin had to do the flying himself.

It was realised from the start that this put the RN's premier contender at a disadvantage compared with its RAF rivals. On the other hand, the naval personnel hoped the speed and acceleration of the twin-engined Scimitar, which was the only jet with enough fuel capacity to avoid the need for drag-inducing drop tanks, would be enough.

The Navy also reasoned that using Paris as the starting point for its main attempt would avoid language problems on the radio and make use of proven landing aids if visibility deteriorated during the flight. Wisley airfield in Surrey was chosen because, being south-west of London, the prevailing winds would assist the helicopter and also because the route from the Thames at Chelsea was straighter and shorter (by a mile) than the route from Biggin Hill.

A special canvas slide was made to enable the pilot to leave the Scimitar's cockpit in a hurry and enable him to be running to the Whirlwind helicopter within four seconds of the Scimitar's wheels stopping.

On the day, Martin climbed up behind Paris newspaper seller Jean Gobat on the pillion of his BSA Golden Flash. Martin claimed he kept his eyes tightly shut as the pair snarled through the Paris traffic at 70 mph.

The trip from the Arc de Triomphe to Issy where a Whirlwind was waiting, quivering at take-off rpm, took three minutes. The following eighty-yard sprint on a hot day in full G-suit left Martin gasping for breath as he hurled himself into the helicopter's cabin. Three minutes later the helicopter landed at Villacoublay where the Scimitar was waiting with its engine running and pre-take-off checks completed.

Martin was encumbered by his oxygen mask when Sub Lieutenant Aitchison handed his passport to officials, made the necessary R/T and G-suit connections and strapped the pilot into his seat. Aitchison's final task was to remove the ejection seat pin and throw it over his shoulder as a signal to the ground crew to remove the ladder while Aitchison was still clinging to the top of it.

The flight to Wisley took twenty minutes. The cockpit canopy was opened on finals and the port engine stopped at touchdown to allow Martin to slide safely from the cockpit past the air intake. The Scimitar squealed to a halt within 1,400 yards. After presenting the necessary documentation to a waiting Customs officer, Martin hurled himself into the waiting Whirlwind where he was handed a welcome cold drink.

The helicopter landed on a lighter moored in the Thames and Martin was transferred to the shore by jackstay. 'From a crimpled heap on the pavement,' Martin wrote later,

> it was a mere two paces to the pillion of Marine Hands' motorcycle. Via a carefully chosen route involving only Hyde Park Corner traffic lights, we arrived at Marble Arch where, with shaking hands, the card was fumbled into the clock and stamped.

Martin's colleague, Lieutenant Commander W.J. Carter, planned to use a two-seat Sea Vixen jet but his first run had to be aborted due to a misunderstanding between Carter and his French motorcyclist. On a later run, Jean Grobar terrified his pillion passenger with his ruthless progress through the Paris traffic.

Theoretically, Carter should have been faster than Martin as he was not piloting the Sea Vixen. However, the aircraft made a straight-in approach to Wisley which meant cutting the throttles far out from the airfield to slow it for the landing. The unexpected result of this run-in at low engine speed was a loss of hydraulic power to operate the control surfaces.

As the aircraft neared the ground one wing dropped and there was scarcely enough rudder control available to correct it. The result was a heavy landing which left the aircraft snaking crazily up the runway. Carter's next ordeal awaited him at Chelsea Embankment. A big crowd had gathered to watch his progress from helicopter to dry land, and particularly the spectacle of him being whisked from motor launch to dry land by sheerlegs. Despite the drama Carter's time was a disappointment.

An unexpected intervention came on 16 July when a Second World War Hawker Hurricane fighter was spotted making frequent visits to Biggin Hill. The aircraft turned out to be 'The Last of the Many', owned by the manufacturers and flown by the company's chief test pilot Bill Bedford. He was preparing for his role as pilot for airline chief Eric Rylands to Paris in the two-seat Hunter lent by the manufacturer.

Of course, most competitors didn't have exclusive use of their own jet fighter. Even the team of eleven men and two women from the nationalised British European Airways had to use public transport – more or less. Well before the race, the BEALine Syndicate published a statement of their aims. In it they made it clear that they were acting on behalf of air travellers frustrated by the obstacles thrown up by bureaucracy.

Their main mission was to prove that the scheduled airline time between London and Paris of three hours and ten minutes could be dramatically reduced by the use of a little common sense and initiative. They set out from Marble Arch in city suits and summer dresses, the only concession being a ban on the wearing of high heels.

The journey from Marble Arch to Paddington station was undertaken by a special double-decker bus driven by William Eldridge who had been a London bus driver for thirty years. Later, he recalled: 'It was the fastest drive I've ever had on a London bus.'

At Paddington, the team transferred to a special train to take them to Ruislip Gardens with cars to take them to Northolt where they boarded a Comet 4B airliner (G-APMA) bound for Le Bourget. Taxis took the team from the airport to the Arc de Triomphe. The syndicate's members took an average of sixty-two minutes fifteen seconds to travel from London to Paris. In doing so they won a special £1,000 prize awarded on the basis of journey time, originality, ingenuity and initiative.

BOAC Comet first officer Bill Neely hedged his bets by having a plan A and a plan B. Both involved the co-operation of British Rail, which was given willingly. Plan A involved flying between the two capitals using a surplus Belgian Air Force two-seat Meteor jet trainer, then by helicopter from Biggin Hill to the railway sidings at Grove Park about six miles away. There he would step from the hovering helicopter onto the roof of a special train to Charing Cross. A motorcycle would take him to Marble Arch.

Neely's second idea involved the construction of a special self-designed helicopter landing platform at Hungerford Bridge, which carries trains over the Thames between Waterloo and Charing Cross stations.

With better luck Neely might have done a lot better than he actually did but a series of misfortunes conspired to delay his runs. On his last, the Meteor pilot, Antoine de Montblanc, fell off the wing while the aircraft was being refuelled, breaking his elbow.

Despite the pain from his injury, de Montblanc insisted on carrying on. Neely said later

> I wanted to call off the attempt but Antoine insisted. He said he could manage and didn't want to let me down. When I got to Villacoublay I expected to find him in the back seat leaving the flying to me. I was horrified to find him in front. But there was no time to argue, so I jumped in behind him and off we went.
>
> His left arm was useless so he could not work the throttle. He used his feet on the rudder bar and I leaned over to handle the throttle. When we got airborne I took over the control column as well while he nursed his broken arm.

Navigation suffered and the radio became unserviceable which cost Neely additional time. But when the Meteor did eventually land at Biggin Hill, a doctor attended to de Montblanc while Neely sped on his next leg of the journey by Alouette helicopter. His time of fifty-seven minutes twenty-eight seconds was a poor reward for his persistence and original thinking. Neely tried again and his final attempt was also the last of the competition, but further mishaps inflated his time to over an hour.

Another civilian who had the use of his own fighter aircraft was Billy Butlin. The sixty-three-year-old holiday camp magnate lost 9 lb in weight but gained the admiration of spectators who dubbed him 'Puffing Billy'.

Butlin had salvaged a two-seat Spitfire together with a supply of Rolls-Royce Merlin engines. He used a heliport floating in the Thames and on one occasion, when it moved from its expected mooring, he was forced

THE GREAT RACE

to jump into the riverside mud. In London he was met by world water speed record holder Donald Campbell who drove him to Marble Arch.

Inevitably the services of the cross-Channel air ferries were much in demand and there was intense competition between the two main operators, Silver City Airways and Channel Air Bridge. Stirling Moss was already a frequent ferry flyer when he drove the seventy-three miles from London to Ferryfield airport, Lydd in ninety minutes on the first day of the contest. He was airborne two minutes after arriving, having driven his Alpine Rally-prepared Renault Dauphine up the ramp into the aircraft himself. Moss achieved a total time of two hours forty-five minutes fifty-six seconds.

He shaved three-point-five minutes off this time on his return trip to London but airline entrepreneur Freddie Laker went even quicker two days later. He drove his own Rolls-Royce and used one of his own ferry aircraft on the Southend-Paris route to stop the clocks at two hours thirty-five minutes twenty-nine seconds.

Silver City fought back on 19 July when motor racing promotor John Webb hustled his Jensen to Paris in two hours twenty-seven minutes seventeen seconds but on his return trip to London, Webb had an accident and ran off the road. Stevenson Pugh commented: 'At this, the two ferries appear to have decided that honours were even.' Other competitors to use the car ferries included Lord Montagu of Beaulieu with his 1909 Humber and also the owner of a Heinkel bubble car.

Most of the contestants were British; French participation looked pretty thin in comparison. But it would have looked even thinner without the support of the country's premier motor manufacturer. Renault made a block entry covering twelve competitors who made twelve attempts on ten of the eleven days of racing.

The team included racing driver Maurice Trintignant, Stirling Moss' teammate, and Pierre Auerbach who participated out of 'a love of excitement and speed'. He used a Morane Saulnier Paris executive jet and set the fastest time for the use of civilian transport in fifty-five minutes nine seconds.

Colette Duval was the big French heroine of the race. The twenty-six-year-old was helped by the French Air Force and even though she failed by three minutes to take the lead in the race, the *Daily Mail* reported on the 'vast, near-hysterical crowd that waited at the Arc to greet the copper-haired Paris model and parachutist'. The paper added

> They cheered her. They toasted her. Not only because she was a woman. Not only because the beautiful Colette was France's

only real hope in the race that has excited two countries. But because, only a few hours after narrowly escaping disaster when her Vautour jet 'plane crashed on the Paris-London outward run she had the courage to try again.

The Vautour's pilot had mistaken the disused Battle of Britain airfield at Kenley in Surrey for Biggin Hill. The rutted and weed-grown runway was too short for the 650-mph jet bomber and it careered through a fence and stopped sixty yards from a 150-foot cliff. Duval was offered another Vautour for a second run. Yet despite help from the police in keeping her route through the centre of Paris relatively traffic free, her time was not quite good enough: forty-four minutes forty seconds.

Jean Salis flew his replica Blériot monoplane from Lydd to Calais, while Christine Blériot, a cousin of the famous aviator, used a three-seat Nord 1203. Derek Piggott flew an Olympia 419 gilder in difficult conditions on 22 July, having made several flights towed across the Channel by a Miles Messenger. Other aircraft used by competitors in addition to those already mentioned included an Auster Aiglet, Druine Turbulent, Jodel D.117, de Havilland Dove, Percival Prentice, Avro 19, Miles Student, de Havilland Vampire and Vickers Viscount.

Hatfield Technical College student Hugh Tansley used a pair of Ransomes ride-on lawn-mowers. It was a long journey. According to the *Daily Mail*

> he cruised 12 miles to Croydon in 2.5 hours then ran to a waiting Tiger Moth for his Channel hop. He finished the race to the Arc de Triomphe on another mower after a leisurely lunch.

Tansley's pilot had been Lewis Benjamin in Tiger Moth G-ACDC. Years later, he recalled that at Croydon 'everyone seemed to be in the grip of madness in their haste to get us airborne in the shortest possible time. We cleared Lympne in an atmosphere of pure panic.' In fact, air traffic control held an arriving DC-3 to enable the Tiger Moth to land first and clear Customs. The result was the biplane was back in the air within minutes. 'It was unreal,' Benjamin recalled.

The aircraft landed at Toussus-le Noble near Paris where a large crowd was waiting. So, too, was a fresh lawn-mower. Tansley was cheered all the way from there to the Arc de Triomphe.

THE GREAT RACE

In fact, the bumpy cobbled French roads played havoc with the mower and Tansley had to summon roadside assistance three times. On one occasion the petrol tank had to be secured with rope. The *Mail* quoted Tansley as saying: 'Apart from that the old girl went like a bomb. At times I passed several pedestrians – older ones, of course. I did up to 6 mph.' The paper added: 'In brilliant sunshine he cut a gay dash round the Arc.' His time was ten hours forty-four minutes.

Another competitor whose achievement really caught the public imagination was Paris housewife Madelaine Rassam. The blonde mother of four had no backers and no pre-arranged plans. Before setting off she explained her reason for entering:

> I know there's no chance of my doing the fastest time, but that's not my idea. It seems to me that the real point of the race is to try to find ways of speeding up the journey for ordinary passengers.

She relied on hailing taxis and scheduled airline services to get her to London in one hour fifty-nine minutes thirty-one seconds. The trip cost her £14. The enthusiasm that greeted her arrival at Marble Arch seemed to surprise and embarrass her. She explained:

It was so easy. I had a taxi booked at the Arc de Triomphe but he didn't turn up. So I just walked to the Champs-Elysees and waved for one ... and he got me to Le Bourget in just over ten minutes. I think the pilot must have hurried too because we were ten minutes early at London Airport.

Perhaps the bravest competitor was Paul Bates, a polio victim who made the trip in a van equipped with an iron lung. He managed the journey between the two capitals in under seven hours.

Ten consolation prizes of £100 were awarded to competitors who had 'emerged with high merit'. They included Bill Aston, chief production test pilot of Vickers who used a Piaggio P.136 amphibian lent by shipping magnate Aristotle Onassis to fly from the Thames at Barking to the Seine in Paris. At the other end of the scale, disabled competitor Owen Dixon drove his two-seat invalid carriage, while Jonathan Hutchinson carried a folding motor-scooter in his Percival Proctor light aircraft. Other winners included Red Rory Walker, Billy Butlin, Pierre Auerbach, Bill Neely and Madeline Rassam.

Most competitors, of course, hadn't a hope of winning outright with the British armed forces taking the event so seriously. So, too, did their political bosses. Secretary of State for Air, George Ward, told the House of Commons that the RAF team had been under the control of Fighter Command and included three officers from RAF Duxford, and one officer cadet from the RAF College, Cranwell. The Hunter and helicopter pilots, motorcyclists and servicing, radar and airfield teams were drawn from units based in the UK and in RAF Germany.

The result was a resounding victory for the RAF. Squadron Leader Charles Maughan, CO of No. 65 Squadron based at Duxford, took forty minutes forty-four seconds to travel from Paris to London. Second was Eric Rylands, chairman of the airline Skyways, who was lent a Hunter by the manufacturers and recorded forty-one minutes forty-one seconds, while Duxford station commander, Group Captain Norman Ryder, who also started in Paris, finished third with a time of forty-two minutes six seconds.

He was just ahead of twenty-year-old Cranwell cadet, John Volkers, who managed forty-two minutes thirty-four seconds. It came at a cost for the 'baby' of the RAF team who injured his hand when it got caught in the winch on Chelsea Embankment. He carried on to the finish in great pain but described the time taken to free his hand as 'five seconds of eternity'.

Eric Rylands had turned out to be the dark horse of the race. A civilian who had split the two fastest RAF runners, he was a canny competitor who understood that split seconds count. He had cut the corners from his competitor's card to make it easier to insert into the stamping machine and arranged for a plank to get him into the passenger seat of his Hunter and save more time. The Royal Navy may have had the fastest aircraft in the competition but Commander Martin's time was forty-three minutes eleven seconds, while his colleague, Lieutenant Commander Carter, took forty-four minutes fourteen seconds.

The prizes were presented to the winners at Marble Arch on 23 July by Lord Rothermere, chairman of the Associated Newspaper Group. Louis Blériot's widow, Alice was also present. The prize money awarded to the RAF contestants was donated to charity.

After the race Stevenson Pugh wrote

> Twenty men and one woman travelled between London and Paris in less than one hour. All of them were professional pilots of the highest standing or they were backed by teams of such ability. The contest to break the hour and beat it down to 40 minutes can now be seen in perspective as the race within the race.

THE GREAT RACE

The race, Pugh thought, had certainly lived up to its promise right from the start and that those who had predicted disaster had been proved wrong. It became 'one of the most exciting stories of speed of modern times,' he said.

And serious lessons had been learned. The RAF discovered some interesting things about operating Hunter jets, while the RN had gained new knowledge about their equipment at peak performance. The helicopter teams from all three services had also benefited from the experience. But overall, the three services counted the race as the year's biggest spur to recruitment.

Perhaps the most important lessons, though, concerned the time to travel between the two capitals by scheduled airline services. The BEALine Syndicate spent just over a minute on the ground for every three spent in the air. What the race clearly demonstrated was that it was possible to get from London to Paris in forty minutes. Every air traveller in the Western world now knew that.

'They are not going to be so easily fobbed off with frustration and delay in the future,' said Stevenson Pugh. 'The fare-paying passenger is now entitled to demand that his journey in future from Arch to Arc can be done comfortably in 90 min.'

Hare and Tortoise

In September 1948 *The Aeroplane* organized a demonstration to show that, by using helicopters and conventional fixed-wing aircraft it should be possible to travel between the centres of London and Paris within an hour.

At the time BEA scheduled services took just over an hour from Northolt to Orly, but passengers had to allow another two hours forty-five minutes for transport to and from the airports and to clear Customs and Immigration controls.

Earlier in 1948, the Nene-Viking (see chapter ten) had averaged thirty-five minutes for the round trip but, amazingly, the record from city centre to city centre had stood at one hour fifty-nine minutes since 1921 when it was set by a Vickers Viking amphibian which had taken off from the Thames and landed on the Seine.

The Aeroplane had been impressed by the capability, demonstrated in 1938 by the German Focke-Achgelis twin-rotor helicopter (see chapter nine), which showed that the problems of hovering flight and control about three axes had been overcome.

The 'hare and tortoise' demonstration, which had been conceived eighteen months earlier by R.F. Dangerfield, chairman of Temple Press, *The Aeroplane*'s publisher, took place on 30 September when a letter from the Lord Mayor of London was delivered to the President of the Municipality of Paris. It attracted considerable public interest but bad weather over Paris meant that departure of the Bristol 171 helicopter was delayed twice.

The BBC provided live coverage of the take off from a car park near St Paul's. The commentator reported 'he's off' as the helicopter, piloted by Eric Swiss, lifted off and headed for Biggin Hill. There, a Gloster Meteor T7, the company's civil-registered demonstrator piloted by test pilot Bill Waterton, was waiting with engines running. 'Transfer of the letter was effected with remarkable rapidity,' *The Aeroplane* reported. 'In less than one minute from the time the helicopter landed beside the Meteor, Waterton was off down the runway.'

The red-painted Meteor jet trainer completed the 214-mile trip to Orly in twenty-seven minutes thirty-eight seconds at an average speed of 465 mph. At Orly, the letter was transferred to a Westland-Sikorsky S51 piloted by Alan Bristow. It headed for the Esplanade des Invalides where a large crowd had been gathering since 09:00hr. The total time for the 237-mile trip was forty-six minutes forty-four seconds.

The Aeroplane said that the demonstration had provided a yardstick 'to measure the services at present on offer to the public'.

Squadron Leader Charles Maughan

In 1959 Charles Gilbert Maughan was CO of 65 Squadron at Duxford flying Hawker Hunter F6s when he and his pilots heard about the *Daily Mail*'s plan to sponsor an air race between London and Paris to commemorate Blériot's flight of July 1909.

Having decided that it would be a 'good idea' to enter, it soon evolved into a major operation involving many Duxford-based units.

To be near London, the race team deployed to Biggin Hill where Maughan's two-seat Hunter T7 was positioned. After numerous practice runs, during which the operation was refined to a high degree, Maughan made his attempt on 22 July.

From Marble Arch he travelled by RAF police motorcycle to a hastily prepared helipad at Chelsea Reach where a Sycamore helicopter was waiting to take him to Biggin Hill. He jumped into the two-seat Hunter and flew to Villacoublay, followed by another helicopter ride to Issy from where he was whisked by RAF motorcycle to the Arc de Triomphe.

According to *The Daily Telegraph*, many techniques and devices had been used to shave seconds off Maughan's time, including the RAF police assuming brief control of traffic lights on the short journey through London.

Maughan was born in London and joined the Fleet Air Arm in January 1942, in which he was commissioned as a pilot the following year. He joined 836 Squadron and initially flew Swordfish torpedo-bombers before being posted to 801 Squadron in the latter years of the war to fly Seafires. After the war Maughan worked for the control commission in Germany before joining the RAF on a short-service commission.

Following his success in the air race, Maughan was appointed to command a Vulcan bomber squadron and flew the big delta with single-minded dedication. Promoted to group captain he commanded the V-bomber base at Honnington. He retired from the RAF as an air vice marshal in 1977. He died in 2010 aged eighty-six.

Third place in the London-Paris air race was taken by Group Captain Edgar Norman Ryder, station commander at Duxford. Born in India in 1914, Ryder joined the RAF on a short-service commission in 1937. He served in the Second World War as a fighter pilot and was credited with destroying eleven enemy aircraft before being shot down and captured in 1943.

After shooting down a Messerschmitt Bf 109 near Ashford the vanquished German pilot gave Ryder his Iron Cross. Ryder returned it in 1960. That year he retired from the RAF and settled in Arizona where he died in 1995 aged eighty-one.

Second place in the 1959 race went to Eric Rylands, chairman of the independent airline Skyways.

Chapter Thirteen

A Lot Less Bovver

The weeds are breaking through the surface, the markings painted on the assembly bays have faded and the vast concrete pad between the sea and where the terminal building used to be is slowly crumbling.

Once Pegwell Bay on the Kent coast between Ramsgate and Sandwich was a thriving transport hub. It may have looked like an airport but it wasn't and nor was it a seaport, not in the conventional sense. This used, in fact, to be a hoverport, a place where giant hovercraft operated, carrying passengers and vehicles across the Channel.

It wasn't that long ago that the hovercraft was being hailed as a great British invention that would revolutionise transport. Yet within half a century it was transformed from the miracle mover that could traverse virtually any surface with ease to a half-forgotten curiosity.

You could even buy a lawn-mower that worked on the hover principle. It was claimed to be easier to operate than a conventional mower, hence the sales pitch that it was 'a lot less bovver with a hover'.

But it was as a public transport vehicle that the hovercraft came into its own, with craft able to carry up to 400 passengers and sixty cars across the English Channel in a fraction of the time taken by conventional ferries. The air-cushion vehicles went into service in 1968 and were the fastest seagoing vessels ever to cross the Channel. It took them just thirty-five minutes to make the journey at up to 80 mph – making them faster than the trains which now use the Channel Tunnel. The quickest-ever Channel hovercraft crossing took just twenty-two minutes.

What was never quite settled, though, was how hovercraft should be categorised and what kind of qualifications were needed to operate them. According to Sir Christopher Cockerell, the man generally credited with inventing the thing, said: 'The Admiralty said it was a 'plane and not a boat, the Royal Air Force said it was a boat and not a 'plane, the Army were plain not interested.'

A LOT LESS BOVVER

It was finally accepted that hovercraft were nearer to aircraft than ships. They had aircraft-style flight decks and cabin seating arrangements with commercial services advertised as 'flights'.

For a while hovercraft seemed to have the answer to so many transport needs. There were drawbacks, of course. They were noisy and couldn't operate in heavy seas. The loss of the duty-free sales that boosted slim profit margins, plus the cheaper travel offered by conventional ferry operators, meant the writing had been on the wall for years. The final nail in the coffin was the opening of the Channel Tunnel. The cross-Channel hovercraft service was finally withdrawn in October 2000.

The hoverport therefore passed into history to rank alongside the area's probable use by Julius Caesar for his first landing in July 54 BC and the top-secret port at nearby Richborough, which was established to ferry supplies to Britain's armies on the Western Front during the First World War.

Britain's Christopher Cockerell is generally accepted as the inventor of the hovercraft – he certainly invented the terminology – but the truth is that like other great inventions several people thought of it at about the same time. Other inventors worked on ways of making boats go faster by using a thin film of air but it's now accepted that Melville Beardsley in the US and Cockerell conceived the idea of the air-cushion vehicle independently and at virtually the same time.

With funding from the National Research Development Corporation, a contract was awarded to Saunders-Roe, the Cowes-based manufacturer of flying boats, to build an experimental prototype to Cockerell's design. This would become known as the SR.N1.

The core of the roughly circular vehicle was a buoyancy tank made of riveted aircraft-grade aluminium alloy sheet coated with a thin layer of pure aluminium to protect against corrosion. The main lift engine was an Alvis Leonides radial piston engine similar to that which powered the RAF's Percival Provost trainer aircraft. In the hovercraft it drove a lift fan housed within a centrally-mounted cylindrical housing.

Air generated by the fan provided forward and backward thrust for propulsion via a series of longitudinal ducts either side of the craft's deck. Simple rotatable aerofoils were installed on the ends of the ducts to exert control forces; the vertical aerofoil on the aft end was extended to form a pair of conventional aerodynamic rudders.

It was quickly discovered that the power of the 435 hp Leonides was sufficient only to produce a top speed of 35 knots and a Blackburn-Turbomeca Marboré turbojet was later added to provide additional power.

This was subsequently replaced by a Bristol-Siddeley Viper III turbojet of approximately double the Marboré's thrust. A flexible skirt which greatly improved the effective depth of the air cushion was added during the development programme.

Despite initial imperfections in its directional control system, this machine made history in the summer of 1959. Displaying the experimental craft registration G-12-4, it demonstrated to the press on 11 June its ability to cross both land and water. While the demonstration was intended to involve only land-based motion, after pressure from enthusiastic journalists, the company decided to proceed with the first water-based flight that day. The demonstration received considerable press coverage in which the craft was inevitably dubbed 'the flying saucer'.

A second sea trial followed two days later with full-power runs and tests of emergency ditching drills. Experience from this trial run resulted in the addition of a hydrodynamic planing bow to reduce the craft's tendency to dip into the waves. Later tests included the first operational transition between land and water to prove the craft's amphibious capability. On the 22nd the SR.N1 participated in its first operational sortie during an exercise with the Royal Marines on Eastney Beach, Portsmouth.

It was Cockerell's idea that the first crossing of the English Channel by hovercraft should be accomplished in the fiftieth anniversary of Louis Blériot's 1909 flight. At first Saunders Roe's management was against it on the grounds that the craft had so far only operated in the protected waters of the Solent and not in the open sea. Its longest voyage to date had been one of just six miles.

By the time it was realised that the publicity value of a successful trip was worth the risk it was almost too late. Hurried preparations included an aerial survey of beaches at Dover on 21 July in the company's de Havilland Rapide to find a site for launching the hovercraft on its historic trip. The most suitable one seemed to be one inside Dover Harbour, but on 24 July there was a last-minute change of plan.

This was due to a weather forecast which predicted strong north-easterly winds for the next few days. This would make a crossing by the SR-N1 hazardous if not impossible. The only alternative was to take the craft to Calais and make the attempt from there. Accordingly, it was hoisted aboard the Royal Fleet Lighter RN 54 and transported to France as deck cargo for its sternest test yet.

Accompanied by the Admiralty tug *Warden* and an RAF air-sea-rescue launch, the SR.N1 arrived in the late afternoon at Avant Dock Calais where

A LOT LESS BOVVER

a large crowd had gathered. But the decision had already been taken to postpone the crossing until the following day. Captain Peter 'Sheepy' Lamb, a Second World War and Korean War Fleet Air Arm pilot who was in command of the SR.N1, had decided the sea was far too rough. A series of demonstrations in the harbour and nearby sands provided some entertainment for the crowd, which was fascinated by the craft and its ability.

Awaking just after 03:00 hr the following morning, Lamb decided the crossing was on. The fuel tanks – one of fifty gallons had been installed to supplement the normal twenty-five-gallon capacity – were filled and as a precaution two eight-gallon cans were also carried.

At 04:55 hr the SR. N1 piloted by Lamb and accompanied by John Chaplin, head of research, and Christopher Cockerell, the craft cleared the harbour entrance just ahead of the RAF launch. It was not an easy journey. For one thing the compass proved unreliable. Lamb later reported

> For the next five miles navigation was made by dead reckoning, with the RAF launch, which had previously agreed to maintain the true track from Calais to Dover, well away on the port side. At approximately 05:30hr the white cliffs of Dover, tinged red in the morning sunrise, were first visible. Up to this time the SR.N1 appeared to have made extremely good progress at a constant setting of 2,700 rpm. However, a slight swell was now apparent, which retarded the progress of the craft … .

The trip proved to be a minor odyssey. Apart from the sea condition, the hovercraft had to survive a near-collision with a yacht whose crew was not keeping a proper look-out and then avoid the four-foot wake a of a large ship which nearly flung Cockerell overboard. Then it was time to top up the SR.N1's tanks from the cans of fuel previously loaded at Calais. Pouring the fuel into the secondary tank then pumping it into the primary tank was a three-man operation. This meant there was nobody at the controls and the pilotless craft had to be set to follow a wide circle.

Just as Lamb began to pour the contents of the first can, the craft lurched as it hit the swell. The fuel slopped into Chaplin's face. Lamb grabbed him by the neck and dunked his head in the sea. The Leonides engine had a reputation for being difficult to start when hot, so the SR.N1's crew was anxious to complete the refuelling before the tanks ran dry. By the time this was accomplished the craft was riding in the lee of St Margaret's Bay, reaching a speed of 30 knots in what Lamb later called 'the last mad dash' before entering Dover harbour. It proceeded the length of the harbour and beached in a cloud of spay next to the Clock Tower. The time was 06:45 hr. The first crossing of the Channel by hovercraft had taken two hours three minutes. Half a century earlier Blériot had taken just thirty-six minutes but then he hadn't had to refuel on the way.

True to form, the first to greet the SR.N1 and its crew were Customs officers. Their inevitable question of 'anything to declare?' was met with the response 'It's good to be back in England'. The officers didn't know about the celebratory magnum of Champagne Lamb had stored in a cockpit locker.

It was still early in the morning but a large crowd had gathered including reporters. The BBC had stationed an outside broadcast van on the lawn of Dover Castle so that the 08:00 radio news started with the words 'they have arrived'. Both Lamb and Chaplin were interviewed but apparently there wasn't time to include a contribution from Cockerell.

The inventor of the hovercraft wasn't too pleased but recovered his composure in time to answer a reporter's question 'what was it like?' with the reply 'A piece of cake, old chap'. Lamb and Chaplin looked at each other and said just one word: 'Christ!'

That September the SR.N1 appeared at the Farnborough Air Show and the following May it arrived on the River Thames opposite the Houses of Parliament to demonstrate its capabilities to MPs..

Now that the principle of riding on a cushion of air was established, other manufacturers began to produce hovercraft. Among them was Vickers, part of the industrial conglomerate whose aviation interests had been merged with others to create the British Aircraft Corporation. By the early 1960s Vickers had developed its twenty-four-passenger VA-3 hovercraft to the point where it was capable of operating commercial services. Accordingly, in June 1962 it was used to launch the world's first hovercraft services across the estuary of the River Dee between Rhyl, north Wales, and Wallasey, Cheshire.

For three months the craft, displaying the livery of British United Airways, operated six services a day and even carried mail. It proved popular but was dogged by unreliability due to troublesome engines and bad weather. As a result, the craft ran no more than thirty-six days out of a planned fifty-nine-day trials schedule. Some of the VA-3's problems resulted from its lack of a skirt which meant a limited hovering height and led to vulnerability in bad weather. On 17 September the craft broke loose from its moorings and was damaged beyond repair.

Meanwhile, the sole example of the SR.N2, developed from the somewhat primitive SR.N1, had been used on an experimental service operated by Southdown Motor Services in August. It was operated in conjunction with Westland aircraft which now owned Saunders Roe.

This service operated between Ryde on the Isle of Wight and Portsmouth on the mainland using unprepared beaches with tickets sold from an on-site caravan. Over a ten-day period during the peak of the holiday season a total of 1,500 passengers was carried. Two year later, following a Canadian interlude during which the craft operated trial services across the St Lawrence, the SR.N2 began another trial. Back in Britain, it was carrying passengers across the Solent. Between June and August 1964 the craft operated eleven services a day. The average time for the crossing was eight minutes.

The greatly improved SR.N6 appeared the following year. It was the first hovercraft capable of sustained commercial cross-Channel operations and arrived as a timely answer to critics who were wondering why the hovercraft had so far failed to realise its commercial potential. The *Financial Times* put it this way

> In many ways it is a pity that the hovercraft more than any other British development has suffered from a surfeit of premature publicity. In the late fifties the headlines rang with promises of low-cost trans-Atlantic trips, 300 mph air-cushioned journeys up the M1 and airborne tanks which could whisk armies across deserts. Like the circus barker and the bearded lady, the facts, impressive as they are, tend to be something of an anti-climax.

The SR.N6 was considerably bigger than its predecessors and did much to restore the hovercraft's reputation. Initially capable of accommodating thirty-eight passengers it was later stretched to carry fifty-eight and had the distinction of being the first production hovercraft to enter commercial service.

Commercial cross-Channel operations began on 30 April 1966. The potential market had been clear to two Scandinavian shipping companies, Swedish Lloyd and Swedish America Line, which were eager to enter it. Dover, the principal cross-Channel port, was already full to capacity with British and continental rail service ferry operations as well as those of private sector operator Townsend.

In 1965 the shipping journal *Lloyd's List* was reporting that the two Swedish companies were hatching ambitious plans to operate 150-ton hovercraft that could carry cars as well as passengers from Ramsgate. This did not go down well with the *Daily Mail* which saw the proposed service as yet another example of the British failing to exploit a British invention. 'If this is allowed to happen with hovercraft,' the paper lamented, 'we shall really begin to despair of the British will to go ahead in the modern world.'

But the *Daily Telegraph* had a different take on the story. It suggested that the Swedish operation might 'speed a decision by the British Railways Board on whether to operate a hovercraft on one of its well-established cross-Channel routes'.

Meanwhile, Townsend Car Ferries, competitor to British Rail at Dover, announced an order for SR.N6s together with plans to launch a pioneering Dover-Calais service. If successful, it would go on to order a giant SR. N4. Westland called it 'the breakthrough we have been waiting for'.

A new venture called Hoverlloyd Limited was formed in November 1965 and began recruiting staff to operate hovercraft services between Ramsgate and Calais using a pair of SR.N6s pending the arrival of bigger SR.N4s. But, before commercial operations could begin, the required regulatory permissions had to be secured from the Air Registration Board, predecessor of today's Civil Aviation Authority.

This seemed to suggest that the authorities had accepted that hovercraft were to be treated as aircraft but ambiguity remained until formally defined by Act of Parliament. The Hovercraft Act of 1968 provided a legal definition of hovercraft as

> A vehicle which is designed to be supported when in motion wholly or partly by air expelled from the vehicle to form a cushion of which the boundaries include the ground, water or the surface beneath the vehicle.

But from 1972, when the CAA was formed, hovercraft were finally regarded officially as vehicles in their own right and not aircraft, ships or motor vehicles. For a while, the CAA maintained a hovercraft department with its own specialists to ensure the safe construction and operation of hovercraft but this was closed in the 1990s with the decline of hovercraft operations. Responsibility then passed to the Department of Transport.

Former Seaspeed captain John Syring joined the CAA in 1974 to become its chief hovercraft test pilot. Recalling the decline of the Authority's hovercraft department, he said: 'It was set up as a fully-fledged department for a big industry but I could see it would eventually disappear.'

Meanwhile, on 6 April 1966, two SR.N6s were used to give journalists a flavour of what fare-paying passengers could expect from cross-Channel hovercraft operations. The sea state was rough on the outward journey but comparatively smooth on the return.

Nevertheless, the *Daily Telegraph*'s Kathleen Welsh verged on the lyrical in her report:

> On the outward run, from Ramsgate to Calais, it was a bumpy ride on a flying switchback as we flew on a cushion of air over waves five to six feet high. On the return run our craft behaved like a gently-moving rocking chair, skimming across the sunlit ripples. Such are the moods of the Channel.

But *The Guardian*'s air correspondent, David Fairhall, a former naval officer, took a professional mariner's view of the trip. He reported:

> although the force 3 to 4 winds were comfortably within the licensed limit for this 38-seat Westland N6, steep six-foot waves piled up by the tide flowing over the [Goodwin] sands gave us a distinctly uncomfortable if exhilarating spell.

The prototype SR.N4 made its first flight on 4 February 1968 with Sheepy Lamb at the controls. There followed several months of trials before the craft was ready to carry fare-paying passengers. But it looked as though Hoverlloyd, the foreign interloper out to exploit a British invention, would have to settle for second place in the race to operate the definitive hovercraft across the Channel.

Dover Chamber of Commerce had been able to circumvent the normal planning processes by constructing a relatively modest facility in Dover's Eastern Dock. A corresponding terminal with dedicated rail line was constructed at Boulogne. The driving force was Seaspeed, a company formed jointly by British Rail and its French opposite number, SNCF, which began fullscale passenger operations on 1 August with the prototype SR.N4 001.

Two days earlier there had been a press preview and the day before a beaming Princess Margaret, accompanied by her husband the Earl of Snowdon, travelled from Dover to Boulogne with a VIP party on board the craft appropriately named *Princess Margaret*.

CROSS-CHANNEL AVIATION PIONEERS

Setting the scene for the start of cross-Channel hovercraft services, the *Financial Times'* respected aerospace correspondent Michael Donne reported on what could be expected from the SR.N4

> Capable of carrying about 260 passengers and 30 cars, it is expected to have a full load for there has been an encouraging public response to the start of the service. In its first week of operation, the SR.N4 will make three round trips daily between Dover and Boulogne. After 7 August it will make six round trips daily at two hourly intervals between 0920 and 1920 hr from Boulogne. In the autumn the number of round-trips will be reduced for the winter period.

Donne permitted himself a little flag-waving by adding

> Nowhere else in the world but Britain has anyone attempted to build such a large craft as the SR.N4 and thus the start of services this week logs another world technological first for the UK.

Success could mean up to 100 orders for the SR.N4 worth over £150 million for Britain. But, he warned, the price of failure would be high. It was a prophetic remark. Seaspeed had beaten its rival by eight months but it was to be a pyrrhic victory. The prototype 001 was notoriously unreliable and vulnerable to damage from heavy seas and 30 per cent of scheduled services had to be cancelled, attracting much negative publicity. *Princess Margaret* was withdrawn from service in October 1968 for modifications which were subsequently applied to later SR.N4s.

Meanwhile, Hoverlloyd's first two SR.N4s were on their way. They were christened *Swift* and *Sure* by Mary Wilson, wife of Prime Minister Harold Wilson, and Mary Soames, wife of the British Ambassador to Paris in ceremonies held in June and July 1969.

Hoverlloyd began commercial services on 2 April when operations manager and senior captain Captain Bill Williamson climbed the ladder to the flight deck thirteen feet above the *Swift*'s car deck and eased himself into the left-hand seat. At 0900 hr he ordered the first officer sitting next to him to open the throttles of the four Proteus gas-turbine engines.

Slowly, the 130-feet long, 165-ton hovercraft with its load of 254 passengers and thirty cars was lifted up on its eight-foot cushion of air as Williamson eased it towards the hoverport's northern ramp. It was high tide and the craft faced crossing over a mile of mud flat before reaching the sea. Under the 13,600 shp, which was the combined power mustered by its four engines, *Swift* crossed the notorious Goodwin Sands and out into the Straits of Dover at over 60 mph.

To ensure *Swift* safely traversed the world's busiest shipping lanes the second officer's eyes were fixed to the screen of the Decca 629 radar as he called out the bearings of the many other ships sailing in the waters of the English Channel. Behind the flight deck in the two passenger cabins six stewardesses served drinks and duty- free goods while on the car deck the five crew members checked the security of the vehicles lashed by their wheels to ring bolts on the car deck.

Experience would show that some cars were easier to handle than others. Because of their small size, Minis could always be accommodated – the record was fifty-two – but the Citroen 2CV could pose problems. Because of its supple suspension, a particular technique was called for to ensure these vehicles were lashed securely for the forty-minute Channel crossing.

After an uncertain beginning, the end of the first decade of commercial cross-Channel hovercraft operations rewarded the operators for persevering through a series of incidents and near disasters to arrive at a highly efficient and successful operation.

Pegwell Bay was in full swing with four SR.N4s carrying full loads of passengers and cars leaving for Calais and returning on a busy twenty-seven-departure schedule from 06:00hr to late in the evening. This equated to one movement roughly every fifteen minutes. The approach road was crammed with arriving and departing vehicles. The car parks were full, as were the check-in area, departure lounges and cafeterias. In the words of two former Hoverlloyd captains, Robin Paine and Roger Syms, 'All was frenetic activity and bustle.'

Hoverlloyd alone was moving 1.25 million passengers and their vehicles, mostly during the peak months between June and September. But that was less than a quarter of the total volume of cross-Channel hovercraft traffic and by 1980 the writing was on the wall as the company's share dropped to 18 per cent. In 1981 Hoverlloyd and Seaspeed merged to form Hoverspeed with four SR.N4s operating from Dover.

Pegwell Bay remained operational for another few years as a maintenance facility but, after a long period of neglect and deterioration, the terminal buildings were demolished, leaving only the concrete foundations. Today only the handling pad, weed-grown and dirt-strewn, remains as a mute reminder of busier times.

CROSS-CHANNEL AVIATION PIONEERS

The competition from the Channel Tunnel and conventional ferries had proved too strong. On 1 October 2000 the final cross-Channel hovercraft service arrived at Seaspeed's facility at Dover's Western Dock. Captain Nick Dunn had been in command of *Princess Margaret*. It was now a substantially bigger craft than the one which had first crossed the channel with such high hopes back in 1968. It had just carried a load of 321 passengers and fifty-two cars. The era of the giant cross-Channel hovercraft, which thirty-one years earlier had been compared with Concorde, was over. Like the supersonic transport the SR.N4 spanned the '60s and the 2000s. And like Concorde the SR.N4 is now a museum piece.

Pegwell Bay

Right from the start it was clear that Ramsgate Harbour was not ideal for the SR.N6, never mind the considerably bigger SR.N4. Negotiating harbour walls meant dealing with strong crosswinds. In any case, what was needed was a wide open area that could provide a large clear space in which the craft could manoeuvre and park. There also needed to be scope for expansion and it had to be as close as possible to Calais.

Pegwell Bay, between Ramsgate and Sandwich, seemed the ideal location. In fact, it seemed the only suitable location. But first the government and public had to be convinced. Inevitably, that meant a planning application had to be submitted and a public inquiry convened to consider it and hear objections. As it turned out, though, there were two public inquiries.

The battle lines were soon drawn. On one side were local residents who feared the hoverport would mean noise, greatly increased traffic and general disturbance. On the other was the local authority and business community which were alive to the potential of such facilities for an area which was hardly replete with employment opportunity. Kent County Council sided with the opponents, as did Dover Harbour Board which claimed it already offered facilities superior to those proposed at Pegwell Bay. Other sites were suggested, including Lydd despite being over a mile inland.

The inquiry opened at Ramsgate on 3 January 1967 and closed seven days later. Its report published in March revealed that the ministry inspector who conducted it accepted Hoverlloyd's case:

Pegwell Bay was the only suitable location for a hoverport and he recommended that the project should be approved.

But a few months later British Rail threw a spanner into the works by announcing it had come to an arrangement with Dover Harbour Board. This led to the inevitable question: was there a need for two hoverports?

The government decided there was only one way to answer this question. Accordingly, the second public inquiry opened on 12 September and closed on the 15th. It was limited to hearing submissions and arguments on the advantages of a hoverport at Dover compared with one at Pegwell Bay. Hoverlloyd insisted that a decision against Pegwell Bay would strike 'a death blow' for the company and also the whole British hovercraft industry.

In the end it was accepted that the construction of both proposed hoverports should go ahead in the national interest. The government's decision was announced on 10 January 1968. The *East Kent Times*, which broke the story by producing a special edition, reported how the popping of champagne corks had greeted Hoverlloyd's victory after 'a long and arduous battle'.

But the battle to operate the first cross-Channel hovercraft services still had to be won, even though construction proceeded rapidly and the terminal's opening came just nine months after work began. It was formally opened by the Duke of Edinburgh on 2 May 1969.

The hoverport was actually owned by Thanet District Council, which had been an enthusiastic supporter of Hoverlloyd, and was operated by a company called International Hoverports Limited, a Hoverlloyd subsidiary. Designed to handle both vehicles and foot passengers, the operators claimed it equalled the standards of any international airport – 'with a little more besides'.

The world's first purpose-built hoverport had cost £1.5 million to build and could handle 1,000,000 passengers a year. It was claimed to offer the fastest and most direct route of any Channel port to London via the M2 motorway. Express coach services from London connected with hovercraft departures while buses linked the Hoverport with Ramsgate railway station and fast, frequent trains to London.

It comprised a handling pad and a single-storey terminal building which contained a shopping centre with a bank, bureau de change, and an automatic photograph machine for passport photos.

Around the well of the Customs Hall ran a balcony where passengers and friends could 'eat quite cheaply at a large cafeteria'. Once through Customs and Immigration controls passengers moved into a departure lounge, with a licensed snack bar and a Duty-Free Shop.

According to the official publicity material,

> there is also a first-class cocktail bar and restaurant where diners can watch the spectacular sight of hovercraft approaching in a storm of spray to berth on the landing platform right outside the windows. It is fascinating to see 177 tons of hovercraft sit down as gently as a feather.

Perhaps with a nod to those who had opposed the hoverport on environmental grounds, the operators' publicity added:

> Pegwell Bay is noted for its natural wild bird reserve and the migration of these wild birds, butterflies and dragonflies can be observed from armchair comfort, together with the panoramic views of Pegwell Bay and the surrounding countryside.

Hoverlloyd's first SR.N4, 002 *Swift*, arrived at Pegwell Bay on 15 January 1969. That week's *East Kent Times* printed a photograph on its front page under the headline 'Here She Comes'. But not everybody would have agreed with the accompanying strapline 'Giant "Hover" Purrs into Pegwell'. Many local residents feared this signalled the end of their peace and quiet. Those living at Cliffsend near Ramsgate called it the noisiest village in England.

The British Hovercraft Corporation SR.N4

The SR.N4 which operated cross-Channel passenger and vehicle services for thirty-one years is now recalled as the biggest hovercraft ever built. It looks as though it will retain that distinction.

Its primary structure comprised a large modular buoyancy tank, the internal structure of which was divided into twenty-four watertight compartments. This produced a rectangular planform with a semi-circular bow. Power was provided by four Rolls-Royce Proteus turboprop engines driving nine-feet-diameter steerable propellers, arranged in two pairs on pylons on top of the craft's roof. On the SR.N4's introduction to service, they were the largest propellers in the world.

Six independent electro-hydraulic systems driven from the main gearboxes, powered movement of the fins and pylons, while a further four units actuated the variable-pitch propellers.

The control cabin was similar to that of an aircraft's flight deck, housing a crew of three, captain, first officer/flight engineer and a second officer/navigator. The latter's main job was to avoid collisions using a Decca 629 radar. Flying controls appeared broadly similar to a typical aircraft although the control yoke altered propeller pitch.

A twelve-ton skirt and its complex supporting structure ran under the perimeter of the whole craft and, on the underside of the buoyancy tanks, a total of five 21-inch platforms (known as 'elephant feet') enabled the craft to rest on three of them. Fuel was contained in flexible bags located at all four corners. The craft could be trimmed by redistributing fuel between the fore and aft tanks to match load with prevailing weather conditions.

The stern featured large doors for loading vehicles on to the car deck and for unloading. There was another set of loading doors in the bow. All four of the exhausts for the Proteus engines were also in the stern.

Initially the craft could accommodate 254 passengers and thirty cars but in 1972 several were converted to Mk II specification with increased capacity. The Mk III conversion, which raised the Mk II's length by over fifty feet, entered service in 1976 and raised capacity to 418 passengers and sixty cars.

Six SR.N4s were built, mostly to Mk I specification:

> 01 - GH-2006 *Princess Margaret* 1968, Seaspeed – prototype, converted to Mk III specification 1979; scrapped March 2018
> 02 - GH-2004 *Swift*, Hoverlloyd – converted to Mk II specification for February 1973; broken up 2004
> 03 - GH-2005 *Sure* 1968, Hoverlloyd – converted to Mk II specification 1972; broken up for spares 1983

> 04 - GH-2007 *Princess Anne*, Seaspeed – converted to Mk III specification 1978; on display at the Hovercraft Museum
> 05 - GH-2008 *Sir Christopher* 1972, Hoverlloyd – converted to Mk II specification 1974, broken up for spares 1998
> 06 - GH-2054 *The Prince of Wales*, Hoverlloyd – built as Mk II, scrapped 1993 following an electrical fire.
>
> **Specification, SR.N4 Mk II**
> **Length** 130 ft 2 in
> **Beam** 78 ft
> **Weight** 200 tons
> **Power Plant** 4 x Rolls-Royce Proteus turboprop engines each generating 3,400shp
> **Speed** maximum of 80 mph in calm sea and zero wind; normal operating speed 46 to 69 mph.

Sir Christopher Cockerell

One of the last in the tradition of lone British inventors, Christopher Cockerell was from the same era as Frank Whittle and Alec Issigonis. His brainchild, however, failed to achieve the same level of ubiquity as the jet engine and the Mini.

The story of Cockerell's early experiments with empty cat food and coffee tins and a vacuum-cleaner motor have passed into legend, but the man who was described as one of Britain's most original scientific minds had a string of inventions to his credit.

Born in 1910 near Cambridge, Christopher Cockerell was the son of Sir Sydney Cockerell, director of the Fitzwilliam Museum. He grew up in a strongly literary environment but when T.E. Lawrence came to call young Christopher was more interested in the hero's Brough Superior motorcycle than in discussing *The Seven Pillars of Wisdom*.

Cockerell read engineering at Cambridge and for a time worked with the Marconi Wireless Telegraph Company. Although his father once called him 'little better than a garage hand,' he was willing to finance his patent applications. But in 1950 a legacy from his wife's father enabled him to buy a boatyard in Norfolk where he pursued his experiments into the creation of a cushion of air to enable boats to pass more easily though the water.

In 1955 Cockerell persuaded the Ministry of Supply to back his invention but the government's response was to place it on the secret list because of its potential for military use. This put its commercial exploitation back four years while Cockerell struggled to remove his invention from the secret list and form a company to develop the idea.

In 1958 the National Research and Development Council agreed to fund development of the Saunders Roe SR.N1 which incorporated Cockerell's ideas. In 1959 the SR.N1 became the first hovercraft to cross the English Channel.

Chapter Fourteen

The *Radio Queen* and other Tales

The high-wing monoplane flew steadily over the choppy waters of the English Channel, the crackle of its single-cylinder engine bravely competing with the roar of the wind at 3,000 feet.

It was 1954 and a little bit – a very little bit – of aviation history was in the process of being made.

Keeping pace with the aircraft was another, a privately-owned Auster. Both were heading for Marc airfield near Calais in northern France. The Auster landed first but of its companion there was no sign. The Auster immediately took off to begin the search. But it was to be six days before the missing aircraft was found, in a beetroot field near Guemps, five miles from Calais harbour. The first non-stop cross-Channel flight by a model aircraft had been completed.

The *Radio Queen* with its seven-feet wingspan had been made from a kit of parts consisting of balsa wood, wire and tissue paper. It was powered by a miniature diesel engine of 3.46cc and guided by a somewhat primitive three-channel radio control unit.

The model had been designed in 1949 by Colonel H.J. Taplin and *Radio Queen* proved so successful that kits are still available in the twenty-first century. It was built by the staff of a Surrey-based company originally called Electronic Developments but more usually known as E.D. It had been formed by a group of people who had built gun turrets for RAF heavy bombers during the Second World War but in 1945 they were out of a job. The company achieved public recognition in 1951 when one of its radio-controlled model boats crossed the Channel.

Three years later it was the turn of the *Radio Queen*. It took off at 13:35 hr on Wednesday 21 September 1954 from the field at Dover where Louis Blériot had landed forty-six years earlier. Sid Allen controlled the model, heavily laden with fuel, from its hand-launched take off and during its climb-out before handing over control to E.D. director George

Honnest-Redlich in the Auster. The model crossed the French coast at 14:15 hr, having reached a maximum altitude of 3,100 feet during its journey.

The 1950s is now seen as a golden age of aeromodelling and E.D. made the most of its achievement. In its subsequent advertising in the journal *Aero Modeller*, the company called its success 'astonishing' and crowed that its latest achievement proved 'beyond all doubt' the reliability and precision workmanship of its products.

The world had to wait another half-century for the next big milestone in model aircraft technology. In July 2006 Nigel Hawes and Brian Collins flew the first electric-powered model to make the Channel crossing. The 54-inch-span representation of the RAF's Short Tucano trainer flew from Dover to Sangatte in just over an hour. The model, weighing 2lb empty, carried batteries weighing 3lb to provide the power for its flight.

With the growing popularity and availability of drones it was inevitable that someone would attempt a Channel crossing with one. It happened on 16 February 2016 when a team led by Richard Gill remotely piloted such a craft from the beach at Wissant in northern France to Dover in seventy-two minutes on an 'unusually sunny and calm morning'.

The quadcopter was provided by Ocuair, a company which uses drones for survey and aerial inspection work. The flight, Ocuair said, 'demonstrates the future potential of commercial drone technology.'

The flight was conducted with the approval of the aviation regulators of both countries. To adhere to current regulations, the pilot had to follow in a boat within at least 500 yards of the drone. But a third of the way through the flight the drone's satellite navigation system stopped working, so the team had to guide it manually for the last twenty minutes, something they described as 'extremely challenging'.

'Given that the team were operating on the very edge of what is practically possible for a quadcopter, the weather conditions were critical,' the team noted in a celebratory blog post. 'Any type of adverse wind would have had a severe impact on the drone, meaning it might not make the distance. Given he was flying over water, there are no second chances or emergency landings.'

Ocuair said the flight would help to develop drone technology further. Richard Gill described the flight as an attempt to 'push the technology in a meaningful way'. He said:

> The UK leads the world in terms of legislation, so I thought it would be good to see us lead the world in commercial

UAV applications too. I wanted to do something meaningful to stand out and show what this technology is capable of. Companies like Amazon have seen the commercial potential of drones. This record is important in the context of future drone activity because it proves that drones can be reliably used over a distance.

Like the *Radio Queen* and the Tucano models, the quadcopter did not carry a pilot. Felix Baumgartner, on the other hand, was the exact opposite, a pilot without a 'plane.

On 20 July 2003, he became the first person to skydive across the Channel using a specially made carbon-fibre wing strapped to his back. Parachutes checked his twenty-mile-long freefall descent during which he reached 220 mph.

Baumgartner's rigid 'wing suit' was designed by inventor and engineer Alban Geissler and the main and reserve parachutes by Daniel Preston and Stane Krajnc. Manufactured by Atair Aerodynamics, the high-performance parachutes had already won numerous awards and set world records

But the Channel crossing was just one step in Baumgartner's career, the highlight of which was his jump from a helium balloon from the stratosphere on 14 October 2012. When he landed in New Mexico he had established world records for skydiving an estimated twenty-four miles and reaching an estimated top speed of 843.6 mph or Mach 1.25.

Baumgartner became the first person to break the sound barrier without vehicular power. He also broke skydiving records for exit altitude, vertical freefall distance with a drogue parachute and vertical speed without a drogue.

Just as spectacular was the achievement of Swiss daredevil Yves Rossy. On 16 September 2008 he became the first person to cross the Channel using only a jet-propelled wing strapped to his back.

The forty-nine-year-old former fighter pilot was taken to a height of 8,000 feet by a Pilatus support aircraft which, once he had jumped out, guided him on his route. Before leaving the aircraft he ignited the four kerosene-burning jet turbines attached to the wing on his back. After a period of free fall, he opened the wing and soared across the water. With no steering controls, the only way to change direction was by moving his head and back.

Rossy developed and built the semi-rigid wing himself. It spanned eight feet, was made of lightweight carbon composite and weighed about

120 lb including fuel. It was powered by four Jetcat P400 jet engines modified from large model aircraft engines.

As he crossed the White Cliffs of Dover just after 13.05 hr, Rossy even had enough fuel for some celebratory aerobatics to entertain the crowds gathered below. He then deployed his parachute and drifted gently downwards, waving his legs excitedly. Rossy's ungainly face-in-the-dirt landing, however, contrasted with the elegance of his high-altitude flight through the crystal blue autumn sky. But he declared that he felt 'great, really great'.

After two previous flights had been postponed because of bad weather, everything went to plan for Rossy's third attempt. He was helped on his way by a tailwind that cut his flight time by around two and a half minutes compared with his calculations. Support was provided by a search and rescue helicopter in case he landed in the sea, and another helicopter to film him in the air. A further aircraft flew above him to relay the pictures.

After his nine minutes thirty-two seconds flight Rossy said: 'I am so happy. With that crossing I showed it is possible to fly a little bit like a bird. I am full of hope there will be many in the near future.' The forty-nine-year-old Rossy told the BBC the tensest moment was when he jumped from the aircraft 'because I did have many problems during exits before'. But this time he made a perfect exit and quickly set the correct course by aiming for the cliffs of Dover.

Rossy was born in the Swiss canton of Neuchatel in 1959. He served as a fighter pilot in the Swiss Air Force where he flew Dassault Mirage IIIs, Northrop F-5 Tigers and Hawker Hunters. After joining Swissair, Rossy piloted Boeing 747s and, later, Airbus A320s for Swiss International Air Lines on the Zurich-Heathrow route.

On 7 May 2011 Rossy flew above the Grand Canyon in Arizona. The United States Federal Aviation Administration had classified his flight system as an aircraft. When it finally granted him a licence, the FAA waived the normal twenty-five to forty hours of flight-testing time, and Rossy acted quickly to complete his flight.

Perhaps the most exotic device used by a cross-Channel pioneer was the flying car which completed the crossing on 14 June 2017. The road-legal machine was a lightweight dune buggy combined with a powered paraglider wing. On the ground it was propelled by a scooter engine and in the air by a micro-light aircraft powerplant driving a ducted fan.

Bruno Vezzoli drove the machine, known as 'Pegasus', from the Champs Élysées in Paris to Ambleteuse airfield between Calais and Boulogne.

'I would say that the biggest risk, just like with any engine-powered machine, would be a breakdown,' Vezzoli told Reuters TV as he made his pre-take-off checks. 'Usually you land on the ground, but in this case we would have to do a sea-landing.'

At 08:00 hr, under a clear blue sky, Vezzoli took off, lurching from side to side as he slowly gained altitude suspended beneath a giant canopy. The journey was expected to take between twenty and seventy minutes depending on conditions but 'Pégase' landed at East Studdal near Dover after flying the thirty-six miles in fifty minutes.

The two-seat 'Pégase' was developed by former journalist Jérôme Dauffy. He said: 'The automotive and aeronautical industries were born around a century ago and it's only now that we are managing to combine the two modes.'

The craft needed around 100 yards in which to take off and thirty yards to land. It was capable of 50 mph, flying at an altitude of 10,000 feet and remaining in the air for about three hours.

Whether or not 'Pégase' represented a glimpse of the future nothing could have been more minimal than the hover-board which French inventor Franky Zapata used to cross the Channel on 5 August 2019. Even so Zapata told *The Times*: 'I think I have taken a step towards the future.'

The paper reported that as he landed at St Mary's Bay near Dover, the forty-year-old aviator clenched his fist, removed his helmet which contained a built-in head-up display, embraced his childhood friend and assistant and wiped a tear from his eye. During his twenty-two minute flight he reached speeds of 105 mph.

Zapata, a former European jet-ski champion, developed his hover-board at a workshop near his home city of Marseilles with the help of a grant from the French army which believed the machine could form the basis of a machine that might one day be used by special forces.

The board was powered by five small jet engines fuelled from a backpack containing 10.5 gallons of kerosene. Horizontal motion was controlled by the pilot leaning in the direction he wanted to go to direct the thrust. Vertical motion was controlled by a throttle on a hand-held controller.

This was Zapata's second attempt to fly the Channel by hover board. Ten days earlier his first bid had ended in failure and an early dip in the sea. But Zapata had already become a household name in France when he flew on his board over the Bastille Day parade in Paris in front of massed crowds and military top brass as well as President Macron and German Chancellor Angela Merkel.

Zapata's successful crossing was not a non-stop one, however, because he had to come down in mid-Channel to refuel. After reaching Dover he reported that he had completed the journey at between 99 and 105 mph but slowed down to 87 mph as he approached the English coast. 'But,' he said, 'my thighs were hurting so I speeded up again to 99 mph. I was telling myself "just enjoy it" and trying not to feel the pain.'

His first sight of the White Cliffs had been 'magnificent'. He added: 'No one will forget this day. It is engraved on our hearts.' He returned to France by ferry, but not before he had shared his vision of the future. His company was developing a flying car based on the hover board's 'endless potential'. He added: 'It will be very safe and very reliable.'

The Birdmen of Bognor

It's quite likely that before 2009 relatively few people were aware that you could earn money by jumping off the end of a pier at one of Britain's more fashionable south coast resorts.

In 2009 one of the participants in the International Birdmen Rally held that year in Worthing disputed the ruling that another contestant had 'flown' further than he had. The matter, which generated considerable publicity locally, came to court five years later.

The International Birdmen Rally was the brainchild of George Abel who saw it as a novel way of raising money for his local branch of the Royal Air Force Association. The first event was held in 1971 at Selsey, West Sussex, and involved contestants strapping on a pair of wings, usually made of wood and fabric, and running up an elevated ramp twenty- to thirty-five-feet high at the end of a pier and attempting to 'fly' the furthest distance before landing in the sea.

Initially there was a prize of £1,000 for anyone who could travel beyond fifty yards. Since then the prize money and qualifying distance increased. The competition was divided between serious aviators flying hang-gliders, inventors with home-designed and built machines and people in fancy dress with little or no actual flying ability, but intent on raising money for charity.

The rally was subsequently held at Eastbourne, Bognor Regis and Worthing. In 2009 at Worthing a £30,000 prize was offered to any competitor who could 'fly' 100 metres. Steve Elkins claimed to have completed the course but the organizers said that he had fallen at 99.8 metres, twenty centimetres short of the 100-metre marker.

Elkins claimed that video footage showed he had exceeded the distance and he took the event organizers to court. But in February 2014 a judge ruled against him, saying that he was 'not satisfied' that the competitor had crossed the mark.

Admittedly, 100 metres is some way short of the total distance to France but who knows? If one of the birdmen actually makes it across, you read it here first.

Chapter Fifteen

Pollution-Free

In 100 years of flying the English Channel it's a fair bet that nobody worked harder to cross the twenty-two miles of ocean than Bryan Allen.

In fact, he was probably the only cross-Channel pioneer to be seriously out of breath at the end of his journey. Allen had reached the limit of his endurance in his struggle with exhaustion, dehydration and cramp as he pedalled across the Channel on what was essentially a flying bicycle.

Allen was an American software engineer who taught himself to fly hang-gliders and was a keen amateur cyclist. He may not have been the first to fly a human-powered aircraft but he was certainly the first to demonstrate that such a craft was capable of controlled and sustained flight.

Allen triumphed over difficult circumstances to become the first man to fly a human-powered aircraft across the Channel but he was not the only hero to emerge from that day in 1979. Dr Paul MacCready was the man who led the team which created the craft that put Allen into the history books. The result of MacCready's efforts weighed as much as the average bicycle yet had a wingspan similar to a Boeing 737 airliner.

Allen was not the first to fly the Channel in an aircraft not powered by burning fossil fuel. Lissant Beardmore was the first to fly the Channel in a glider four decades earlier. On 19 June 1931 he was towed aloft from Lympne airport by a powered aircraft and during his ninety-minute flight he reached an altitude of 14,000 feet before landing at Saint-Inglevert.

The next day Austrian Robert Kronfeld made the first double crossing by glider. His craft, called 'Wien', was aero-towed from Saint-Inglevert to 5,000 feet and landed at the former RAF airfield at Swingfield near Dover. From there he received another aero-tow to an altitude of 10,000 feet which enabled him to return to Saint-Inglevert. Kronfeld received a £1,000 prize from the *Daily Mail* for his flights, which were verified by the British Gliding Association.

There was little new about human-powered aircraft but most were too heavy for sustained flight. It was not until the 1960s that lightweight materials became available. Encouraged by the Royal Aeronautical Society, industrialist Henry Kremer offered a £5,000 prize for the first human-powered aircraft to fly a figure-of-eight course round two markers half-a-mile apart. The designer, entrant, pilot, place of construction and flight had to be British but, to stimulate wider interest, Kremer opened it to all nationalities in 1973 and increased the prize to £50,000.

The first officially authenticated take off and landing by a human-powered aircraft was recorded at Lasham airfield on 9 November 1961 when Derek Piggott flew a craft designed and built at Southampton University. In forty attempts the longest flight was 650 metres. The craft was later rebuilt by Imperial College with a new transmission system but was damaged beyond repair in November 1965.

A week after Piggot's first flight, employees of the de Havilland aircraft company made the first flight of the 'Hatfield Puffin'. The Hatfield Man Powered Aircraft Club had access to company support and eventually achieved a flight of 993 yards, a record which stood for ten years.

A new fuselage and wing were subsequently built around the transmission recovered from the original 'Puffin'. 'Puffin 2' flew in August 1965 and made several flights over a half-mile, including a climb to seventeen feet. After 'Puffin 2' was damaged, it was handed over to Liverpool University who used it to build the 'Liverpuffin'.

Further attempts were made but none was as successful as the Woodford, Essex, Aircraft Group's 'Jupiter'. Designed and built by Chris Roper, it was piloted by serving RAF officer John Potter. In June 1972 Potter flew 1,355 yards but due to Roper's ill health, the project was continued at RAF Halton.

In the early 1970s Paul MacCready and Dr Peter B.S. Lissaman took a fresh look at the challenge and came up with an unorthodox aircraft called 'Gossamer Condor', which evolved through three distinct versions. The first, a proof-of-concept machine, flew just once, in the parking lot of the Rose Bowl in Pasadena. The next, lacking pilot fairings and other refinements, was flown at Mojave airport on 26 December 1976. The third was the record-breaking 'Gossamer Condor 2' which included such improvements as a pilot nacelle and double-skin aerofoil sections, allowing the aircraft to fly long distances as well as to manoeuvre.

On 23 August 1977 Bryan Allen flew it over a 1.4-mile figure of eight at Shafter, California, to win the first Kremer prize. Although the craft reached only 11 mph, it achieved that velocity on just 0.35 hp generated by Allen's muscles alone.

POLLUTION-FREE

The success led MacCready to build the improved 'Gossamer Albatross'. Test flights began in the summer of 1978 at Shafter and yielded positive results. Eventually, the 'Albatross' was able to make fifteen-minute flights and, following further improvements, including a new propeller design, Allen took it for a 13-mile, sixty-nine-minute flight over Harper Lake in April 1979. But Allen's next challenge was the sternest yet: the Channel crossing. To prepare himself he trained by cycling over forty to eighty miles a day.

The years of development and months of training came to a head that June. It was still dark as news media representatives began to gather at around 02:30 hr on 12 June 1979 to watch the Albatross being prepared for its historic flight from England to France. 'There was no drama or uncertainty. Paul always had a fundamental grasp of what's possible and what's not,' Allen recalled

Just before 06:00 hr, with Allen pedalling at the planned 75 rpm, the Albatross lifted off the makeshift runway at RAF Manston and headed out over the Channel. Calm seas and lack of wind suggested a potentially worry-free flight lay ahead. But trouble began soon after take-off. 'I got a triple-whammy of failures,' Allen recalled.

First, the transmit button on his radio failed, leaving him unable to talk to the rest of the team in the escorting boats below. This meant relying on hand signals and head movements. Then Allen's water supply began running out. Due to unexpected headwinds, the flight was taking forty-nine minutes longer than planned and Allen was suffering leg cramps from dehydration due to lack of fluid.

On top of all that, the airspeed instruments and acoustic altimeter failed as their batteries expired. Without these instruments, Allen didn't know his height above the water or his speed.

As the headwind increased, so, too, did uncertainty that the flight would be successful. With the French coast not yet in sight and turbulence taking its toll, the escorting Zodiac inflatable boat prepared to hook on to the aircraft and abort the flight. But when he increased altitude to allow the Zodiac to manoeuvre underneath the Albatross, Allen discovered the air was less turbulent higher up. As the Zodiac got closer Allen kept moving away. For over an hour he kept asking to continue for another five minutes.

During this time, the surface wind calmed slightly and the Albatross plodded on. After careful negotiation of the rocky coastline, Allen landed safely on the beach at Cap Gris Nez. He had triumphed over headwinds, equipment failure and exhaustion. He said later: 'There were so many unknowns on that flight that I couldn't be certain we'd make it, but I was certain I'd use every resource in trying.'

Seventy years after Louis Blériot, Bryan Allen had completed the twenty-two-mile crossing from England to France in two hours and forty-nine minutes without burning an ounce of fossil fuel. He had achieved a maximum speed of 18 mph and an average altitude of 5 feet.

This success earned MacCready the title of 'father of human-powered flight'. Now his thoughts turned towards another form of motive power. In 1980 MacCready formed a team to design and build a solar-power aircraft and seek sponsorship to fund it.

But MacCready was under no illusions that solar energy could ever become a significant source of power for aircraft. Solar cells were too heavy, cost too much and produced energy only under bright light.

'The least useful application of solar cells I can think of is powering an airplane,' MacCready declared.

> I felt that a long-distance flight with the *Solar Challenger* would focus public attention on solar cells and help stimulate the public awareness and support which would speed their development and utilisation. Rapid growth of the solar cell field would lessen our dependence on imported oil.

Ray Morgan took a leave of absence from Lockheed Aircraft Corporation to manage the project. He and his group completed the Gossamer Penguin, which had been designed as a possible back-up aircraft for the cross-Channel flight but wasn't completed.

Gossamer Penguin was similar to Gossamer Albatross but 75 per cent of its size. Now it was to be used as a test-bed for the solar power system and to gain experience of the new power source. Gossamer Albatross made a series of test flights using battery power with MacCready's thirteen-year-old son Marshall at the controls.

The Solar Challenger first flew with battery power, using 120 Nicads which were expected to weigh as much as the solar arrays then under construction for the craft. Petite Janice Brown was appointed project pilot and she made a 1.5-hour flight in August 1980. Brown made the first flight with solar arrays installed in November but in a series of subsequent tests Brown's longest flight was thirty miles; the team had been hoping for 100.

The following spring, engineering test pilot Stephen Ptacek, who had been slimming down to fly the Solar Challenger, made a six-hour flight that covered 200 miles, while Brown reached 16,000 feet.

POLLUTION-FREE

One of MacCready's team, Robert Boucher, wrote in 1984: 'We figured we were now ready for the English Channel so we packed up our gear and headed for Paris, France.'

The airfield at Pontoise, twenty miles north-east of Paris, was established as the team's base for the cross-Channel flight to RAF Manston from where Gossamer Albatross had started its journey. 'Many of the lads at the base remembered the MacCready crew,' Boucher recalled.

But the weather was unfavourable with northerly winds and overcast weather that persisted until midday. As Solar Challenger's top speed was 46 mph there would not be enough time to complete the 200-mile flight in daylight. In desperation the team moved to Manston in the hope that the weather would be better for a run in the reverse direction. It wasn't. After sixteen days they moved back to Pontoise on the expectation of favourable conditions.

On 6 July the team erected Solar Challenger and prepared it for flight. The following morning the weather was ideal – like 'a perfect California day', Boucher recalled – and Ptacek climbed aboard. The craft was then walked out to the runway, watched by thousands of spectators. But ground haze made take-off difficult and it took Ptacek 'six or seven' attempts before he was able to take off and head for England.

He was escorted by several aircraft including one with MacCready and a support team from sponsors Du Pont on board. Morgan and Boucher followed in a van towing a trailer. By the time they reached Calais, Ptacek had landed at Manston. He had been airborne for five hours twenty-three minutes, flying at an average speed of 50 mph. According to Boucher, he had circled Manston for an hour to let all the chase 'planes land and accompanying reporters clear Customs and be ready to photograph Solar Challenger as it landed.

That night, Boucher recalled,

> The RAF at Manston threw a big party for us all. We were treated like heroes. The Challenger sat silently and proudly in an RAF hangar. It had just made the world's first international solar flight.

It had indeed, but the next step in crossing the Channel without burning fossil fuel had to wait two decades and the arrival of hydrogen power. Gérard Thevenot had already achieved fame building ultra-light aircraft and as a championship-level hang-glider pilot. In 1974 he and his brother, Jean-Marc, began building versions of the American Seagull hang-glider which they called 'La Mouette'. In 1979 they produced the Atlas which remained in production until 2012 with over 8,000 examples still flying.

In 2002 he formed a company called Helite which makes airbags, not just for aircraft and cars but motorcycles and pedal cycles as well. It also makes air vests and jackets and its UK distributor supplies many of Britain's police and rescue services.

Meanwhile, Thevenot had become interested in the potential of hydrogen fuel cells as an alternative power source for light aircraft. In 2006 he won the Shell Eco Marathon with a hydrogen-powered car, which he co-designed, but by 2009 his attention had returned to aviation.

The result was a hydrogen-powered ultralight machine using a seven-kilowatt (11 horsepower) Geiger-Eck HP-10 electric motor, controller and propeller powered by three hydrogen fuel cells. Thevenot explained, 'Weighing less than 130 kilograms including the pilot, our hydrogen-fuelled aircraft is extremely light. This allows it to fly powered only by the fuel cell and without the assistance of an auxiliary battery.'

The craft had a simple wooden tricycle frame to which was attached a wing spanning thirty-seven feet. It had a one-gallon tank, enough for approximately one hour of flight. This equates to an average fuel consumption at 300 feet above sea level of 550 gm per flight hour. The aircraft's only emission was pure water vapour. On 6 August Thevenot flew his hydrogen-powered 'La Mouette' hang-glider over roughly the same route as Louis Blériot to cross the Channel in one hour seven minutes.

The race between two Frenchmen to be the first to fly the Channel in an electric-powered aircraft echoed that between Hubert Latham and Louis Blériot to make the first crossing by aeroplane 106 years earlier.

On 9 July 2015 stunt pilot Hugues Duval, flying a tiny single-seat machine, was bidding to beat Didier Esteyne, test pilot for the giant Airbus aerospace group, to the honour. Duval claimed victory, telling the Associated Press that his successful cross-Channel flight was a 'relief' and an 'important moment' after years of developing the aircraft plus numerous flights over land.

But the *Daily Telegraph* reported that Duval had needed 'a little help getting airborne'. It turned out that he'd actually needed quite a lot of help and this was to be the source of controversy as to which of the pilots should take the honour.

Duval was already well-known as an active member of an aerobatic group called Tranchant, based at Rennes St Jacques Airport. He set a new speed record for an electric-powered aircraft in 2011 flying a

POLLUTION-FREE

Colomban Cri-Cri. Designed in the 1970s by French aeronautical engineer Michel Colomban and named after his daughter, Christine, the Cri-Cri was world's smallest twin-engine aircraft. It featured a cantilever low-mounted wing, single-seat cockpit enclosed by a bubble canopy, and a fixed tricycle undercarriage.

Construction was of aluminium sheet glued to Klegecell foam. The two JPX PUL 212 single-cylinder piston engines, each generating 15 hp, were mounted on pylons attached to the aircraft's nose. Wingspan was a miniscule sixteen feet and the aircraft, which could reach 140 mph, was capable of aerobatic flying.

In June 2010 an electric-powered Cri-Cri appeared at the Green Aviation Show at Le Bourget. It was claimed that the modified airframe with composite components could fly for thirty minutes at 68 mph under the power of four brushless electric motors with counter-rotating propellers. The following September a version known as Electravia with two electric motors each producing 25 hp set a world speed record for lithium-polymer-powered aircraft of 162.33 mph.

On 9 July 2015 Duval eased himself into the tiny cockpit of his Cri-Cri which was actually mounted on top of a rugged Max Holste Broussard single-engine utility aircraft. The *Financial Times* quoted Duval as saying he'd decided on the unorthodox take-off from another aircraft to keep his attempt to cross the Channel secret. 'If people had found out, it is possible I might have had a few problems,' he said. Some reports said that his Cri-Cri had been banned from taking off from Calais airport.

According to the *FT*, 'it was catapulted from another aircraft in the middle of the Channel.' The `plane then circled over Dover and headed for France. Film from a camera mounted on the Broussard's wing showed the tiny aircraft separate and arc away from the carrier aircraft to complete the rest of the journey, taking twenty-one minutes to fly across the water.

'By contrast,' the *FT* reported,

> the two seat electric aircraft made by Airbus and flown by Mr Esteyne took off from Lydd airport in Kent and landed in Calais. With a barely noticeable whirring sound, Mr Esteyne set out on Friday morning under sunny skies to cross the Channel, landing about 36 minutes later in France. That was roughly the same time that it took Mr Blériot to make his ground-breaking flight in 1909.

Quietly and without fuss the Airbus team had trailered their machine by road and ferry to Lydd airport where they had assembled it. The *FT* noted that the only indication that Esteyne had started the E-Fan's two electric motors 'was a man suddenly clutching his hat because of the blast from the shrouded fans'. Esteyne added, 'If you compare it with a classical airplane, there's not a lot of noise.'

The *FT* observed that light aircraft with internal-combustion engines were often so noisy that the occupants needed ear-defender-type headsets to preserve their hearing as well as to talk to each other and air traffic control. 'Not so with the E-Fan,' Esteyne said: 'There's also no vibration so it's very comfortable.' Less comfortable, though, was its limited endurance. 'The E-Fan has 53 minutes of autonomy,' said Mr Esteyne. 'For this flight we needed something like 40 minutes.'

After his forty-five-minute flight, Esteyne landed in Calais to cheers and whistles from an admiring crowd. He parked the E-Fan next to a replica Blériot and explained what it was like to fly the E-Fan. 'It is closer to a glider because there is less noise than an aeroplane,' he said. 'It's smooth and very quiet.'

Airbus developed its E-Fan to investigate the feasibility of using electricity to power aircraft. The E-Fan was demonstrated at the Farnborough and Paris air shows to make impressive near-silent displays.

The E-Fan 1.0 had made 100 flights. The project had taken eighteen months from paper to its first flight, said Simon Bradley, head of global innovation network at Airbus Group.

A bright future was predicted for the E-Fan. It was expected to appeal in particular to flight schools because of its lack of annoying engine noise. Its limited endurance was unlikely to be tested by student pilots who would not be venturing far from their home airfield. Soon after production plans were announced, Airbus changed its corporate mind to concentrate instead on a proposed hybrid-electric, regional jet-sized aircraft, with an initial service date of 2030.

Whether or not the flight of the E-Fan offered a glimpse into the future of aviation remains to be seen. Perhaps it will be electric power alone or a combination of sources. But one thing remains clear: there's no limit to human ingenuity in finding new ways to fly across the twenty-two miles of water separating England and France. There will be plenty more cross-Channel pioneers.

MacCready's Masterpieces

Paul MacCready was a Second World War US Navy pilot who gained a doctorate in aeronautical engineering. He took up gliding and became the first American to win the world championship.

It was when MacCready found himself responsible for a $100,000 debt after he had guaranteed a relative's business venture which subsequently failed that he decided to try to win the £50,000 prize put up Henry Kremer

His first craft, known as 'Gossamer Condor', was inspired by hang-gliders but with increased wing area. A gondola accommodating the pilot was suspended beneath the wing with a canard control surface mounted on an extension to the front fuselage. Construction was largely of lightweight plastics with aluminium spars.

From this evolved the Gossamer Albatross with its very long, high-aspect-ratio wing much like a glider's to permit flight with a minimum of power. In still air the required power was in the order of 300 W (0.40 hp), although even mild turbulence made this figure rise rapidly.

The Solar Challenger was designed as an improvement on the Gossamer Penguin, which in turn was a solar-powered variant of the Gossamer Albatross. Challenger was powered entirely by the photovoltaic cells on its wing and stabiliser, without even reserve batteries.

Designed to withstand sustained high-altitude flight and normal turbulence, it was the first such craft capable of long-distance flight. Its two motors, each three-inches wide and seventeen-inches long, operated in tandem on a common shaft to drive a single, controllable-pitch propeller.

The design incorporated advanced synthetic materials with very high strength to weight ratios and included Kevlar, Nomex, Delrin, Teflon and Mylar, supplied by sponsor Du Pont. Gossamer Albatross and Solar Challenger are preserved at the Smithsonian National Air and Space Museum, Washington DC.

In 1991 Paul MacCready was inducted into the Aviation Hall of Fame. He retired as chairman of AeroVironment due to ill health in August 2007, eight days before his death.

'Gossamer Albatross' - Specification
Length 34 ft
Wingspan 97 ft 8 in
Height 16 ft 0 in
Wing area: 488 sq ft
Weights empty 70 lb; gross 215 lb
Maximum speed 18 mph
Range 35 miles.

'Solar Challenger' - specification
Length 30 ft 4 in
Wingspan 46 ft 8 in
Powerplant two Astro 2500 solar-powered electric motors generating 2.5 hp each
Weights empty 220 lb; gross with pilot 339 lb
Maximum speed: 46 mph
Range (estimated) 400 miles; endurance (estimated) 11hr (645 projected km)

The Airbus E-Fan

Although the Airbus E-Fan wasn't actually the first battery-powered aircraft to cross the English Channel it was the first to do so entirely under its own power and therefore deserves its own special place in aviation history.

Airbus Group developed it in conjunction with Aero Composites Saintonge. It used on-board lithium-ion batteries to power its two electric motors and could carry a pilot and passenger in tandem. It first flew in April 2014 at Bordeaux-Merignac airport and, at that year's Farnborough Air Show, Airbus announced that the E-Fan would go into production by 2017 but with a side-by-side seating layout.

The E-Fan was of all-composite construction with the two 60 kW electric motors mounted on either side of the rear fuselage driving ducted fans. Power came from a series of 250-volt lithium polymer battery packs mounted in the inboard section of the wings. They had enough power for one hour and would take an hour to recharge.

An onboard back-up battery was available to make an emergency landing if power ran out while airborne.

The aircraft featured a T-tail and a retractable tandem undercarriage with outrigger wheels. Unusually, the main wheel was powered by a 6-kW electric motor, which not only allowed the craft to be taxied without using its main motors but also accelerated it to 37 mph for take-off.

Two production variants were planned initially, a two-seater E-Fan 2.0 for use as a trainer, and the stretched E-Fan 4.0 four-seat touring aircraft. To increase flight duration the E-Fan 4.0 would have had a hybrid-electric system with a small engine to charge the battery and increase flight duration from two to three-and-a-half hours. The first flight of the E-Fan 2.0 was originally planned for 2017 and the E-Fan 4.0 for 2019.

Airbus had invested €20m in developing the technology and in 2015 announced plans to build production models at a new facility at Pau in south-west France. First deliveries were expected at the end of 2017 or early 2018. But in April 2017 Airbus cancelled production to pursue other avenues of research.

Airbus E-Fan - Specification
Length 21 ft 11 in.
Wingspan 31 ft 2 in.
Max take-off weight 1,213 lb
Powerplant 2 x Electric motors each generating 30 kW (40 hp) each powered by Lithium-ion batteries producing 29 kWh and driving eight-blade ducted fans each producing 266 lb static thrust
Maximum speed (estimated) 140 mph; cruise 99 mph
Endurance 60 min.

21st Century Aeronauts

It was in 1981 that the world's first solar-powered hybrid hot-air balloon crossed the English Channel. It was piloted by Julian Nott, a noted innovator in the field.

Its envelope was designed with a special black panel which absorbed the heat from the sun. On the other side was a panel of silver insulating fabric, which helped retain the heat in the envelope. Built by Cameron Balloons, it was the first balloon to be certificated to use the hybrid solar concept. It made its first flight in August 1981.

Nott was an expatriate Brit who lived in California. He spent many years working with NASA engineers developing balloons to operate in planetary atmospheres. His achievements include the first balloon crossing of the Sahara Desert and the first crossing of Australia. He died at the age of 74 in a ballooning accident in 2019. At the time of his death Nott was experimenting with his patented design for a balloon using cryogenic helium.

In May 2010 Jonathan Trappe made the first Channel crossing by helium balloon cluster. Dangling beneath a cloud of brightly coloured balloons, Trappe, 36, controlled his altitude by cutting the balloons free one by one with a pair of scissors. He landed in a field near Dunkirk.

Trappe, who had already set several records for helium balloon flights, took off at 05:00 hr into a clear blue sky, from the Kent Gliding Club airfield at Challock near Ashford about ten miles from the coast. Trappe was using a slightly sturdier basket than he normally used and he carried a GPS system to work out his location, but he had no immersion suit to save him if he crashed into the Channel.

Cheered on by spectators, Trappe lifted off and rose to a maximum height of 11,000 feet during the crossing. 'We are the least manoeuvrable of aircraft, so we have right of way,' he said before taking off. Later, he described his flight as a classic challenge. 'There is adventure to be had even in our modern times.'

Asked by a reporter what it felt like to have conquered the channel. 'We have not conquered the channel,' he replied. 'We have only had the honour to float in the skies above the cold waters for one quiet day. Today and forever, the English Channel remains unconquered.'

In April Trappe secured his place in the *Guinness World Records* for the longest cluster balloon flight when he covered more than 109 miles in an overnight flight which lasted almost fourteen hours over his home state of North Carolina with his confection of balloons christened 'The Spirit Cluster'.

At 07:00 hr on 7 April 2017 eighty-two hot-air balloons were launched from Lydden Hill Race Circuit near Dover and headed for the

POLLUTION-FREE

famous White Cliffs of Dover and the open water. The crossing earned a new Guinness World Record. The previous record, coincidentally set on 7 April 2011, saw forty-nine balloons complete the flight.

In 2017 the participants came from ten different countries. The attempt required specific weather conditions both on the ground and at altitude and these do not frequently occur. As a result the flight had been on standby since 5 March.

Organizer James Strickland said it was a 'fantastic flight in perfect weather conditions'. He added: 'Having flown across the channel in 2011 this time it was truly amazing to break the Guinness Book of Record. Of all the flights I have ever done this has to be the number one.'

Once all teams had returned to their home countries, the GPS flight tracks from each balloon were submitted to Guinness for the flight to be officially ratified as a new world record and with BBC *Breakfast* broadcasting live from a balloon to transmit pictures around the world.

Cross-Channel Chronology the Key Pioneers – From Blanchard to Zapata

07 Jan 1785 Jean-Pierre Blanchard and John Jeffries make the first-ever aerial crossing of the English Channel from Dover to Calais in a balloon

15 Jun 1785 Jean-Francoise Pilâtre de Rozier and Pierre Romain both die in their attempt to fly a balloon from France to England

19 Jul 1909 Hubert Latham makes first of two attempts to cross by aeroplane but fails due to engine failure

25 Jul 1909 Louis Blériot makes first aeroplane crossing using a Blériot XI monoplane with 40 hp engine

2 Jun 1910 Hon. Charles Rolls makes first double crossing from Swingfield Downs, Kent to Sangatte, France using a Short-Wright biplane

23 Aug 1910 John Moisant of the USA makes first cross-Channel aircraft flight carrying passengers, mechanic Albert Fileux and his cat, from Calais to Dover

12 Apl 1911 Pierre Prier becomes the first pilot to fly non-stop from London (Hendon) to Paris (Issy-les-Moulineaux), in 4 hr 55 min

02 Apl 1912 Eleanor Trehawke Davies becomes the first woman to fly the Channel as passenger to Gustave Hamel in his 70 hp Blériot

16 Apl 1912 Harriet Quimby of the USA becomes first woman pilot to make the crossing from Dover to a beach near Neufchatel-Hardelot, France in a Blériot XI

25 Aug 1919 Air Transport and Travel makes world's first scheduled international passenger flight, from Hounslow to Le Bourget, Paris in a de Havilland DH 16

26 Apl 1925 Imperial Airways begins services from Croydon Airport

18 Sep 1928 Juan de la Cierva makes first channel crossing by autogyro (Cierva C.8)

CROSS-CHANNEL CHRONOLOGY THE KEY PIONEERS

19 Jun 1931 Lissant Beardmore makes first crossing by glider, having received an aero tow from Lympne airfield, to land at Saint-Inglevert airfield, Calais

20 Jun 1931 Austrian Robert Kronfeld makes first double crossing by glider

6 Sep 1945 Captured German Focke-Achgelis Drache makes first crossing by helicopter, from Cherbourg to RAF Beaulieu, flown by a German pilot accompanied by two Allied officers

14 Jul 1948 Silver City Airways operates first cross-Channel car ferry service, from Lympne to Le Touquet

25 July 1948 Experimental Vickers Nene-Viking makes first crossing by jet airliner between London Airport and Villacoublay, Paris

29 Jul 1950 Vickers Viscount becomes first turbine-powered aircraft to fly commercial services in a trial operated between London (Northolt) and Paris Le Bourget by British European Airways using Ministry of Supply-owned prototype

Jul 1952 Supermarine test pilot Dave Morgan sets a new record by taking 18 min 3.3 sec to fly from London to Brussels in the Supermarine 541, prototype of the Swift jet fighter

18 Apl 1953 BEA begins regular passenger services using Viscount 700 Series aircraft

21 Sep 1954 E.D. 'Radio Queen' becomes the first radio-controlled model aircraft to fly the Channel

13-23 Jul 1959 *Daily Mail* stages air race between London and Paris to commemorate Louis Blériot's flight; the winner, Sqn Ldr Maughan, RAF, takes 40 min 44 sec to travel from the Arc de Triomphe, Paris to Marble Arch, London.

24 Jul 1959 Saunders Roe SR-N1 makes first cross-Channel by hovercraft from Calais to Dover

27 Jul 59 1959 Air France operates first cross-Channel passenger services using pure-jet Caravelle aircraft on Nice-Paris-London route

30 April 1966 Seaspeed launches cross-Channel hovercraft services using SR-N6s

02 May 1969 first purpose-built hoverport opens at Pegwell Bay, Ramsgate

1 August 1969 Seaspeed launches car and passenger ferry services with 400-seat SR-N4s

CROSS-CHANNEL AVIATION PIONEERS

12 Jun 1979 Bryan Allen makes first human-powered Channel crossing in pedal-powered MacCready 'Gossamer Albatross'

07 Jul 1981 Stephen Ptacek makes first crossing in electric-powered aircraft, the MacCready 'Solar Challenger', which draws its energy from the sun

02 October 2000 Seaspeed SR-N4 makes final passenger-carrying cross-Channel hovercraft service

31 Jul 2003 Felix Baumgartner of Austria makes crossing in 20-mile freefall wearing a wingsuit with carbon-fibre wings

26 Sep 2008 Yves Rossy of Switzerland makes first crossing with a jetpack

6 Aug 2009 Gérard Thevenot makes first crossing with an electric-driven aircraft with an on-board energy source using hydrogen fuel cells

28 May 2010 Jonathan Trappe of the USA takes 4 hr to cross the Channel beneath a cluster of helium balloons, using scissors to cut the balloons free to control his altitude

09 Jul 2015 Hugues Duval makes first crossing in battery-powered aircraft, but his Colomban Cri-Cri is carried aloft on a conventional aircraft and then released

09 Jul 2015 Didier Esteyne makes first crossing a battery-powered aircraft (Airbus E-Fan) taking off under its own power

16 Feb 2016 first Channel crossing by remotely-controlled quadcopter drone

14 Jun 2017 Bruno Vezzoli and Jerome Dauffy make first crossing by flying car using a lightweight dune buggy suspended from a paraglider wing

04 Aug 2019 Franky Zapata makes first crossing by jet-powered hover board.

Bibliography

Books

Andrews, C.F. and Morgan, E.B., *Vickers Aircraft since 1908*, Putnam 1969/1988

Bluffield, Robert, *Imperial Airways, The Birth of the British Airline Industry 1914-1940*, Ian Allan Publishing, Hersham, 2009

Brabazon of Tara, Lord, *The Brabazon Story*, William Heineman, London, 1956

Brett, R. Dallas, *History of British Aviation 1908-1914* Vol. I, The Aviation Book Club, London, *History of British Aviation 1908-1914* Vol. II, The Aviation Book Club, London

Collyer, David G., *Lympne Airport in old photographs*, Alan Sutton Publishing Limited, Stroud, 1992

Gardner, Robert, *From Bouncing Bombs to Concorde, The Authorised Biography of Sir George Edwards OM,* Sutton Publishing, 2006

Handley Page Limited, *Forty Years on, 1909-1949,* Fonthill Media, 2012

Holmes, Richard, *The Age of Reason,* Harper Press, London 2009, *Falling Upwards*, William Collins, London 2013

Jackson, A.J., *de Havilland Aircraft Since 1909*, Putnam, 1962, *Avro Aircraft since 1908*, Putnam 1965/1990

King, John, and Tait, Geoff, *Golden Gatwick, 50 Years of Aviation*, The Royal Aeronautical Society and the British Airports Authority, 1980

Lithgow, Mike, *Mach One*, Allan Wingate, London, 1954

Mackersey, Ian, *The Wright Brothers, the Remarkable Story of the Aviation Pioneers who Changed the World,* Little, Brown, London, 2003

Masefield, Sir Peter, with Bill Gunston, *Flight Path*, Airlife Publishing, 2002

Ord-Hume, Arthur W.J.G., *Hovercraft, The Story of a Very British Invention,* Stenlake Publishing, 2016

Paine, Robin, and Symes, Roger, *On a Cushion of Air, The Story of Hoverlloyd and the Cross-Channel Hovercraft,* Writersworld, Woodstock, 2012

Pugh, Stevenson, *The Daily Mail Blériot Anniversary Race,* 1959

Reese, Peter, *The Men who Gave us Wings, Britain and the Aeroplane 1796-1914,* Pen & Sword, Barnsley, 2014

Rolt, L.T.C., *The Aeronauts,* Alan Sutton Publishing, 1966

Smith, Graham, *Taking to the Skies, The Story of British Aviation 1903-1939,* Countryside Books, Newbury, 2003

Thomson, Adam, *High Risk, The Politics of the Air,* Sidgwick and Jackson, London, 1990

Wall, Robert, *Airliners,* Collins, London, 1980

Walsh, Barbara, *Forgotten Aviator, Hubert Latham, a High-Flying Gentleman,* Tempus Publishing, Stroud, 2007.

Periodicals

The Times
The Daily Telegraph
Financial Times
Daily Mail
Flight
Aeroplane

Websites

flightglobalarchive.com
vickersviscount.net
doverhistorian.com

Index

Abel, George, 189
Achgelis, Gerd, 111
Aero Club de France, 17–18, 37, 110
Aero Club *see* Royal Aero Club
Aerofoil principle, 10
Aeroplane, The, 39, 87, 96, 115, 131, 153, 155, 165–6
Aéroplanes Deperdussin: Monoplane, 64–5, 72
Air accidents and investigations, 4, 15, 25, 41, 46–7, 53, 55, 57, 59, 67, 70, 71, 85, 97–8, 99–100
  BAC One-Eleven, 148
  Fa 223, 114
  KLM DC-2, 118
Air Council, 89
Air meetings and shows:
  Aerial Derby Day Hendon (1914), 66
  Belmont International Aviation Tournament, The, 49
  Blackpool, 26
  Bournemouth, 53, 55
  Doncaster, 26
  Farnborough Air Show, 140, 172, 198, 200
  Green Aviation Show (2010), 197
  International Air Congress (1910), 49
  Paris Aero Salon (1908), 41, 55
  Rheims Aviation Meeting (1909), 16, 25, 46
Air Ministry, The:
  Air Traffic Control, 98–9
  Cross-Channel Committee, 87–8
  Radio Position Fixing, 97
Air Registration Board *see* Civil Aviation Authority
Air Traffic Control:
  Jeffs, 97–8
  Mayday distress signal, 98
  World's first Air Traffic Control Tower, 98
Airborne Forces Experimental Establishment, 114
Airbus Group, 196
  A320, 187
  E-Fan, 197–8, 200–201
Airlines and cross-channel services:
  Air Charter, 131–2, 133
  Air France, 146
  Air Transport & Travel (AT&T), 80–5, 90
  Air Union, 101
  British Airways, 146, 148
  British Caledonian Airways, 127, 148–9
  British Eagle, 138
  British European Airways (BEA), 115, 121, 127, 136, 140–3, 146–8, 159, 165
  British Marine Air Navigation, 95

British Overseas Airways
  Corporation (BOAC), 124
British United Air Ferries, 132
British United Airways (BUA),
  132, 148–9
British World Airlines, 144
Channel Air Bridge, 131–2 161
Channel Islands Airways, 133
*Compagnie des messageries
  aériennes* (CMA), 84
*Compagnie générale
  transaérienne*, 84
Daimler Airline, 90, 94, 98, 104
Dan Air, 149
Deutsche Aero Lloyd, 96
Deutsche Luft Hansa, 96
Grandes Express Aériennes, 97
Handley Page, 82–5, 87, 89–90,
  93–4
Imperial Airways, 90, 95–6,
  99–105, 122
Instone Airline, 85, 90, 95, 104
*Koninklijke Luchvaart
  Maatschappij voor Nederland
  en Kolonien* (KLM), 85
Lignes aérienne farman, 84, 100
Scandanavian Air System, 146
Silver City Airways, 124–34, 161
Skyways, 163, 167
*Societé Anonyme Belge
  d'Exploitation de la
  Navigation Aérienne*
  (SABENA), 96, 115
Swiss International Air Lines, 187
Swissair, 187
*Syndicat National pour L'étude
  des Transports Aériens
  (SNETA)*, 85
Trans-Canada Air Lines, 146
United Airlines, 147
Airports & aerodromes:
  Ambleteuse, 187

Barajas (Madrid), 115
Biggin Hill, 155, 157, 159–60,
  162, 166–7
Bordeaux-Merignac, 200
Brooklands, 62, 68, 73, 140–1,
  144–5
Buc (Versailles), 73, 75–6, 80
Calais, 197
Chilbolton, 137
Croydon, 86, 88, 95, 96–7,
  99, 100, 102, 106–107, 110,
  118, 121
Crotoy, 65, 67
Ferryfield (Lydd), 115, 128,
  129–30, 132, 161, 197–8
Gatwick, 122, 130, 132
Heathrow, 122, 137, 144
Hendon, 47, 59–61, 65–9, 73–7
Hounslow Heath, 79, 81, 86
Lasham, 192
Le Bourget, 48, 79, 81, 82, 84, 97,
  110, 142, 143, 144, 159, 197
Le Touquet, 115, 124–6, 128–30
Lympne, 124–9, 191
Marc, 184
Mojave, 192
Rennes St Jacques Airport, 196
Schiphol, 85
Swingfield, 191
Paris Villacoublay, 66, 138,
  156–8, 160, 167
Wisley, 137, 140, 142, 145,
  157–8
Aircraft Manufacturing Company
  (AIRCO), 80
DH16, 81
DH4, 80, 82–3, 85
Airspeed Ltd:
  Ambassador, 140–1
Alcock, John, 17
Allen, Bryan, 191–3
Amiens, 40, 71, 73, 91

210

INDEX

Antoinette Company, 17–18, 24–5, 27–8
  IV, 18–19
  VI, 21–4
  VII, 24–6, 28
Anton Flettner, Flugzeugbau GmbH: Fl 282, 114
Armstrong Whitworth and Co:
  AW 154 Argosy, 100
  Atlanta, 104
  Ensign, 104
Atair Aerodynamics, 186
Aviation firsts:
  first aeroplane to fly the Atlantic non-stop, 86
  first aircraft to cross the Channel under its own power, 200
  first aircraft to make two return trips between Croydon and Le Bourget in one day, 90
  first airliner with a lavatory, 86
  first car ferry service, 126–7
  first Channel crossing by helium balloon cluster, 202
  first Channel crossing with a passenger, 59
  first cross-Channel air terminal (Britain), 106–107
  first cross-Channel flight, 16, 37
  first crossing of Australia, 202
  first crossing of the Channel by airship, 85
  first crossing of the Channel on a hover board, 188–9
  first daily international service London to Paris, 81
  first double crossing by glider, 191
  first drone to cross the Channel, 185–6
  first electric-powered model to cross the Channel, 185
  first female pilot to cross the English Channel, 62–3
  first flying car (Pegasus) to cross the Channel, 187–8
  first heavier-than-air craft to cross the Channel, 16
  first helicopter to fly the Channel, 113
  first human crossing of the Channel, 193–4
  first human-powered aircraft to fly a figure-of-eight course round two markers half-a-mile apart, 192
  first London to Manchester flight, 16
  first man to fly a human-powered aircraft across the Channel, 192
  first named air service, 102
  first non-stop Atlantic crossing, 16
  first non-stop cross-Channel flight by a model aircraft, 184
  first non-stop double crossing of the English Channel, 50–2
  first officially authenticated take-off and landing by a human-powered aircraft, 192
  first person to break the sound barrier without vehicular power, 186
  first person to cross the Channel using a jet-propelled wing, 186–7
  first person to fly non-stop from London to Paris, 59–60
  first person to skydive across the Channel, 186
  first pilot to be licensed to command a turbine-powered aircraft, 142–3
  first scheduled London-Paris international airmail service, 83

211

first to fly the Channel in a glider, 191
first to fly the Channel in an electric-powered aircraft, 196–7
first woman to cross the Channel, 61–2
first woman to loop the loop, 62
world's first air traffic control tower, 98–9
world's first international solar flight, 194–5
world's first scheduled flying-boat service, 95
Aviation Traders, 134
  Carvair, 134–5

Baden-Powell, Major Baden, 38
BAe Systems, 68, 148
Ballooning:
  Aîné Robert, 3, 6
  Blanchard Balloon Academy, 13
  Cadet Robert, 3, 6–7
  Charles Sadler, 8
  Francois Pilâtre de Rozier, 5–6, 9, 11, 14–15
  Globe, The, 3–4
  Hubert Latham, 14, 16–17
  Jacques Charles, 3, 6–7
  Jacques Faure, 17
  James Sadler, 9, 14–16
  James Tytler, 8
  Jean-Pierre Blanchard, 1, 7, 8–14
  John Jeffries, 1, 8–14
  M. Collin-Hullin, 7
  Montgolfier family, 2–5, 7, 12
  Pierre Romain, 14–15
  Vincent Lunardi, 8
Balloon flights:
  England's first balloon ascent, 8
  first balloon crossing of the Sahara Desert, 202
  first Channel crossing by helium balloon cluster, 202

first manned flight in the New World, 13
Guinness World Records, 202–203
London to Paris, 17
world's first solar-powered hybrid hot-air balloon crossed the English Channel, 201–202
Banks, Sir Joseph, 7–8
Baracca, Francesco, 48
Battery-powered aircraft, 197–8, 200–201
Baumgartner, Felix, 186
Beardmore, Lissant, 191
Blanchard, Jean-Pierre, 1, 7–14, 37
Blériot, Christine, 162
Blériot, Louis, 1, 17–18, 29–43, 44, 45–6, 60, 62
  100th anniversary, 42
  cross-channel flight, 24–5, 29–43, 56, 153
  publicity, 36–7
Blériot/Voison:
  II, 41
  III, 41
  IV, 41
  VII, 41
  XI, 41–2, 46, 59–60, 62, 66, 74
Boeing:
  247, 104
  727, 147
  747, 187
Books and papers:
  Age of Reason, The, 9
  Experiments and Observations on Different Kinds of Air, 3
  Goldfinger, 135
  High Risk, 127
Bossoutrot, Lucien, 79
Bouche, Henri, 110
Boucher, Robert, 195
Boulogne, 15, 73, 76–7, 92
Boyle, Colin, 23–4, 26

212

INDEX

Breguet-Dorand helicopter, 111
Brett, Dallas, 51, 57, 74
Brie, Wing Commander Reggie, 115–18
Bristol Aeroplane Company:
  Freighter, 124–7, 129, 131–4
  Scout, 74
  Superfreighter, 129
British Aerospace *see* BAe Systems
British Aircraft Corporation, 148, 150–1
  BAC One eleven, 148–9
British Aviation Services (Britavia), 123, 130
British Deperdussin Company, 47
British Government:
  Airline subsidy, 86–9, 94
  Brabazon Committee, 139
British Rail, 130, 159, 174–5, 179
British Wright Company Limited,
Brock, William L., 74–7
Brooklands, 68, 73, 140
Bryce, Jock, 140–1, 144–5, 148, 151
BSA Group, The, 84
Butler, Frank, 38
Butlin, Billy, 160–1, 163

Calais, 19, 23–4, 34, 63, 65, 71–3
Campbell, Donald, 161
Capper, Lieutenant Colonel John, 38
Car ferry services, 124–35
Carbery, Lord, 74–6
Carr, R. H., 74
Cars:
  Jensen, 161
  Renault Dauphine, 161
  Rolls-Royce, 161
Carter, Lieutenant Commander W.J., 158–9
Caudron Aircraft Company:
  Monoplane, 65
Cavendish, Henry, 2
Channel Tunnel, The, 169, 177–8

Charles, Jacques, 3, 6–7
Churchill, Winston, 80, 86–7, 94, 123, 131
Cierva Autogiro Company, 109–10, 117
  C.6, 109
  C.8, 109–11, 117
  C.19, 117, 119
  C.30, 118–19
Ciro's Aviation, 122
Civil Aviation Authority, 125, 174
Claisse, Maurice, 111
Clark, Captain Storm, 127
Cockerell, Sir Christopher, 168–9, 170, 182–3
Cody, Samuel Franklin, 44
Collin-Hullin, M., 7
Colomban Cri-Cri, 197
Competitions and races:
  Aerial Derby, 74, 76
  Baron de Forest, 57, 67
  Circuit of Europe (1911), 71–3
  Daily Mail (Blériot Anniversary Race) 153–67
  Gordon Bennett International Gold Cup, 25
  International Birdmen Rally, 189–90
  King's Cup (1928), 109–10
  London-Brighton-London, 68
  London-Manchester, 74, 76
  London-Paris-London (1914), 71, 73–7
  MacRobertson Trophy (1934), 154
  Mildenhall-Melbourne (1934), 104
  Royal Aero Club Gold Medal, 38, 51
  Ruinart Prize, 49
  Schneider Trophy, 67
Concorde, 147, 149, 151, 177, 178
Cornu, Paul, 108
Crandall, Sir William, 21
Cross-channel airliners, 92–3

D'Arlandes, François Laurent, 5–6
Da Vinci, Leonardo, 108
Daily Mail, 16, 19, 32, 35, 44, 56, 82, 174,
  prizes, 17, 20, 191
    Blériot Anniversary Race, 153–167
    first cross-Channel flight, 16, 37
    first heavier-than-air craft to cross the Channel, 16
    first London to Manchester flight, 16
    first non-stop Atlantic crossing, 16
    Grand Prix d'Académie des Sports, 110
    Lahm Prize, 110
Daily Telegraph, The, 33, 167, 174–5, 196
Darwin, Erasmus, 7, 15
Dauffy, Jérôme, 188
de Forest, Baron Maurice, 56–7
de Havilland Aircraft Company,
  4B Comet, 147, 159
  Albatross, 104
  DH104 Dove, 136
  DH16, 93
  DH18, 89–90, 98
  DH34, 89–90, 95–6, 104–105
  DH4, 92–3
  Hatfield Puffin, 192
  Tiger Moth, 162
de Havilland, Geoffrey, 80, 92
de la Cierva, Juan, 108–109, 110, 111, 116–18
de Lambert, Comte Charles, 17, 20
de Lesseps, Jacques, 48–9
de Montblanc, Antoine, 160
de Rozier, Francois Pilâtre, 5–6, 9, 11, 14–15
de Vaisseau Conneau 'Beaumont', Lt, 72–3

Deperdussin, Armand, 47
Donne, Michael, 176
Dorand, Rene, 111
Dornier Flugzeugwerke:
  Do 217, 112
Douglas Aircraft Company:
  DC-2, 104
  DC-3, 136
  DC-4, 134
Dover, 1, 12, 19, 21–2, 25, 29, 31, 33, 35, 38, 48–51, 54, 57–9, 63, 65–6, 71–4, 77, 91, 92, 174–9, 185, 187–9, 197, 202–203
  Castle, 9–10, 29, 33–4, 48, 63, 172
Duval, Colette, 161–2
Duval, Hugues, 196–7

Eastbourne, 62, 65
Eastchurch 50, 57, 65, 91
Edwards, George, 138–40, 144–6, 148–51
Elder Hearn, T., 74
Elkins, Steve, 189–90
Engines:
  Alvis Leonides, 114
  Anzani W-3, 42
  Armstrong-Siddeley:
    Lynx, 109
    Mamba, 139
  Bramo Sh 14a, 119
  Bristol Hercules, 136
  Bristol-Siddeley Viper III, 170
  Centaurus, 140–1
  Gnome, 43, 61–2, 66, 74,
  Jetcat P400, 187
  Le Rhone, 74, 76
  Leonides, 169
  Napier Lion, 10
  Pratt and Whitney JT8D, 148
  Rolls-Royce:
    Avon, 146
    Dart, 139–41, 143
    Eagle, 93

INDEX

Medway, 147
Merlin, 160
Nene, 136
Proteus, 176, 181, 182
Spey, 147–8
Tyne, 144–5
Turbomeca Marboré, 169
Esteyne, Didier, 196–8
Evening Standard, 81–2
Ewen, W.H., 65

Fairey Aviation, 155
  Fairey Rotodyne, 115–16, 155
Farman Aviation Works:
  F180, 100
  F60 Goliath, 79, 97, 99
Farman, Henri, 25
Farnborough, 44, 91, 109
Faure, Jacques, 17
Fay, John, 114–15
Feber, Captain Ferdinand, 18
Federation of Airline Pilots, 96
Feltes, Goy, 49
Films and TV programmes:
  Lost World, The, 101
  Those Magnificent Men in their Flying Machines, 42, 71
Financial Times, 173, 176, 197–8
First World War,
  Blériot XI, 46–7
  Morane-Saulnier Type G, 78
Flanders, Howard, 1
Flight, 19–23, 26, 29, 32, 35–9, 45, 48–51, 57–8, 61, 74–7, 81–2, 100, 110–11, 126, 128, 141, 143, 147, 153–4
Flights:
  Brooklands-Wisley (Bryce), 145
  Calais-Deal (Moisant), 59
  Calais-Eastbourne (Prevost), 64–5
  Cricklewood-London-Paris, 83
  Crotoy-Dover (Ewen), 65

Croydon-Le Bourget, 110
Cruden Bay-Jaeren (Tryggve Gran), 43
Douai-Arras (Blériot), 29
Double crossing of the Channel (Rolls), 50–2
Dover-Calais (Blériot), 29–41
Dover-Calais (Quimby), 62–4
Dover-Cologne (Hamel), 66
Dover-Sangatte (first electric-powered model), 185
Dover-Wissant to Hendon to Paris (Valentine), 65
Eastchurch-Beaumont (Sopwith), 58
Étampes-Artenay (Blériot), 29
Heathrow-Le Bourget (Lithgow), 151–2
Hendon-Brooklands (Hamel), 68
Hendon-Paris (Salmet), 59–61
Hendon-Paris Hamel), 61–2
Hendon-Windsor (Hamel), 68
Juvisy Aerodrome-Paris (de Lambert), 21
Le Havre-RAF Beaulieu (Fa 223 *Drache*), 113
Les Baraques-Dover (de Lesseps), 48–9
Les Baraques-Dover (Kremer/Feltes/van Hoorn), 49
Les Baraques-Sangatte, (Blériot), 31
London-Le Bourget (Lawford), 81
London-Manchester (Paulhan), 52
London-Paris (Fairey Rotodyne), 115–16
London-Paris (Prier), 59–60
London-Paris (Summers), 136–7
London Gatwick-Genoa (BAC One-Eleven), 148
Lydd-Calais (Salis), 162
Lydd-Le Touquet (S.51 Dragonfly), 115

Marble Arch-Arc de Triomph
  (*Daily Mail* Blériot
  Anniversary Race), 153–67
Montreal (de Lessups), 49
New York-Le Bourget (Charles
  Lindbergh) 48
Newfoundland-Eire (Powell),
  122–3
Northolt-Le Bourget (Rymer),
  142–3
Orleans-Étampes (Blériot), 29
Paris-Ambleteuse (Pegasus/
  Vezzoli), 147–8
Rotterdam-Brussels (Cierva), 110
Toronto (de Lessups), 49
Flights, luxury:
  Golden Ray (Air Union), 102
  Silver Arrow (Silver City), 13
  Silver Wing (Imperial Airways), 102
Flying schools:
  Blériot:
    Étampes, 47
    Hendon, 59
    Pau, 47, 68
  Brooklands, 47, 67
  Ewen, W. H., 65
  Hendon, 47
  Issy-les-Moulineaux, 49
  Wright Brothers Flying School
    (Pau), 20
Focke, Heinrich, 108, 111, 118–20
Focke-Achgelis: 119
  Fa 223 *Drache* (Kite), 111–14,
    120, 165
Focke-Wulf Flugzeubau AG, 111,
  118–20
  Fw 19, 119
  Fw 190, 120
  Fw 200, 120
  Fw 61, 111, 119
  Fw Stieglitz biplane, 111
Fokker, Anthony, 78
Folkestone, 73, 75–6

Fonck, René, 47
Fontaine, Charles, 33
Franklin, Benjamin, 7–8
French Aerial League, 38

Garros, Roland, 72–5, 77–8
Geddes, Sir Eric, 95
Geissler, Alban, 186
Gill, Richard, 185–6
Gloster Aircraft Company:
  Gloster Meteor, 160, 166
Gorell, Lord, 89
Grace, Cecil, 55, 57–9
Grahame-White, Claude, 57–8, 65,
  76–7
  Factory, 74, 78
Gran, Tryggve, 42–3
Greswell, Clement, 57
Grey, C. G., 87, 96
Guardian, The, 175
Guynemer, Georges, 47

Hafner:
  Rotachute, 114
  Rotorbuggy, 114
Haldane, Richard, 38, 45
Halliwell, Lieut. E., 85
Hamel, Gustav, 61–3, 65–9, 77
Handley-Page:
  HP 42, 103
  HP 42/45, 105–106
  O/400, 82
  W8, 83, 95, 101
Harper, Harry, 16, 19, 24, 29, 31,
  33–4, 40, 45–6
Hawker Aircraft, 67
  Hurricane, 159
Hawker, Harry, 17
Hawker Siddeley:
  Hunter, 157, 166
  Trident, 147
Helicopteros SA, 115
Helicopters, 108–120

216

INDEX

Commercial services, 115
de la Cierva, Juan, 108–11, 116–18
Fairey Rotodyne, 115–16, 155
Focke-Achgelis Fa 223 *Drache*, 111–14, 120, 165
Focke-Wulf-Flugzeugbau, 111, 118–20
Fw 61, 111, 119
Igor Sikorsky, 116
Luftwaffe, 112–113
Westland S.51 Dragonfly, 114–15
Helite, 196
Hirth, Helmuth, 7
Hives, Lord, 139–40
Hoare, Sir Samuel, 94–5
Hollingsbee, Bob, 50–1
Holmes, Richard, 9–11, 14
Hovercraft, 168–83
  first crossing of the English Channel by hovercraft, 170–2
  Hovercraft Act 1968, The, 174
  Pegwell Bay, 178–80
  SR.N1, 169–72, 183
  SR.N2, 173
  SR.N4, 175–8, 180–2
  SR.N4 001, 175
  SR.N6, 173–5
  VA-3, 173
Hoverlloyd Limited, 174–7, 180,
Hoverspeed, 177
Howard Wright biplane, 57–8
Human-powered aircraft, 191–4, 199–200
Humphery, G. E. Woods, 90, 96
Hunting Aircraft:
  Jet Provost, 156
Hydrogen-powered aircraft, 195–6

Illustrated London News, 81
In-flight entertainment, 101
In-flight meals, 101, 103
Ingham, Bruce, 81–2
Isle of Grain, 65

Jarrett, Philip, 20–1
Jeffries, John, 1, 8–14
Jeffs, G. J. H. 'Jimmy', 97–8
Johnson, Amy, 17

King George IV, 12
King George V, 51
King Louis XVI, 4–5, 11
Kremer, Henry, 192, 199
Kremer, Pascal, 49
Kronfeld, Robert, 191

L'Aéronautique, 110
Laker, Freddie, 131, 134–5, 148, 161
Lamb, Captain Peter 'Sheepy', 171–2, 175
Lamplugh, Capt A. G., 123
Latham, Hubert, 14, 16–27, 31, 37, 44, 49
  Prix Ambroise Goupy, 19
Lawford, Lt E.H. 'Bill', 80
Le Matin, 33, 36
Leblanc, Alfred, 30–1
Les Baraques (Calais), 31, 48, 59
Levavasseur, Léon, 17–19, 24–5, 27
Lindbergh, Charles, 48
Lioré et Olivier:
  213, 101
  LeO 21, 102
Lithgow, Lt Commander Mike, 148, 151–2
Loraine, Robert, 57
Luftwaffe:
  Lt Helmut Gerstenhauer, 112–13
  Transportstaffel 40, 113
Lunardi, Vincent, 8

MacCready, Dr Paul, 191–2, 194, 199
MacCready/Lissaman:
  Gossamer Albatross, 193–4, 199–200
  Gossamer Condor, 192, 199

MacCready/Morgan:
  Gossamer Penguin, 194, 199
  Solar Challenger, 194–5, 199–200
Mackenzie Grieve, Kenneth, 17
Macmillan, Harold, 154
Marconi Company, The, 31, 97, 182
  Air Traffic Control, 99
Martin, Commander Ian, 157–9
Martinsyde:
  Martinsyde S1, 74
Masefield, Peter, 115, 140–5, 151
Maughan, Sqn Ldr Charles, 163, 166–7
McLean, Frank, 57
McMullin, Lt J., 82–3
Messerschmitt:
  Bf 109, 111
Millinship, Rob, 39–40
Mitchell, Reginald, 95
Mockford, F. S. 'Stanley', 98
Moisant, John, 56, 59, 69–70
  First airman to cross the Channel with a passenger, 59
Montgolfier, Étienne, 2–4
Montgolfier, Jacques, 12
Montgolfier, Joseph, 2–3, 5, 7, 12
Montgolfier, Pierre, 2
Moore-Brabazon, John, 17, 50, 53, 55
Morane, Leon, 77
Morane, Robert, 77
Morane-Saulnier, 66, 74
  MS 406, 78
  Type G, 77–8
Morgan, Ray, 194–5
Moss, Stirling, 155, 161
Museums:
  Brooklands, 144
  Calais, 11
  Hovercraft Museum, 182
  Shuttleworth Collection, The, 39
  Smithsonian National Air and Space Museum, 199

National Research and Development Council, 183
Neely, Bill, 159–60, 163
Noel, Louis, 74–5
Northcliffe, Lord, 16, 21, 37–8, 44
Nott, Julian, 201–202

Ocuair:
  Ocuair quadcopter (drone), 185–6
Oddey, W. R. M., 65–6
Orde-Hume, Arthur, 110

P&O, 130
Paris, 4, 6–7, 17, 36–7, 59, 62, 65–6
  Vincennes, 71, 73
Patterson, Maj Cyril, 81
Paulhan, Louis, 17, 52
Pegwell Bay, 178–80
Perrin, Harold, 38
Perry, Lady Victoria, 62
Pickles, Sydney, 65–6
Pierson, Rex, 139
Piggott, Derek, 192
Pilot, 34
Poulet, Étienne, 79
Powell, Griffith, 122–31, 135
Prevost, M., 64–5
Prier, Pierre, 59
  First to fly non-stop from London to Paris, 59–60
Priestley, Joseph, 3
Primrose, Wg Cdr W. Harold, 80
Pugh, Stevenson, 153, 154, 161, 164, 165

Quimby, Harriet, 62, 69–70
  First female pilot to cross the English Channel, 62–3
Quinron, M., 38

INDEX

Radar:
  Decca 424, 129, 176, 182
Radio Position Fixing, 97
Radio Queen, 184–5
Rassam, Madelain, 163
Rawson, Flight Lieutenant Arthur, 109–10
Renaux, Eugene, 74, 76
Reserches Aéronautiques Louis Blériot, 46
Rheims, 16, 25, 46, 72
Rickenbacker, Eddie, 48
Robert, Aîné, 3, 6
Robert, Cadet, 3, 6–7
Robinson, W. S., 123
Rolls, Honourable Charles, 38, 49, 54, 67
  Death and obituary, 53, 55
  First non-stop double crossing of the English Channel, 50–2
Rolls-Royce Limited, 55, 139
Romain, Pierre, 14–15
Roper, Chris, 192
Rossy, Yves, 186–7
Rothermere, Lord, 164
Royal Aero Club, 21, 50, 55
  Gold Medal, 38, 51
Royal Air Force:
  Stations:
    RAF Beaulieu, 113–14
    RAF Duxford, 164, 166–7
    RAF Kenley, 79, 80, 162
    RAF Manston, 193, 195
    RAF Northolt, 121–2 128, 136, 142–4, 159, 165
  Units:
    No. 2 (Communications) Squadron, 86 Wing, 80
    Transport Command, 123
    Versailles Peace Conference, 80
Royal Flying Corps, 65, 91–2

Royce, Frederick, 55
Ryder, Group Captain Norman, 163, 167
Rylands, Eric, 163, 167
Rymer, Captain 'Dickie', 142–3

Sadler, Charles, 8
Sadler, James, 8–9, 14–16
Sadler, Windham, 16
Salis, Jean, 162
Salmet, Henri, 56, 60
  Double crossing of the English Channel, 59–61
Saulnier, Raymond, 77
Santos-Dumont, Alberto, 38
Saunders-Roe,
  SR.N1, 169–72, 183
  SR.N2, 173
  SR.N4, 175–8, 180–2
  SR.N4 001, 175
  SR.N6, 173–5
Seaspeed, 175–6, 178
Second World War:
  Focke-Achgelis Fa 223 *Drache* (Kite), 112–13
  Morane-Saulnier 406, 58
Selfridge, H. Gordon, 36, 38
Seymour, Arthur, 20
Shackleton, Ernest, 38
Shaw, Captain Jerry, 84
Sheerness, 66
Sheldon, John, 8
Short Brothers, The, 50, 55
  C Class Empire Flying Boat, 103–104, 122
  Short Tucano, 185
Sikorsky, Igor, 116
Skene, R. L., 74, 91
SNCASE, 120
SNCF, 175
Solar-powered aircraft, 194–6, 199–200

Sopwith Aviation Company, 67
Sopwith, T.O.M., 17, 56–7, 59, 67–8
SPAD:
  VII, 47
  VIII, 47
Stack, Robert, 77
Sud Aviation, 146
  Caravelle, 146–7
  Vautour, 162
Summers, Joseph 'Mutt', 137–8, 140
Supermarine Aviation Works (Vickers) Limited, 95
  Scimitar, 157–8
  Sea Eagle, 95
  Spitfire, 95, 150, 160
  Swift, 151–2
Swingate, 50–1, 57, 59
Sykes, General, 88–9
Syring, John, 174–5

Tabuteau, Maurice, 72–3
Tansley, Hugh, 162–3
Taplin, Colonel H. J., 184
Thaxter, Dave, 127
Thevenot, Gérard. 195–6
  'La Mouette', 196
  Atlas, 196
Thompson, Adam, 127
Times, The, 20–1, 23–4, 36–8, 55, 188
Townsend Car Ferries, 174
Trappe, Jonathan, 1, 202–203
Treehawk Davis, Eleanor, 61–2, 65
  First woman to cross the Channel, 61–2
  First woman to loop the loop, 62
Trenchard, Air Marshal Sir Hugh, 87
Trubshaw, Brian, 145
Tytler, James, 8

Union pour la Sécurité en Aéroplane, 110

Valentine, James, 65, 72–3
Van Hoorn, Henk, 49
Védrines, Jules, 72–3
Verdon Roe, Alliott, 17
Vezzoli, Bruno, 187–8
Vickers:
  Vimy Commercial, 86, 95
Vickers-Armstrong Aircraft, 144, 150
  Nene-Viking, 136–8, 151–2, 165
  VA-3 hovercraft, 172
  Vanguard, 101, 144–6, 149–50
  Viking, 121, 136–8, 142–3, 150, 165
  Viscount, 138–44, 146, 150, 154
Vidart, René, 72–3
Voison, Gabriel, 40–1
Vought-Sikorsky:
  VS-300, 116

Webb, John, 161
Weir, Lord, 88
Westland Aircraft, 114, 173–4
  S.51 Dragonfly, 114–15, 166
Weyman, Charles T., 72
Whitten Brown, Arthur, 17
Whybrow, Douglas, 131
Williamson, Captain Bill, 176
Willows, Ernest, 85
Wolff, Kurt, 91
Woodford Essex Aircraft Group Jupiter, 192
Woolston, 95
Walker, Captain Roderick 'Red Rory' Bamford, 155–6, 163
Walsh, Barbara, 16, 18–20, 26, 32, 37
Wright Brothers, The, 20–1, 47, 50, 55
  Flyer, 50–1
Wright, Wilbur, 16, 20, 55
Wulf, Georg, 118–19

Zapata, Franky, 1, 188–9

Also by Bruce Hales-Dutton and Published by Air World
www.pen-and-sword.com

PIONEERING PLACES OF BRITISH AVIATION
The Early Adventures of Powered Flight in the UK

From as early as the beginning of the nineteenth century, Britain was at the forefront of powered flight. Across the country many places became centres of innovation and experimentation, as increasing numbers of daring men took to the skies.

It was in 1799, at Brompton Hall, that Sir George Cayley Bart put forward ideas which formed the basis of powered flight. Cayley is widely regarded as the father of aviation and his ancestral home the 'cradle' of British aviation.

There were balloon flights at Hendon from 1862, although attempts at powered flights from the area later used as the famous airfield, do not seem to have been particularly successful. Despite this, Louis Bleriot established a flying school there in 1910.

At Brooklands attempts were made to build and fly a powered aircraft in 1906 even before the banked racetrack was completed but these were unsuccessful. But on 8 June 1908, A.V. Roe made what is considered to be the first powered flight in Britain from there – in reality a short hop – in a machine of his own design and construction, enabling Brooklands to claim to be the birthplace of British aviation.

These are just a few of the many places investigated by Bruce Hales-Dutton in this intriguing look at the early days of British aviation, which includes the first ever aircraft factory in Britain in the railway arches at Battersea; Larkhill on Salisbury Plain which became the British Army's first airfield, and Barking Creek where Frederick Handley Page established his first factory.

ISBN: 978-1-52675-015-0

AIR WORLD

Also by Bruce Hales-Dutton and Published by Air World
www.pen-and-sword.com

THE TRANS-ATLANTIC PIONEERS
From First Flights to Supersonic Jets – The Battle to Cross the Atlantic

To cross the Atlantic by air was a feat that took all the guts and determination that the two men involved could muster, but there was something else. Alcock and Brown were true professionals. Both had thought very deeply about the challenges facing them and both were determined to leave nothing to chance. In the background was the £10,000 prize offered by Lord Northcliffe, whose generosity represented a potent incentive for pioneer aviators.

Inevitably, the names of Alcock and Brown have become synonymous with that first trans-Atlantic flight. They were the first but by no means the last of the trans-Atlantic pioneers. His Majesty's airship *R-34*, for example, made the first flight from east to west and followed that up with the first return crossing. Charles Lindbergh made the first flight from the North American mainland to that of Europe. Amelia Earhart was the first woman to make a solo crossing.

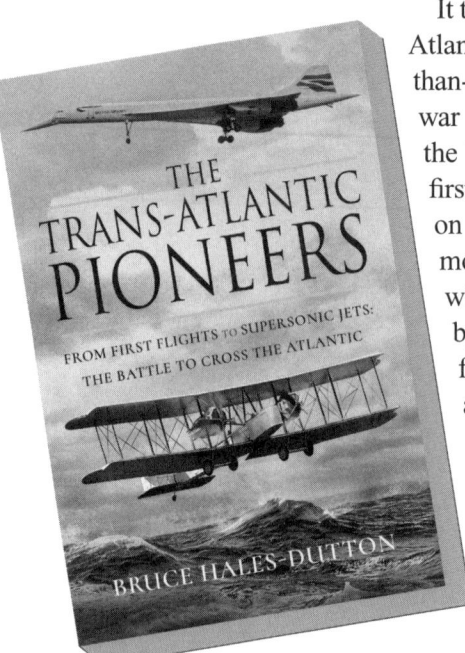

It took the demands of war to prove that the Atlantic could be crossed regularly by heavier-than-air craft and pave the way for the post-war commercial operations that followed. In the 1950s came the first jets, followed by the first supersonic airliners. And the pioneering on what is still the world's busiest and most prestigious intercontinental air route will continue. Who, the book concludes by asking, will operate the first airliner featuring hybrid power, the first fully autonomous machine, the first to use other than fossil fuel?

Will the next hundred years be exciting as those truly pioneering days of the past?

ISBN: 978-1-52673-217-0